D1881129

CASTE AND DEMOCRACY IN INDIA

CASTE AND DEMOCRACY IN INDIA

A Perspective from Below

Vivek Kumar

GYAN

Published by

Gyan Publishing House
5, Ansari Road
Daryaganj, New Delhi-110002
Phone: 011-47034999, 9811692060
E-mail: books@gyanbooks.com

Distribution Network
gyanbooks.com
India, USA, Canada, UK, Australia, France

© Author

All rights reserved. No part of this work may be reproduced, stored, adapted, or transmitted in any form or by any means, electronic, mechanical, photocopying, micro-filming recording or otherwise, or translated in any language, without the prior written permission of the copyright owner and the publisher. The book is sold subject to the condition that it shall not, by way of trade or otherwise, be lent, resold, hired out, or otherwise circulated without the prior publisher's written consent in any form of binding or cover other than that in which it is published.

ISBN: 978-93-6280-885-1 (PB)

First Published, 2024

Printed at: Gyan Press, Delhi.

The views and opinions expressed in this book are author(s) own and the facts reported by them have been verified to the extent possible, and the publishers are not in any way liable for the same.

Caste and Democracy in India: A Perspective from Below
Author: Vivek Kumar

To

Dear Sir

Prof. Nandu Ram

Contents

Foreword 9

Acknowledgements 11

Introduction 13

PART I: UNDERSTANDING CASTE

1. Caste and Hindu Social Order: Some Pedagogic Issues 53
2. Caste: Views from the Field 75
3. Caste: Views of Ambedkar and Lohia 89
4. Epistemology of Caste Based Social Exclusion 105
5. Caste and Politics of Reservation 127
6. Untouchability in Uttarakhand: Views from the Field 135

PART II: CASTE MOBILISATION AND DEMOCRACY

7. Caste Mobilisation in Uttar Pradesh: A Survey of 2002 Assembly Elections 141
8. Politics of Change: A Case of Uttar Pradesh 147
9. Strengthening of Indian Democracy: BSP's Experiment in Uttar Pradesh 153
10. Celebrating Birthday for 'Swabhiman' A Perspective from Below 159
11. Understanding Patterns of Mobilisation: A Case of BSP 169

PART III: DEMOCRACY AND INDEPENDENT AGENDA FOR YOUTH

12. Problems of Youth in Era of Globalisation 179
13. Violence and Youth: An Independent Agenda for Youth 189

14. Dalit Youths: Construction of Different Personality 199

PART IV: DEMOCRACY AND ISSUES OF REPRESENTATION

15. Democracy and Self-Representation 213
16. Representation of Marginalised Sections and Indian Political Parties 219
17. Indian Democracy and Personality Cult 251
18. Presidential Election in World's Largest Democracy: The Issue of Representation 257
19. Saffronisation in Democracy 261
20. How Representative are Social Sciences in India? 267
21. Literature and Self Representation: A Case of Dalits 273

PART V: DEMOCRACY AND DEVELOPMENT

22. Social Development and Planning in Developing Countries 289
23. Caste Development and Corruption 301
24. Cultural Heterogeneity and Exclusion in India 315
25. The Reformists Role of Buddhism: Dalits and Their Development 321

List of Acknowledgements 329

Index 331

Foreword

The journey of a deeply hierarchical society as a democratic polity in the early years was observed from the outside with considerable trepidation. This gave way to hailing India as the world's largest democracy despite its deep social and economic inequality. Views from the inside too changed and importantly were varied. It could not be otherwise, given India's inequality and the fact that different castes and communities were differentially located. The Constitution was constitutive of this fundamental discrepancy of political equality and social inequality. It could be thus read both as a document of liberalism as well as of social justice. In other words the relationship between caste and democracy seen as essentially antithetical by dominant groups, widely evident in popular media and mainstream discourse, need not necessarily be so. This purportedly flows from the influence of liberal individualist ideas in which the self is constituted not by a place within a group, but abstracted from it.

It is in this context that Vivek Kumar's book on Democracy and Caste acquires special significance. The collection of essays in this book demonstrates the dynamic aspect of democracy and its enabling role in mobilising the marginalised castes from 'below'. This self-representation and assertion of Dalits for instance in Uttar Pradesh has been of critical significance for deepening Indian democracy. At the same time the expansive logic of democratic principles have led to greater and great participation. The book is important not only for debates on Indian democracy but also for its debates on caste. The scholar has engaged with conceptual questions relating to matters of defining caste and why this needs to be taken into account for understanding the relationship between caste and democracy. This book is a welcome addition to contemporary debates on caste and democracy.

The significant aspect of this book is that an attempt is made to rethink dominant modes of understanding caste: as evident in the prevalent popular discourse; to dominant academic conceptualisations of caste which the author argues is both erroneous and misplaced. He draws from the writings of thinkers such as Babasaheb Bhimrao Ambedkar and Ram Manohar Lohia to restate the fact that caste was integral to any understanding of Indian society and therefore genuine democracy would be possible only with the annihilation of caste.

There are two aspects to this perspective: one, in terms of caste mobilisation by marginalised sections to strengthen Indian democracy; and two, in terms of views from the 'field'. In both cases the effort is to re-conceptualise ideas about a formal notion of democracy that ignores questions of structural inequalities or persists with an idea that caste is a 'colonial construct', ignoring the long and complex history of the persistence of jati as a core 'given' identity.

Professor Maitrayee Chaudhuri
Chairperson
Centre for the Study of Social Systems
School of Social Sciences
Jawaharlal Nehru University,
New Delhi-110067

Acknowledgements

I acknowledge the contribution of my teachers Prof. T.K. Oommen, Prof. Nandu Ram, Prof. Anand Kumar, who shaped my critical understanding about institutions like caste and democracy. I am happy that my journey with them is still on. My special thanks are due to Prof. Maitrayee Chaudhuri who not only agreed to write the foreword of the book but also gave me constructive suggestions to reorganise the arguments discussed in introduction so that the book can cater to both general readers and Sociologists alike.

In the Center for the study of Social Systems, JNU, I immensely benefitted from the discussions with my colleagues specially Prof. Surinder Singh Jodhaka, Prof. Tilput Nongbri, Prof. V. Sujata, Dr. Amit Kr. Sharma Dr. Bimol Akoi Jain, Dr. G. Srinivas, Dr. Arshad Alam, and Dr. DiyaVaid; I thank them all for their valuable academic support.

Outside the Centre but in JNU my arguments were sharpened because of discussions with Prof. P.S. Khilarp Prof. Subodh Malakar, Prof. Govind Prasad, Prof. Shusma Yadav, Dr. Lobiyal, Dr. Y.S. Alone, Dr. Manindra Thakur, Dr. S. Srinivas Rao, Dr. Y. Chinna Rao, Dr. Aqlakh Ahmad, Dr. Ajay Kumar, Dr. Madho Govind, Dr. Ram Chandra, Dr. Pradeep Shinde, Dr. Milind Awad, Ms. Jyoti Athwwal and Dr. Prachin; I sincerely thank them for their contributions.

I express my gratitude to Prof. Shyam Lal, Pro. R.K. Kale, Prof. G. G. Wankhede, Prof. P.G. Jogdand, Prof. A. Ramaiah, Prof. S.L. Gaikawad, Prof. Kameshwar Chaudhry, Dr. Harish Wankhede, Dr. Raj Kumar (Eng. Lit), Dr. Raj Kumar (Pol. Sc.), Dr. Narendra Kumar, Dr. Shantanu Das, Dr. Sukumar, Dr. Vijay Pal, Dr. Pravesh Kumar, and many others who gave their valuable suggestions during the evolution of the book.

I thank my students Dr. Suresh Babau, Dr. Shailesh Darokar, Dr. Naresh Kumar, Dr. Sailendra Kumar, Mr. Sanjay Ingole, Mr. Pradeep

Kumar (KNIT), Mr. Vinod Arya, Mr. Rakesh Patel, Mr. Babu Waghmare, Mr. Anil Kumar, Mr. Swapnil Moon, Mr. Amol Madame, Mr. Kshirod, Ms. Reena Gautam, Ms. Nilima Nagrale, Ms. Shipra Singh, Ms, Shaeen Praveen, Ms. Mamta Bairwa, Ms. Prachi Patil, Mr. Anurag Bhushan, Ms. Navita, Mr. Shashwat; and many other students, who have directly and indirectly been part of discussions, by way of king Perplexing question or being patient listeners to my ideas, in the completion of this book.

My thanks are also due to my office staff (CSSS, JNU) for their assistance in the completion of the book. I take this opportunity to thank Gyan Publishing House for accepting the manuscript for publication.

My wife Jaya has always been a patient and serious listener giving me her critical comments which have been helpful in taking my arguments forward, I thank her for valuable contribution. I remember my daughter Abhivyakti and son Pratham for showering their love and affection during this exhausting journey and never complained about my neglect.

October 14, 2013

Vivek Kumar
CSSS/SSS,
JNU, New Delhi.

Introduction

This book makes two claims about caste and democracy in India. The first claim is that social scientists have only partially understood the realities entrenched in the institution of *Jati* (caste). Second, due to lack of understanding about *Jati* (caste), they have propagated a distorted picture of the relationship between caste and democracy. Hence, this book is about the apparent paradoxical relationship between democracy and caste. One is seen as modern, while the other is seen as traditional; one as equal, the other as hierarchical. These dichotomies are only partially true as this book would show. The widespread view, evident in public discourse, is that caste is pernicious for democracy. On the contrast developments in India since independence would show not just the close relationship between caste and democracy but also the double-edged nature of this relationship. At the same time, however, democracy has a liberating potential.

This suggests that society, to start with, is casteless and democracy ideally also operates on the assumption that all individuals are equal and marked. However to reiterate B.R. Ambedkar's observation that while the Constitution ensures one man one vote, one vote, one value, the unequal social and economic structure of Indian society would not make this an automatic possibility in the truest sense of the term (Ambedkar 1994: 1216). Sociologically this implies that democracy in India, and elsewhere, never emerged in an undifferentiated society. Race in western societies is an illustrative example (Myrdal 1944, Muse 1970). Gender is the other contested category. In the Indian context caste defined the structure for most parts, making some sections unequally poised *vis-a-vis* the modern instruments of democracy. My central argument therefore is to question the dichotomy posed between caste mobilisation and democracy as false. This, I argue, can be traced to basic social science flaws in understanding caste and the limits of perception by dominant sections. My critique therefore draws from both theoretical understandings as well as historical developments on ground.

It is my contention that four main currents can be found in the discourse on *Jati* (caste) system in India. First, partial understanding of the realities embedded in the institution of *Jati* (caste); second, erroneous assumption of characteristics of *jati* as its intrinsic characteristics; third, blackout of intrinsic characteristics of *Jati* (caste) and fourth, State as the creator of *Jati* (caste) ideology and identity as it is seen today. Through these currents, in turn the Savarna *jati* social scientists have produced a narrow structural-functional approach (that there is inter-dependence and inter-connectedness between each *jatis*) to understand *jati* (caste) system. However, the empirical data suggests that these very social scientists hold caste as divisive, degenerate and antithetical to the development of democracy.

On the other hand a totally opposite view, based on experiential reality of the *Jatis* (castes) placed at the lowest ebb of the social structure, always found Jati (caste) as an institution, which is exclusionary, discriminatory, and devoid of social justice. But these very strata found *Jati* (caste) system very conducive to democracy. As we will see in the following pages, they have interacted with democracy to assert their legitimate constitutional rights against hierarchy, exclusion, discrimination, etc. It is through democracy that they have been continuously demanded equality and social justice. Further, the empirical data reveals that the aforesaid strata have successfully changed the mobilisation pattern in the democratic politics of India. A number of articles in the book will validate that ex-untouchable *jatis* have established their own independent political organisations which was not possible earlier. Today, they mobilise not only people from their own jati but also mobilise the *Shudra Jatis* (OBCs) and *Savarna Jatis* (Brahmins, Kshatriya and Vaishyas). I have called this mobilisation *Arohi* mobilisation. *Arohi* is a Hindi term which means 'in ascending order'. Mobilisation from below hence, assumes significance because it has never been recorded earlier in the functioning of Indian politics. Even Rudolph and Rudolph (1987) while studying caste mobilisation in Indian politics did not notice such a phenomenon or this phenomenon did not exist at that time (See Part II, Chapter 7-11).

Therefore, we can observe that two opposite views on the relationship between Jati (caste) and democracy come to fore. These are one, Jati (caste) as functional for society but antithetical to Indian democracy and second, Jati (caste) as dysfunctional to the ex-untouchable Jatis but functional for Indian democracy. So, the moot question is that if there are two views regarding caste and its relationship with democracy, then why is it that one view gets privileged over the other? As we can see there is a plethora of writings justifying caste as functional for society, but dysfunctional for the onward march of democracy, but we do not find any study on the other view. Hence, it is pertinent to understand and analyse how and why the first view gets privileged over the other. Why have social scientists failed to understand and identify an effective methodology to understand the nature of social exclusion suffered by ex-untouchable Jatis (See Part I, Chapter 4)? In this context, this book would help us to understand the causes of one view being privileged over the other. One answer can be found in Chapter 1, where the author tries to grasp that apart from partial understanding of caste, this privileging is also a result of the composition of the Social Scientists in the academia.

Use of *Jati* (Caste) in Indian Democracy

Another related issue discussed in the book is use of *jati* in Indian democratic politics. Who were the main groups who used caste in democracy? Two main groups involved in the process can be identified. These are the 'beneficiaries' of the jati system and the 'victims' of the system. The field view of Jatis, from a perspective from below, divides the whole Indian society (Hindu society, to be precise) into two broad categories – the beneficiaries of the *Jati Vyavastha* (caste system) and the victims of the system (Ram 1982). Beneficiaries of the system included the *Savarna Jatis* – the *Brahmans, Kshatriyas* and *Vaishyas* who have benefited from the ritual and religious Hindu social order. The victims of the system included the ex-untouchable Jatis and the Shudra Jatis (OBCs in modern parlance) who were excluded from any privileges but given every duty to serve the *Savarna Jatis*. Both the 'beneficiaries' and the 'victims' of the *Jati Vyavastha* have, over the years, especially after the advent of Parliamentary democracy, negotiated with the Jati system in their own ways.

Why was caste used by these two groups in modern democracy in India? The higher social strata and established power were the bases of usage of caste in Indian democracy by the so-called *Savarna jatis*. Hence, they came down to so-called *Ashprishya* (ex-untouchable) and *Shudra jatis* to mobilise them, by using their ritual status and offering allurement (Rudolph and Rudolph 1987). On the other hand, the lower echelons, especially the *Ashprishya jatis*, used their humiliation, exploitation, exclusion, deprivation, discrimination, and their pain and agony, to mobilise the similar *jatis*. Apart from this, what were the main reasons of using caste in politics by the *Savarna* and *Ashprishya jatis*? First and foremost reason for use of caste in democratic politics by the 'beneficiary *Jatis*' was lack of numerical strength. After the advent of democracy, the *Savarna jatis* needed numerical strength to maintain their ritual power through secular politics. They did not have numbers and, used caste to garner support of the lower strata. This was a mechanical relationship as many of the political parties led and dominated by so-called *Savarna Jatis* maintained a relationship with the *Ashprishya and Shudra jatis* on the same basis. The second reason for using caste in democratic politics by beneficiaries of *jati* system was to maintain their domination and hegemony. Contrarily, the victims of the jati system used *jatis* to dismantle the domination and hegemony of the Savarna jatis.

It will not be an exaggeration to argue that as longas only the beneficiaries of the *Jati Vyavastha* kept on using jati for mobilising people in the modern politics, there were noostensible problems in the society. However, as soon as the victims of the *Jati Vyavastha* started using jati for mobilising the exploited, excluded, discriminated and humiliated people, the whole society, including Savarna Social Scientists, literate gentry, politicians, laymen and now-a-days, media started launching scathing criticism of this type of mobilisation. Without understanding the differences in the processes of mobilisation they have termed it process of 'Casteism'; in Hindi it is called as '*Jativad*'. However, if we examine this process of mobilisation bycombining both the *Ashprishya* and *Shudra Jatis* and also the ex-untouchable castes converted to Sikhism, Islam, and Buddhism we would call it as caste assertion (*Jati Drahata*). Let us elaborate a little bit on this issue of Casteism and Caste Assertion to make sense of these processes to understand the relationship between caste and democracy.

***Jativad* (Casteism) vs. *Jati Drahata* (Caste Assertion)**

It is evident from mere observation of the composition of modern institutions of governance that the so-called Savarna Jatis have monopolised them. So, they had enjoyed monopoly on the socio-economic and political institutions because of their ritual status in the Jati hierarchy with religious legitimacy. However, after modernisation and emergence of secular institutions like Bureaucracy, Army, judiciary, education, etc., they also started dominating and virtually monopolised each of the modern institutions. For instance, take polity – the upper castes not only dominate the structures of the political parties led and dominated by the upper castes, but when those political parties come to power – whether in States or at the Centre, they dominate the government as well (Zoya Hasan 1998 and Jafferlot 2003). How does it happen? It is not that they were extraordinarily gifted and suited for managing these institutions. It happened because of life-chances, social networks which the Savarna *Jati* individuals enjoyed. It was because of social and cultural capital, to use Bourdieu's language. Further, their lineage, pedigree and of course their association with English education also helped them to create this monopoly. The primordial identities played a dominant role in getting someone access to the Government, Public Sector or any other secular Jobs. I call this whole process of monopolisation of the modern secular institutions on the basis of social and cultural capital as 'Casteism', which has negative connotation. It is so because discrimination and exclusion is the essence of this process. The so-called Savarna Jatis not only monopolised these aforesaid institutions at the cost of other jati representation but they also monopolised them through discrimination against the ex-untouchable and Shudra Jatis also. The monopolisation is done so that they should not get access to these institutions. The lakhs of pending cases of discrimination of Scheduled Caste employees in Scheduled Caste Commission proves the point.

If the beneficiaries of the caste system practice casteism for monopolising the resources, rights and privileges in the modern institutions in contemporary India, the victims of the caste system-the Scheduled Castes (Dalits), Scheduled Tribes (*Adivasis*), Other Backward Castes (*Pichri Jati*) and converted minorities (*Dharmantarit Alpsankhayaks*) are retorting to 'caste-assertion' in contemporary period. Assertion analytically is a neutral term. A group wants to assert for its legitimate rights enshrined in the Constitution. They are not usurping the rights of the others. They do not want to monopolise the rights and privileges as the so called upper castes do in spite of the fact that they were realistically denied ever right and privileges. The society in accordance with sacred texts did not accord to them any rights whatsoever. Hence, it was all the more necessary for the victims of the system to assert for their rights. But the irony is that when the *Dalits/ Adivasis/Pichri Jatis*, etc. assert for their rights they are ridiculed and criticised that they are spreading the poison of casteism in the society.

Not only that but also because of political, bureaucratic, and reservations in education they are being termed as beneficiaries of the system – caste system. The so called upper castes have never tried to understand that reservation is only a tool for ensuring the representation of those groups who were denied representation in the institutions of governance for millennia. Reservation in polity, bureaucracy and education is not a poverty alleviation programme. In a way it is a compensation for the wrongs combined by the whole society for millennia. So when Dalits and other marginalised groups mobilise themselves on the basis of an ideology of a political party how can it be called as casteism? This is just another way to dismantle the existing caste monopolies of so called upper castes in the different institutions of governance. Hence, when Dalits and OBCs mobilise their brethren it cannot be termed as casteism. There is fundamental difference between the two–one is associated directly with the monopoly of the minority in the aforesaid institutions; the other is associated with sharing of the democratic institutions by the majority of deprived population leading to their own representation.

Relationship between *Jati* (Caste) and State Today

Laymen and intellectuals alike argue that State is perpetuating Jati. State has reified caste and sustained caste divisions between castes because of policies run by it. Politics like identification of caste-like establishment of Scheduled Castes (SC) list, Other Backward Castes (OBCs) category, and general Caste categories is the handiwork of State. These categories are visible at least in the application forms for different types of competitive exams and government employments. This is done to ensure quotas of jobs under Articles 16(4) and 335 of Indian Constitution for SCs and OBCs. We have also reservations for SCs and OBCs in educational institutions and professional institutes – engineering, medical, management etc. Apart from this SCs also enjoy reservations in politics– from local bodies (Art. 244D and 244T), State Assemblies (Art. 330) and the Parliament (Lok Sabha) (Art. 332). Caste has manifested also when different Commissions were appointed to identify Other Backward Castes; Kaka Kalelkar Commission and Mandal Commission which were appointed after independence to identify these castes played important role in it.

To answer whether Jatis were created and sustained by State or not we will have to answer the question whether Castes (*Jatis*) came first or state policies like reservation. Obviously, caste existed much before reservation policy came into existence. Secondly, Caste does not exist only with the victims of the Social System (which are getting some compensatory policies) but it exists among those which have been the beneficiaries (those who have been enjoying privileges for thousands of year) of the system-the so-called twice born *Varnas*, as discussed earlier. So it becomes clear that State has only attempted to identify the already existing groups of people to provide them some compensatory facilities; it has not invented them afresh. Further, in this context, another point should be kept in mind that there have always existed at least four *Varnas* since time immemorial (see Chapter I). As time went by, a fifth Varna *panchama* was added. A rough estimate tells us that there are more than six thousand castes. For instance the *Mandal* Commission has identified 3743 castes. Moreover, there are 1031 Scheduled Castes. Above all there are thousands of castes and sub-castes within the three twice-born castes – Brahmins, *Kshatriyas* and *Vaishyas*. However, what State has done is that, first of all it has dismantled the ritual Varna classification in its functioning which was hierarchical and exclusionary. Now these, twice-born hierarchically arranged *Varnas–Brahmans*, *Kshatriyas* and *Vaishyas* have been reduced to a horizontal secular category – called as 'general category'. In a way state has principally annihilated the ritual Varna category in public life.

Another ritual category which existed in the society was of *Panchamas* (the fifth Varna) or "untouchables", *Asprishyas*, *Antyaj* (last born), *Antvsin* (last to reside) *Antvarna* or Outcastes. The state has also given them a very secular identity – Scheduled Castes or SCs. This is the Constitutional identity for some One thousand and thirty one Castes. The ex-untouchable and general category castes alike use this nomenclature for addressing the ex-untouchables now. This has at least two very positive impacts, one, it has obliterated the stigmatised primordial caste identities in public usage at least in urban areas and among educated middle class. Secondly, it has created a sort of unified category of number of castes – i.e., Scheduled Castes giving them new identity and solidarity. The Scheduled Castes certificates do mention their names, but the names are used by the state to identify the historicity and cumulative nature of exclusion suffered by that caste so that they can avail certificates. Hence, we can safely argue that State has in reality dismantled individualised caste identities of ex-untouchables of India and given them a secular and collective nomenclature.

The next identity which state has created through their Commissions is 'Other Backward Castes' (OBC). We all know that most of the members of this category were known as *Shudras*; the fourth category in the Varna hierarchy. Now according to Mandal Commission 3743 castes have been lumped together and declared as 'OBC', i.e., educationally and economically backward castes. The criteria to identify their backwardness have been economic and educational. Above all another economic rider was placed for their identification, i.e., creamy layer. Hence by drawing a list, what state has done is that it has lumped three thousand seven hundred and forty three castes and thereby it has obliterated the internal differentiation for providing them state facilities. Again as in the cases of SCs the State has succeeded in obliterating the stigmatised *Shudra* identity for so many castes and given them the secular identity of OBC.

In a way then we may conclude that Indian state has successfully negotiated with the contemptuous, stigmatised and ritually privileging caste and Varna identities. Instead it has propagated secular identities of groups like general category, OBCs and SCs. However, the civil society has not given up its fixation with the ritual social identities. The matrimonial columns and matrimonial websites are testimonies to the aforesaid fact. Hence we have to affirm once and for all that State never created Caste System in Indian society. However, the members who constitute state and implement the policies of the state do practice caste prejudices. Moreover members of civil society still practice casteism and members constituting State are recruited from their only. Hence they bring their social practices in the secular realm as well, perpetuating Caste and Caste prejudices in public life.

Jati (Caste) and Personality Cult: The case of Indian Polity and Civil Society

The relationship between *jati* and democracy has strengthened the phenomenon of 'Personality Cult' in Indian society. Personality cult is prevalent although in most of the spheres of Indian society but it is rampant in the functioning of Indian democratic politics. Moreover it has now started getting extended to civil society organisations also as the book will make it clear. The relationship between *Jati* and Politics producing 'Personality Cult' has benefitted the *Savarna Jatis* the most. However, it has not been analysed by any social scientists till date. Therefore, we need a brief discussion here to analyse the relationship between *jati* and democracy. The slogans at the time of the *Savarna Jati* leader's ascendance to a position, in their own political party, at the time of occupying some office in the government or at the time of their death will further demonstrate the claim of the book. In the same vein, to prove the point, we can take examples from practical political field to show how the *Savarna Jati* politicians have dominated the Indian politics after independence. Whether in government or in opposition it is they who have dominated the democratic politics. Pandit Jawaharlal Nehru, Pandit Govind Ballabh Pant, C. Rajagopalachari Achyra Kriplani, Atal Bihari Vajpayee, Jai Prakash Narayan, Venkat Raman, etc., to name just a few, can be called as the first generation leaders just after independence who hailed form Savarna Jatis and dominated the Indian Politics.

The Brahman essence of the ruling elite can be easily observed when Prime Minister Jawaharlal Nehru on 14th August 1947 sat a *yajna* performed by the Brahmins to celebrate the event of a Brahmin becoming first Prime Minister of India and wore the *Raja Dand* given to him by the Brahmins (Ambedkar 1979: 149). In the same vein Anderson has described the ceremony in his own words, "To hallow the solemn occasion, Nehru and his colleagues sat cross-legged around sacred fire in Delhi while ...priests ...chanted hymns and sprinkled holy water over them...Three hours later, on a date and time stipulated by Hindu astrologers, the stroke of mid-night on 14th August 1947, Nehru...assured his broadcast listeners ...their 'tryst with destiny' "(Anderson 2012: 103). It was not surprising that once Pt. Jawaharlal Nehru became the Prime Minister of India most of the offices of Government of India were dominated by Brahmins".

By mere observation one can argue that the domination of Brahmins grew more as the time went by in Indian Politics. Indira Gandhi, Morarji Desai, Uma Shankar Dikshit,Shankar Dayal Sharma (President of Indian National Congress 1972-74), Chandra Shekhar, Parnab Mukherjee, Narain Dutt Tewari, Arjun singh, etc., can be called as the second stage leaders who dominated the Indian politics in early 1970 till the demise of Indira Gandhi. How can one forget the Charisma which she carried after the creation of Bangladesh in 1971-the slogan says it all, 'India is Indira and Indira is India'? In the third epoch of democracy after independence-say after 1984 with the demise of Indira Gandhi were Rajeev Gandhi, Arun Nehru, P.V. Narsimharao, Vishwanath Pratap Singh, Natwar Singh, K.C. Pant, Madhavrao Scindia, Rajesh Pilot; V. C. Shkula, S. C. Shukla, Dig Vijay Singh, to name just a few; in opposition we saw the emergence of BJP with its Savarna *Jati* leadership led by Vajpayee, Murli Manohar Joshi, Yashvant Singh, Yashvant Sinha, Arun

Jately, Shushma Swaraj, Annant Krisha, again to name just a few, came to centre stage of the Indian democracy. In contemporary times Rahul Gandhi and his so-called young brigade- Jyotiraditya Madhavrao Scindia, Jatinn Parsad, Millind Deora, Sachin Pilot, Sandeep Dixit R P N Singh etc., again come from Savarna jati and are likely to dominate in future.

How is it possible, in democracy, that member of numerically less dominant *Jatis* dominate the national politics in such a big numbers? On the other hand members of *Jatis* with high numerical strength are sidelined. Even if a handful leaders, of the numerically dominant *Jatis* like Jagjivan Ram, Buta Singh, Bangaaru Laxman, Kalyan Singh, Uma Bharti, to name just a few, occupy some positions and try to assert their independent position in the Indian politics they are unceremoniously thrown out of their parties. The main difference between the members of numerically less dominant and more dominant *Jatis* is their social status in the established social order. The social status enjoyed by the Jatis in the local area bring them the whole cultural capital of their *Jatis*- the networks, jati icons, language, the festivals, etc., which gives them Charisma and translate it into personality cult. The local population starts revolving their personality as they can sit with them, eat with them, drink from their utensils, and enter their courtyards. The whole interactional process helps them to mobilise people. On the other hand there is no cultural capital for the *jatis* located at the lower echelons of the caste hierarchy. For them it is *Jati* stigma. Therefore nobody wants to associate themselves with them. Further there are very few people who would like to annoy the local *Savarna Jati* politicians. Sometime it is because of fear and sometime it is uncertainty of lower strata candidates' chances to win an election.

Further, the *Savarna Jati* individuals with less numerical strength use their pedigree, historicity, life chances and networks to get access to different administrative functionaries and the political organisations. Things become very easy for them. This further enhances their status. The local people throng to them to get their petty and day to day works done, further giving them clout. The ritual status of the less numerically dominant *Savarna Jati* mixed with secular status gets further lift when their members exploit their *Jati* identity by extending it to print and visual media. The media persons oblige because they find *Jati* affinity with the politicians. This role of Indian media in magnifying the impact of a political act of *Savarna Jati* leaders is enormous. Small little deeds of the Savarna *Jati* political leader, are, more often than not, blown out of proportion. The example of Bhartiya Janata Party's 'Shining India Campaign' in 2004 General election and Aam Aadmi Party's campaign in 2013 elections amply prove the point that how media blows things out of proportion. Contrary to this, the numerically dominant *Jatis* suffering from stigma because of ritual status do not have any pedigree, neither any network nor secular power; most of them may be first time politicians. They, individually neither can influence local administration, functionaries of the party nor the media. Their most significant political achievements are blacked out or given a negative spin (Kumar 2009). The sum total of these processes is that the members of numerically dominant castes cannot cultivate 'personality cult' which cuts across their own *Jati* and is accepted even by members of *Savarna Jatis*.

'Personality Cult' is also produced in the relationship between *Jati* and Civil Society Organisation (Non- Governmental Organisation {NGO}) in contemporary India. In this context it is significant to note that 'Civil Society in India is seen by most theorists as a fluid association of social groupings which are based on caste and kinship linkages or on religious mobilisation' (Chndhoke 1995).'Tenth Five Year Plan 2002-2007 (Chapter 6)' include: people's participation, decentralisation, civil society involvement, using information and technology, empowerment of the marginalised etc. to list a few as it main goals. In this light we can observe that the number of CSOs, today, is going more and more. However, the empirical data suggest (Annual Report 2003-2004 and 2008-2009, Ministry of Social Justice and Empowerment, Government of India) that most of the NGOs registered with government of India for uplifting the Dalits are all dominated by the *Savarna Jati* members. The same is true for the International NGOs. The main issue involved here is the conditions for establishing a NGO laid down by the government of the day. The statuary conditions for establishing an NGO is heavily tilted towards the elite of the society. For stance to get financial help from the government a NGO should be functioning for at least three years. It should have proper papers of its audit by Charted Accountant, filing of Income Tax Returns etc., then the proposals for working will be forwarded by the District Magistrate office. The member running Dalit NGOs at the grassroots have revealed rampant discrimination against them while the *Savarna Jati* proposals are dealt favourably. In this manner the *Savarna Jati* members who run the NGOs at the grassroots acquire Charisma and develop networks which cut across the local, regional, national and international forums. It is no coincidence that most of the foreign funded NGOs are domintted by the *Savarna*

Jati members and it is they who have got *Magsaysay* awards producing 'Personality Cult'. Few of these very personalities have joined political parties and few have them launched their own.

Relationship between Caste and Corruption in Democracy

Is there any relationship between caste and corruption in Democracy? It is important to ask this question because most of the rules, informal or formal, have been formulated by the so-called *Savarna Jatis*. Moreover, they dominate the formal and informal institutions of law and governance. As has been told earlier that it is they who dominate-Polity, Judiciary, Bureaucracy, Industry, University, Civil Society, and Media Industry. Yet, in analysing the nature and causes of corruption we never take cognizance of caste of the lawbreakers. However, when it comes to the *jatis* placed lower in the *jati* hierarchy there is labelling and stereotyping that they are corrupt. That is what one social scientist, without any empirical data dubbed the 90 per cent of the Indian population-the SCs, STs, and OBCs as the most corrupt. Astonishing part of the debate was instead of analysing the statement on methodological and epistemological basis most of the *Savarna* Social Scientists and few Dalits as well defended the social scientists in the name of freedom of speech and expression. But the fact remains that nobody could remove the existing stigma and stereotyping of the *jatis* placed lower in the jati hierarchy. It is in this biased state of affairs the book (Chapter 23) analyses the structural location of corruption in Indian society. Can we sociologically define Corruption? No doubt there exists a narrow definition of corruption propounded by the law of the land, that is, misuse of public office for personal gain. But this definition does not reveal much and does not take us too far in finding the solution of eradication of corruption from the society. That is why we have to ask is corruption inbuilt mechanism in the informal and formal structures of society or it emerges with the time? Secondly, we have to also ask whether the levels of corruption increase as the development also increases. Thirdly, we have to also analyse whether there are certain institutions in the society which socialise the members of the society in corrupt activities? EASEREWRE

Once understand the broader definition of Corruption we can understand the structures of the corruption also. Second, we will come to know how the roles and statuses distributed in the society produce corruption. It is here *Jati* as the core structure of the Indian society unknowingly socialises its members in certain practices which can easily be termed as corrupt. However, when the Indian social scientists or administrators try to fight with corruption they never consider the nature of social structure, based on *Jatis*, as the real basis of corruption. For instance, they never take cognizance of the fact that certain *Jatis* have survived on the labour of other *Jatis*. They are socialised to look down upon the work done by hand and only survive on the labour of mind. This in turn has produced the institution of bonded labour. Similarly, origin of institution of dowry, a corrupt practice, can be traced back to *jati*. The search of a spouse from the same *Jati* restricts the supply and in turn the demand of dowry goes up. We can observe that many fathers and daughters have committed suicide because of their incapacity to pay the dowry demanded by the groom's side. Further, we have also cases of bride beating and bride burning because of dowry. One can add a long list of such processes which can be kept in the category of crime. But their origin is in caste.

Caste Conceptualisation of Communalism

Communalism, in India, has been analysed through perspective of religion. However, it can be analysed through perspective of *Jati* also. Social scientists have argued that Communalism does not emerge as a natural process it is artificially created because of competitive politics (Brass 2003). In general parlance we can argue that 'communalism' can be defined as a process through which a historically dominant group invents an 'Other'. This 'othering' may be done at any pretext-religious, economic, social etc. In this context therefore one can imagine who constructs an 'other' in Indian society. It is obvious the deprived and excluded *Jatis* will not construct the 'idea' of the other. It is also a fact that the Rashtriya Swayam Sevak Sangh (RSSS) differentiates between population who have both father and holy land in India and those who have father land in India and holy land outside India. In this background it also becomes clear that who are the functionaries of RSSS who have framed this communal ideology. Off Course the so-called *Savarna Jatis* as they can only be the head of the organisation. Therefore, it becomes obvious that the so-called *Savarna Jatis* are only capable of constructing the 'other' against whom battle can pitched.

But the irony is that although, the *Savarna Jatis* can only formulate the ideology to produce an 'Other' but they do not have numerical strength to wage a battle against them. Therefore, they need the *Jatis* located lower in the *Jati* hierarchy. But why do these join hands with the *Savarna Jati*? The answer is because of want of acceptance. As the lower Jatis have been excluded from every sphere of life they get an opportunity to prove the point that they are part and parcel of the Hindu Social Order. Second, these Jatis live in the vicinity of the minorities and more often than not they have similar occupational status also. That is why we see that the epicentre of Communal violence is always aforesaid place in the city. However, as the communal violence is spreading from urban to rural areas the *Jati* relationship is becoming stronger because it is only *Savarna Jatis* may have weapons and courage to attack the minorities. This is not one way process. The so-called Upper-Castes among minorities do the same. Hence, on the above analysis of Communalism we may put this preposition that the explanation of Communalism through caste perspective is must.

II

Having discussed broad contours of the book we would like to discuss here some specific aspects which have direct bearing on the nature of debate carried out in the book. Two specific issues are deliberated here. One is Jati (Caste) and other democracy. We have explained, in this, the way caste still has a very limited influence on people. Based on empirical data we have observed; at least, in rural areas of North India including Bihar and Madhya Pradeshthat people use *Jat*, *Jati*, exact *jati* name or place of residence in the village to identify the individual. Further, we have also tried to analyse how erroneously social scientists have added certain characteristics as intrinsic to *Jati* (Caste) and on the other hand they have blacked out certain other which they should have defined as intrinsic to *Jati* (caste). Last but not the least based on methodology and epistemology an analysis has been done here to understand the issue of relationship between *Jati* (Caste) and British State. In sum the idea behind doing this exercise is to highlight the fact how discourse on caste (*jati*) has restricted our vision to understand the realities embedded in this institution. Let us analyse *Jati* first.

Recognising Individual's Identity: *Jati* or Caste

At the outset the term 'Caste' came to India with the Portuguese only in 15th Century. It has/had particular connotation and was developed by the Europeans to make sense of the native population for their own-self (Dumont 1999). However, when Caste is literally translated it is equated with *'Jat'* or *'Jati'* in Hindi. But it is an empirical reality that the institution of *'Jati'* when translated into English as Caste does not provide us the exact nature and total repertoire of functions its members perform in the society. For instance *Jati 'Nai'* or *'Naou'* translated into

English would mean 'Barber'. However, the English term cannot capture the number of functions a *Nai* or *Naou* performs – viz. besides cutting hairs and nails; he acts as messenger, as match-maker and also solemnises marriages in number of castes. In effect the term Barber gives us one caste one occupation equation. Contrary to this most of the Castes do not survive only on one occupation. Apart from their certain assigned occupations by Hindu social Order based on their birth most of them work as agricultural labourers or have been working on their own land. If their settlement is nearer to a city then many of them go to work as cycle-rickshaw puller or as mason. For doing the same they may go to city early in the morning and get back home by evening leading to circulation of population.

Further, individuals in the rural areas still do not use the term caste and may not understand the meaning of the term 'caste'. My own field work in northern part of India suggests that most of them were not familiar with the term caste and instead use the term *Jat* or *Jati*. But even the term *'Jat'* or *'Jati'* is used by them in a generic sense. It is used in terms of 'Adam Jat'-meaning Human Species. The term *Jat* is also used in denoting gender – *'Mard Jat'* or *'Aurat Jat'* (men and women). Of course it is also used to denote the type of specific job/ occupation which people practice. In Hindi there is no term for sub-caste. They refer people only with his *Jati* name. Therefore it becomes clear that in rural areas people do not use the term caste but use their own *jati* identity to refer to each other. Apart from using particular *jati* names villagers interact with each other or identify individuals on other bases also. As far as the members of the same village are concerned the villagers are aware of each other's identity. If they have any confusion, in order to ascertain the identity of the individual they would ask which part of the village he or she lives.

The field view of Indian villages will prove the point that, even today; most of the villages have segregated settlements based on names of *Jatis*/Varna. For instance, the geographical space, in the village, where Chamars live will be known as Chamrauti, Chamartolia, Chamkat, etc. Similarly, the part of village where Brahmins and Thakurs (Kshtriyas) live is termed as Bamnauti and Thakuraiah respectively. In the same vein Dhobi, Pasi, and Ahir localities are called as Dhubiana, Pasiana, and Ahirana respectively. But I have no hesitation in saying that no sociologist has written or analysed the identities of the localities where different jatis live. Hence, as soon as a villager comes to know the residence of a person he comes to know his jati identity. However, the way caste, with its characteristics has defined been defined, does not capture the identities of individuals through their residential patterns.

Apart from knowing the identity of persons through their residence in the village there is another way to know the *jati* of strangers. A Savarn jati person can ask the unknown visitor, 'Kaun Manai ho!, Or Kaun Log ho!, Or Kaun Biradar ho!' (Literally translated it would mean which people you are or which community you belong or latently which *jati* you belong). If some people want to differentiate themselves with others they would argue that this man is not 'Lotiya Shareek' (meaning one cannot take water from their utensils). Further in some areas the so-called lower castes are also addressed as Chot Jati or Naan Jati (meaning lower jati or people without *jati*). There are internal dereferences within Jatis which are widely prevalent in the oral history of the geographical a locality in which that *Jati* exists. For instance in western Uttar Pradesh-among Kanyakubji or Kanujia Brahmins there is a saying – Nau Kanujia Terah Chulhe (nine Kanujiua Brahmins need thirteen hearths). In the same vein in eastern UP and in parts of Bihar among the Mushars Jati there is a saying, *'Sab Ghar Khaun Dhob Ghar Na Khaun'* (I will eat at every one's house except Dhobi's {Washer man Community}). This further highlights the internal differentiation within the so-called higher and lower Jatis. Added to these, some *Jatis* are also associated with stigma while for some others there is pride and Charisma. This contempt and stigma for some *Jatis;* pride and charisma for others is perceived as based on deeds performed in past incarnation (Karma and Dharma).

Caste: Division of Labour or Division of Labourers?

In addition to the narrow perspective to understand the reality existing behind the institution of Caste the sociologists have propounded an erroneous understanding of caste also. They have been arguing that the 'Division of Labour' is intrinsic characteristic of caste system. Further, Jajmani system was highlighted as part of caste system to substantiate the point that caste system stands on division of labour. In doing so, sociologists do not reveal that caste is not a system of 'division of labour' but 'division of labourers'. This fact can be proved by number of interrelated and interconnected processes associated with the division of Labour. One, any system of division of labour is an open system facilitating upward and downward mobility of the members belonging to that system. But caste system is a rigid system. Whoever is born into a caste cannot change his/her occupation and thereby status (see chapter II in this book). Secondly, in a system of division of labour, individuals enjoy the choice of occupation and profession. However, the caste system does not allow such freedom and hence mobility. Thirdly, division of labour is essentially based on 'individual' – a person has capacity and choice to choose an occupation. But, it is a fact that, Caste is based on collective identity. There is no choice of an individual. The capacity of an individual to discharge the duty of caste does not matter at all. It is just the accident of his birth that pushes him to undertake take jati occupation. Fourthly, same types of occupations exist world over. But nowhere other than in India occupations have produced such elaborate caste system (see chapter II). Last but not the least, it has been observed in the society that even if a group of individual have left their hereditary occupation or they have not performed it for generation even then caste stigma remains attached with them. Hence, one is forced to argue that the way contemporary sociologists define caste and the way they have done in the past is erroneous.

Caste and its Blacked out Characteristics

I have raised only one point about the misrepresentation of the characteristics of caste. However, there are number of other characteristics which the Sociologists have not been able to highlight and blacked out (see Chapter I). Both misrepresentation of some characteristics of caste and blackout of certain others go hand in hand. One of the most important blacked out characteristics of caste is its exploitative nature. No sociologist tells explicitly that basic nature of caste is exclusionary, exploitative, and discriminatory and lacks democracy and social justice. Sociologists have failed to highlight how caste pervades the modern institutions like – polity, bureaucracy, judiciary, university, industry, communication industry and even civil society to name just a few modern institutions. The composition of each of the aforesaid modern institutions, in terms of human resources, will prove the point that only certain castes have monopolised them, and in turn others have been excluded. The case is so glaring that 85 per cent of the Indian population has only 10 to 15 per cent representation. According to a rough estimate SC/ST/OBC and religious minorities are 85 per cent of the Indian population but their representation in these aforesaid institutions is only 15 per cent. Contrary wise, those castes which constitute only 15 per cent of India's total population (Brahmins,

Kshatriyas, and Vaishya) dominate most of the aforesaid institutions. How has it happened? No sociologist has revealed that caste as a system creates jealousy, hatred and animosity between castes. These further, results in prejudice, especially against those castes which are considered as ritually impure and are placed lower in caste hierarchy. This prejudice leads to exclusion and results in discrimination and atrocities, etc. In this manner, we can observe how such an important characteristic – caste is exploitative, exclusionary, discriminatory, and devoid of social justice has escaped the imagination of the social scientists or sociologists in particular in India.

Is Caste a Colonial Construct?

Along with the narrow framework to understand the existing reality behind the institution of caste, hiding many more characteristics of castes, and erroneously adding some other characteristics; few social scientists argue that 'caste as we see it today' did not exist before colonial period. This perspective further restricts the historicity of caste institution and there nature of exclusion and exploitation in different epochs. Therefore it is pertinent to deconstruct this established view of Dirks that, "...Caste (as we know it today) is modern phenomenon, that it is, specifically, the product of an historical encounter between India and Western colonial rule" (Dirks 2004). By this he did not "...imply that it was simply invented by the too clever British" *(ibid)*. However he argues that, "... I am suggesting that it was under the British" "Caste" became a single term capable of expressing, organising, and above all "Systematising" India's diverse forms of social identity, community and organisation" (Dirks 2004: 5). How was this achieved? In this regard Dirk observes that, "This was achieved through an identifiable (if contested) ideological cannon as the result of a ... colonial modernity during two hundred years of British domination. In short, colonisation made caste what it is today" (ibid: 5). In the same vein he emphasises that, "under Colonialism, Caste was thus made out to be more – far more pervasive, far more totalising and far more uniform ... at the same time ... it was defined a fundamentally religious order" (Dirks 2002: 13). To prove his point Dirks candidly points that he will follow the following Methodology and epistemology to trace the carrier of caste. In his own words, "In the pages that follow I will trace the carrier of caste from the medieval Kingdoms of southern India to the textual traces of early colonial archives; from the Commentaries of an eighteenth century Jesuit missionary to the enumerative obsessions of the late nineteenth century Census; from the ethnographic writings of Colonial administrators and missionaries to those of twentieth century Indian scholar" (Dirk 2002: 6).

The aforesaid premise for tracing the career of caste raises a few methodological and epistemological issues. As far as methodological issue is concerned it can be argued that the premise limits the nature and scope of the understanding of caste without logically forwarding specific justification–why will the author trace the career of caste only from the medieval Kingdoms of South India. In fact the author has not specified where his medieval period begins and where it ends. Secondly, he again adopted a very narrow approach as far as epistemology of caste is concerned. In other words the sources of foundation of knowledge about 'caste as we know it today' is modern phenomenon is very-very narrow. To begin with if you restrict the regional history for tracing career of caste only to kingdoms of southern India then what about nature, origin and development of caste in different parts of India. As if other parts–East, West, North and Central Indian regions of India were not having caste or they were casteless? It is important to understand the nature and development of castes in these regions because Dirks has tried to generalise regional reality of caste for whole India although it is a well-known fact that there exist different types of stratification system in different parts of the country. For instance Rudolph and Rudolph (1987) have argued that the stratification system in south is discrete and that in north India is continuous. Vincent A. Smith had also argued that, "No four original castes ever existed at any time or place…in northern india the names Vaisya and Sudra are not used except in books…In the south all Hindus who are not Brahmans fall under domination of Sudra, while the designations Kshatriya and Vaisya are practically unknown" (Smith 1958:62). In the same vein Dirks did not bother to analyse and understand history the oral history and culture which was associated with each caste (*jati*) which had taken long period to develop and had acquired deep roots in the people's vocabulary and psychology.

It is evident from above that with regard to historicity of Caste Dirks has restricted it to medieval ages; happily leaving the ancient period of Indian Society. The significance of tracing the carrier of caste since ancient period is that in this ancient India in all pervasive caste milieu that Buddha launched the movement of the 'abolition of castes to emancipate four hundred million men' *(ibid)*. In the same vein Bougle quoted Max Muller to show that, "thieves and bankrupts, brigands, beggars, cripples, slaves, prostitutes and road sweepers through (ing) around the Buddha ... The evil spirit of Caste seems to have vanished" (*ibid:* 68). Further, Bougle tells us that, "... Certainly, Buddhism, more than any other sect, must have appeared formidable to the Brahmans ... Buddhist community worked to undermine the Brahman's clientele" (Bougle 1971: 73). It is in this context we should also know that around 4th Century BC there emerged Maurya dynasty which had extended its boundaries a great deal. Especially under the Kingship of Ashoka the great. After ascending the throne Ashoka made Buddhism as the state religion. According to Ambedkar, because of this, "The Brahmins had not only lost state patronage but they lost their occupation ... The Brahmans therefore lived as the suppressed and depressed classes for nearly 140 years during the Mauryan empire lasted" (Ambedkar 1987: 268). Hence to avenge their plight of the Brahmans, Pushyamitra a military general in the army of Mauryan empire, revolted against the King to capture the power and declared his state religion as Brahminism (Ibid: 268-9). No doubt Ambedkar also accepted advent of Islam as another reason for the downfall of Buddhism. But for us in the light of the discussion Bougle (1971: 76) looks to be more appropriate. According to him "... the caste system, because it has deprived India of the sense of active hope, is itself responsible for the inertia that Buddhism displays in the matter of social reform, however egalitarian its doctrines may be" (Bougle 1971: 76).

Further even in the medieval ages Dirks did not also take note that, had the caste system not been so widespread, exclusionary and so exploitative; people would not have converted to Islam and Sikhism in so many numbers. For instance in Punjab people, especially from the lowest strata embraced Sikhism (Webster 2002) to save themselves from Brahmanical caste tyranny. In his one point agenda Dirks also forgot to discuss number of revolts that took place in the history against the Brahmanical caste system. For instance Bougle (1971: 67) wrote, "... Indeed, Hinduism has seen the rise of its protestants, ... Muslims like Kabir, Low caste prophets like Ramdas the tanner or Dadu the cotton carder – all ... have tried to emancipate the voluntary slaves, reunite the enemy brothers ... But ... in the majority cases, ... the Brahmans once again monopolise the sacred office in Sects that were originally the most anit-Brahmanic" (Bougle 1971: 67). In this regard Bougle further argued, "that in the moral atmosphere generated by the Caste system, ideas which are hostile to the system, in particular egalitarian ideas, cannot survive" (*ibid:* 68). The aforesaid description itself proves the pervasiveness of Caste System.

Another omission in tracing the carrier of caste is the Bhakti Movement specially the movements of saints professing formless god (Nirgun Bhakt). Dirks did not take note of lower caste Bhakti saints who were raising the revolt against the Brahminical caste system which had excluded them from the religious and social realm. The couplets of Ravi Das, a 15th Century saint poet belonging to caste placed out-side the Varna hierarchy reveal how caste identities were important and invoked for assertion during medieval ages in India. Ravi Das belongs to Bhakti tradition which revered formless god. How caste identity is important and why caste should be annihilated has been highlighted in the following couplets of Ravi Das:

Kah Ravi Das Khalas Chamara
Jo Hum Sahari So Meet Humara

[Translated literally the concept says that Ravi Das who is pure Chamar (name of the caste) says that those who live with us they are the real friends]. In fact, the aforesaid couplet reveals the existing nature of caste exclusion and lack of social solidarity in the North Indian society during that period. That is why Ravi Das had to make a plea about the social nature of natives where members can live amicably. In the same vein Ravi Das is depicting the vicious nature of caste and virtually demands annihilation of caste for emancipation of humanity. The couplet goes like this: –

Jat Jat Mein Jat hai Tin Kelan ke Pat
Raidas Na Manukh Ban Sake Jab Tak Jat Na Jat

[Meaning thereby, there is caste within caste within caste like Banana leafs and human being will not be Human unless and until caste is annihilated].

In the same vein we can prove the pervasiveness and belief in caste identity before the colonial period from another couplet by Kabir, another saint of formless god stream from UP. In this couplet Kabir is also not shy of disclosing his caste identity. He says:

Jat Julaha Nam Kabira
Ban Ban Phiru Mai Masi

[Literary translated Kabir argues that his Caste is Julaha (weaver) and his name is Kabir]. Similarly, we can take number of examples of Saint Poets who were very critical of all pervasiveness of caste in the existing social structure which was based on caste system. These saints virtually launched protest and emancipatory movements against the exploitative and exclusionary nature of caste.

Analysing Development of Caste through Census

Let us now turn to 'enumerative obsession of the nineteenth century census' to understand the carrier of caste as traced by Dirks. In this regard Dirks himself has written that, "The first census of India took place over a two-year period between 1871 and 1872, though it ... was subsequently seen as so flawed in its conception and its execution that it has never attained the status of the subsequent decinal censuses ... The most difficult task was the establishment of general classificatory categories for the population around the important issues of religion and caste" (Dirks 2004:200-1), Further, "In the 1881 census ... although it was originally intended that the caste should be classified by their social position, great difficulty was experienced in carrying this out ... The total population was broken into Brahmin, Rajputs, and other caste. The bulk of the members of "other-castes"... were listed in alphabetical order" (Dirks 2004: 208). With regard to 1881 census Ambedkar narrated that, "beyond listing the different castes and creeds and adding up their numbers so as to arrive at the total figure of the population of India, the Census of 1881 did nothing" (Ambedkar 1989: 231). According to Dirk, "The 1891 Census formally abandoned Varna as the Central classificatory structure for enumeration in favour of occupational criteria, ... The 1891 Census broke sixty sub-groups into six broad categories; agricultural and pastoral, professional, commercial, artisan and village menials" (Dirks 2004: 211-12).

Again we can observe that there is no attempt to classify population on the basis of caste in a hierarchical form. It was in the 1901 Census a new principle of classification of population was adopted (Ambedkar 1989: 231). According to Dirks, in 1901 Risley as the Census Commissioner insisted the principle of "social precedence as recognised by native public opinion ... the ... Varna as the basis for enumeration and classification" (Dirk 2004: 220-21). A point should be noted here that this Varna classification emanates from Rigveda Purushsukta tenth Mandal hymn and has existed since ages in public psyche. So what was new being done by the Census now? Dirks explains that Risley's scheme of classification by social precedence was abandoned in the next Census. He argues that although the 1911 Census continued to collect caste information, it was decided ... not to classify Castes by status (Dirks

2004: 237). It is astonishing to note that Dirk abruptly finishes his discussion on "The enumeration of Caste" by Census after 1911. He did not write anything of what happened in 1921 and 1931 Censuses. We know that 1931 was year when the last Caste based Census of India took place.

The details of 1921 and 1931 Census apart, the problem arises from the claims made by Dirks that, "... Risley's ... vision gave the Census ... significant role in the production of modern caste identities in India; it also provided the ideological basis" (Dirks 2004: 26). How can one make such an emphatic claim that such profound Caste identities and ideologies in a civilisation which is 2500 years old can be established in small span of 20 years or even 30 years. Even if we accept that, social identities can be created with the help of State within such a small span of time, then a logical question is that since 1931, 82 years have passed without caste Census, then why Caste identities have not died down? One can argue that caste identities and ideologies are not dying because the State provides compensatory policies to the lower strata of the Caste hierarchy. Granting this position, we need to explain why caste ideologies and identities among the upper castes are not being obliterated – specially the Varna ideology and identity. That means there is much more in the "caste" as it exists today than being just a colonial construct.

III

Having discussed the issues related to Jati (Caste) we will now discuss another specific issue 'Democracy' which has bearing on the themes analysed in this book. At the outset we will give the etymological meaning of the term and then will go on to have an overview of the meaning of democracy as it has grown in the western societies. Apart from philosophical and empirical explanation of democratic development in west we will also analyse development of democratic system of politics in India as well. Here we are specifically interested in tracing the evolution of democratic rights and contest between the ex-untouchable *Jatis* and society in general, British government, the then Indian National Congress and now the political parties in power.

Defining Democracy

The word 'democracy' is formed through a combination of two Greek words – Demos (populace) and Kratos (power), meaning thereby 'people's power'. Political scientists have argued that "In classical Greek polis, democracy was the name of the Constitution in which the poorer people (demos) exercised power in their own interest, as against the rich and aristocratic" (Kenneth Minouge 1985: 186). However, Kenneth argues that Aristotle thought that this type of Constitution is debased. Instead, different other philosophers were of the opinion that, "Only mixed and balanced Constitutions (incorporating monarchies, aristocratic and democratic elements) could be stable" *(ibid)*. We are aware that monopolistic tendencies never liked the idea of democracy because 'Democracy' means sharing, representation and entitlements. We all know that by late 20th Century 'Democracy' became not only a contested concept but also a remarkably ambiguous one. The final definition of democracy is yet to arrive. We are also aware that Aristotle, John Stuart Mills, Tocqueville, Jean Jacques Rousseau, Robert Dahl to name just a few have tried to analyse democracy in their own times and articulated its different characteristics. Aristotle wrote, "that the citizen of our definition [one holding the indeterminate office of judge in a court and member of an assembly] is particularly and especially the citizen of a democracy" (as quoted in Philip Green (ed.) 1993:2).

Apart from Aristotle, John Stuart Mills and Alexis de Tocqueville argued that a democratic citizenship is necessary for both the development of individual character and for the vitality of political life *(ibid)*. Further, Rousseau discussed democracy in the form of "administration". According to Green, Rousseau is concerned with the manner in which laws are made or what we call legislation and concludes that in democracy "Law must be formulated by the entire body of the people, meeting in general assembly" *(ibid)*. He argues that this process of legislation is the essence of classical model of direct democracy. However Green puts a caveat that, "Rousseau's is essentially a vision for small, pre-modern city-states, or even town, which were about to lose ... independence ... to the sway of the modern imperial nation-state" *(ibid)*.

As against the philosophical arguments put forth by the classical thinkers, it was after World War II that according to Green American social scientists defined 'institutions of representative democracy' differently. Robert Michel and Max Weber's works were cited as the basis of 'Empirical Democratic Theory'. According to Green "Empirical democratic theorists have argued that direct democracy is logistically impossible beyond the scale of the small town or commune" (Green 1993:6). In addition another drawback with this institution of representative democracy is that, "In practice ... government by the people" actually consists of governments by elites ... Thus political elites and experts govern; but they do not dominate, in that in the last analysis elections are controlling" (*ibid*:5). Refuting the 'government by the elite' argument Robert Dahl give us hope in democracy. He argues that no doubt inequalities in representation do exist. However, the, "Elites do not Pyramid their power but compete with and check each other, on behalf of the various minorities" (*ibid*: 6). In other words, on the basis of his study in New Haven, USA, Dahl claims that power is dispersed among various interest groups and that this plurality of elites does not form a unified group with common interests. Dahl claims that the evidence shows that local politics is a business of bargaining and compromise with no one group dominating decision making. Of all S.M. Lipset has defined "democracy in a complex society" as ... a political system which supplies regular constitutional opportunities for changing the governing officials, as a social mechanism which permits the largest possible part of the population to influence major decisions by choosing among candidates for political office" (Lipset as quoted in Green: 1993:6).

Democracy in India

However, when we come to India, we have another picture. It is a fact that 'Representative Democracy' as an institution did not evolve from within as it has, in the western society. India did experience democracy since millennia, but a representative democracy was imposed from above in the process of the colonial encounter with the British. According to Oommen (2005: 62), "Both in Greece and India, direct democracy existed for millennia at the grassroots level; in the former in the form of town-meetings and in the latter as gram sabha meetings. But these direct democracies were imperfect. In Greek city states only the patricians were full-fledged participants, the plebeians had access to these meetings but scarcely participated and the slaves were totally excluded from them. Similarly, in Indian villages the full-fledged participants were only twice-born caste-Hindus, the Shudras, broadly co-terminus with today's Other Backward Classes (OBCs) had only limited participation and the Dalits, the ex-untouchables were completely denied participation. At any rate, direct democracy is not a feasible project at higher macro levels. Thus, when one talks of democracy the reference is to representative democracy".

In India according to Kaviraj (1999: 13), "... democracy came through the colonial contact with Britain; the presence of British power delayed the institutions of genuine democracy". Hence the Parliamentary democracy in India had to wait till after independence it created a Constitution based on universal suffrage under the Chairpersonship of Dr. B.R. Ambedkar. Further, according to Kaviraj (1999), "Representative democracy was only the political aspect of the process of creating modernity, of which development planning, secularisation, elimination of caste practices in favour of a common modern citizenship, were the other, equally necessary elements". At a different place Kaviraj argues, "...democracy in ordinary language is meant at least two different things. It means first fundamental constitutional order based on political equality which is meant to be inflexible and constant. But it also refers to a fluid category electoral process and its long-term process" (Kaviraj 2001:289).

Democracy: Issue of Citizen's Rights and Self Representation

In the light of philosophical and empirical forms of democracy we will highlight, in the following pages, how did democracy take shape in hierarchical Indian society with special reference to *jatis* (Castes)? There were Protest/ movements against the rigidity and exclusion of Jatis (castes) since 15th century. However since 1848 with the emergence of Jotiba Phooley in Maharashtra there have been continuous movements against jati (caste) exclusion and discrimination. However, with the intervention of British and introduction of more democratic rights, especially after 1919, socially discriminated *jatis* (castes) on the one hand launched movement against the total domination of so-called Savarna Jatis in the secular institutions of the British government and for their legitimate democratic rights with renewed vigour on the other (Kumar 2010, 2003). With the advent of Ambedkar as the undisputed pan-India leader of ex-untouchables their demands for the democratic rights as citizen became a reality. It was he who for the first time demanded citizens rights for the ex-untouchable *Jatis*. Ambedkar on his part tried to highlight that ex-untouchables were without any social or human rights and without rights how can a democracy function. In this regard he opined that:

> The untouchables are usually regarded as objects of pity but they are ignored in any political scheme on the score that they have no interest to protect. And yet their interests are the greatest. Not that they have large property to protect from confiscation. But they have their very persona confiscated. The socio-religious disabilities have dehumanised the untouchables and their interests at stake are therefore the

> interests of humanity. The interests of property are nothing before such primary interests... The untouchable is not even a citizen. Citizenship is a bundle of rights such as (1) personal liberty, (2) personal security, (3) right to hold private property, (4) equality before law, (5) liberty of conscience, (6) freedom of opinion and speech, (7) right to assembly, (8) right of representation in a country's Government and (9) right to hold office under the State ... These are the interests of the untouchables (Ambedkar 1979: 255-6).

The aforesaid paragraph of Ambedkar proves the point how *jatis* exclude certain groups from the aforesaid rights (see chapter IV) which mainstream sociologists, baring few, did not include as an intrinsic characteristics of Jati system. Further, contrary to Indian National Congress Ambedkar highlighted, that problem of the ex-untouchables was essentially political in nature. In this regard he opined that:

> "it is wrong to say that the problem of the untouchables is a social problem. For, it is quite unlike the problems of dowry, widow remarriage, age of consent, etc., which are illustrations of what are properly called social problems. Essentially, it is a problem of quite a different nature in as much as it is a problem of securing, to a minority, liberty and equality of opportunity at the hands of a hostile majority which believes in the denial of liberty and equal opportunity of the majority and conspires to enforce its policy on the minority. Viewed in this light the problem of the untouchables is fundamentally a political problem" (Ambedkar 1991: 190-191).

Ambedkar after establishing the need of citizens' rights for ex-untouchables and their problems are genuinely political went on to ask for self-representation of the excluded Jatis in the government. In 1919 when the British introduced far reaching political reforms on behalf of depressed classes (as the ex-untouchables were know at that time) Ambedkar opined in his written statement submitted to the Committee on franchise that:

> As the government is the most important field for the exercise of individual capacities, it is in the interest of the people that no person as such should be denied the opportunity of actively participating in the process of government. That is to say popular government is not only government for the people but by the people. To express the same in a different way,

> representation of opinions by itself is not sufficient to constitute popular government. To cover its true meaning it requires personal representation as well. It is because the former is often found without the latter that the Franchise Committee has to see in devising the franchise and constituencies for a popular government in India, it provides for both, i.e., representation of opinions and representation of persons (Ambedkar 1979:247).

Ambedkar also raised the moral issues for self–representation of excluded communities' from the public service by quoting Gopal Krishna Gokhale, who had raised the same issue of exclusion from of Indians in general from the public services Indians. Emphasising the exclusion of Indians from public services, Gokhale had opined that:

> "A kind of dwarfing or stunting of the Indians is going on under the present system. We must live all days of our life in an atmosphere of inferiority and tallest of us must bend in order that the exigencies of the existing system may be satisfied. The upward impulse…is denied to us. The full height to which our manhood is capable of rising can never be reached by us under the present system. The moral elevation which every self-governing people feel cannot be felt by us. Our administrative and military talent must gradually disappear, owing to sheer disuse, till at last our lot, as hewers of wood and drawers of water in our own country is stereotyped" (quoted in Ambedkar 1982: 397).

Drawing an analogy between the Brahmins and allied castes with the foreign agency, i.e., the British, Ambedkar argued that:

> "Is it not open to the backward classes to allege against Brahmins and allied castes all that was alleged by the late Mr. Gokhale on behalf of Indian people against the foreign agency? Is it no open to the Depressed Classes, the non-Brahmins and the Mohammedans to say that by their exclusion from the Public Service a kind of dwarfing or stunting of their communities is going on? Can they not complain that as a result of their exclusion they are obliged to live all the days of their lives in an atmosphere of inferiority, and the tallest of them has to bend in order that the exigencies of the existing system may be satisfied? Can they not assert that upward impulses which every school-boy of a Brahmanical community

feels that he may one day be a Sinha, a Sastri, a Ranade, a Pranjpe, and which may draw forth from him the best efforts of which he is capable is denied to them? Can they not indignantly assert that the full height to which their manhood is capable of rising can never be reached by them under the present system? Can they not lament that the moral elevation which every self-governing people feel cannot be felt by them and that their administrative talents must disappear owing to sheer disgust till at last their lot as hewers of wood and drawers of water in their own country is stereotyped? The answer to these queries cannot but be in the affirmative. If to exclude the advanced communities from entering into public service of the country was a moral wrong, the exclusion of the backward communities from the same field must be a moral wrong and if it is a moral wrong it must be righted" (Ambedkar 1982: 395-6).

The moot question is that why could Ambedkar only plead for the self-representation of the ex-untouchable *jatis*. What did stop leaders of the so-called privileged *jatis* to demand the self-representation for the deprived and discriminated *Jatis*. The question assumes significance in the wake of emerging democracy, however it was.

Self-Representation and Opposition of Gandhi

It is astonishing, but a fact, that Congress and Gandhi were opposed to the self-representation of ex-untouchables in the emerging democracy. First, of all Congress was pressing the idea that it was the only genuine body to represent the ex-untouchables in the negotiation for their political rights with British. This claim was rejected by Ambedkar at the 'Round Table Conference'. Second, the Congress was convinced that mere nominations of representatives of ex-untouchable *'jatis'* in the legislature both at the state and the Centre would suffice. Against all odds, Ambedkar pleaded for separate electorates for them and had also acquired them. However, those who did not understand the essence of *'jatis'* exclusion vehemently opposed separate electorates for victimized *'jatis'*. Mohandas Karamchand Gandhi who was ardent supporter of *'Jati'* system initially and later of Varna system (Ambedkar 1991) opposed separate electorates first at the second Round Table Conference in London in 1931 and then in 1932 in India by going on a 'fast unto death'. Gandhi took the plea that separate electorate will divide Hindu religion. He further suggested to ex-untouchables that if they want they can convert to Islam or

Christianity but in no case he would accept separate electorate for them (quoted in Ambedkar, 1991).

Replying to this version of the Congress and Gandhi, Ambedkar argued that:

> The reasoning ... appears to be correct. But it is only a superficial view of the matter. These elections take place once in five years. It may be asked how can social solidarity between the Hindus and the untouchables be advanced by one day devoted to joint voting if for the rest of the five years they are leading severely separate lives. Similarly, it may well be asked how can one day devoted to separate voting in the course of five years make greater separation than what already exists or contrariwise how can one day in five year devoted to separate voting prevent those who wish to work for union from carrying out their purposes. To make it concrete how can separate electorate for the untouchables prevent intermarriage or inter- dining being introduced between them and Hindus? It is therefore futile to say that the political recognition of the untouchables as a separate element and granting them constitutional safeguards will perpetuate separation between them and the Hindus if the Hindus desire to put an end to it. (Ambedkar 1991: 191)

However, ultimately, Ambedkar had to concede to Gandhi and separate electorate for ex- untouchable *'jatis'* was converted to joint electorate with reserved constituencies. In these constituencies, ex-untouchable members were to be elected by both members of ex-untouchable *'jatis'* and the so-called Savarna *'jatis'*. But Ambedkar was very critical of this arrangement and argued that this arrangement of electoral constituencies have rendered the ex-untouchable *'Jati'* representatives ineffective. In effect, it has reduced them as the tools in the hands of the so-called Savarna *'jatis'*. So, in a way the dream of self-representation of the ex-untouchable *'jatis'* remained unfulfilled in the emerging democracy.

Broadening the Base of Indian Democracy

With the passage of Government of India Act 1935, British took a step further in broadening the base of representative democracy. British introduced adult suffrage for Indians. Through this Act, the ex-untouchables also got the right to participate in the democratic elections, based on adult suffrage to elect their own representative for the first time in Indian history. In addition, they also got their 'Scheduled Caste' constitutional identity. In 1937, this was a totally new experience for a subjugated and excluded group. A historical beginning was made by Ambedkar when he floated the first political party by any ex-untouchable in the history of modern Indian politics. It was the Independent Labour Party in 1936. Later, he established the Scheduled Caste Federation in 1942 and thereafter laid the foundation of the Republican Party of India which was founded after his demise, in 1957. Through his political mobilisation, Ambedkar succeeded in bringing more and more excluded masses in the ambit of democracy which broadened its base. I call this phenomenon elsewhere as the beginning of 'Independent Dalit Political Leadership' (Kumar 2003). However, the political scientists and sociologists have failed to understand this process of mobilisation. They view it as divisive and caste-ist act, which I have discussed earlier, and they also call it identity politics. Two important facts should be noted here: one, when Ambedkar was organizing the ex-untouchables, the term' identity politics' did not exist at all. The concept emerged only in the 1970s. Second, Ambedkar was not organizing people on the basis of exclusive *'Jati'* identity. Although, initially he had started mobilising people of his caste only, but that was because he felt that they have been deprived of their citizens' rights. Later, when he was accepted as an all India leader, then also he did not go on mobilising people on their' Jati' identity; rather, it was based on their exclusion, deprivation and discrimination, as discussed under the heading 'caste assertion' earlier. Nobody answers that why he was accepted cutting across the *'Jati'*, linguistic and regional boundaries. How can he be blamed for practicing identity politics?

Yes, there is a difference between his leadership and Gandhi's. This is in the sense that Gandhi paratrooped into the already established Congress movement, while Ambedkar had to start from scratch.

Development of Democracy after Independence: Can it be Called Identity Politics

After independence specifically Republican Party of India tried to mobilise ex-untouchables and some OBCs at all India level. However, it could gain influence only in certain pockets of the country-Maharashtra, Uttar Pradesh, Punjab, Madhya Pradesh, Andhra Pradesh and Tamil Nadu (Kumar 2003). Soon Congress co-opted the leaders and the agenda of RPI and left it redundant in the democratic mobilisation of ex-untouchable *'jatis'*. This is a cruel face of Indian democracy where political organizations of the excluded communities are desecrated deliberately by the political parties led and dominated by the members of the Savarna *'jatis'*, and literate classes backed by big business houses. The irony is that no political scientist has analysed this phenomenon critically. None of them have either condemned it as breach of constitutional morality in an emerging democracy. Rather, they have blamed the victim 'Jatis' and their organizations as degenerate and open for sale. But even then the 'independent politics' of ex-untouchable castes has survived. After RPI was fragmented, Dalit Panthers Party carried on the legacy of Ambedkarite movement based on constitutional rights enshrined in the Constitution for ex-untouchables. In 1972, Dalit Panthers propounded a class definition of Dalit, which included Scheduled Castes, Scheduled Tribes, Other Backward Classes (OBCs), Women and all those who were exploited in the of name of religion and economy (Manifesto of Dalit Panthers Party). Again, we can observe that the Dalit Panthers were not mobilising people in the name of each *'Jati'*; rather, they were mobilising people on the bases of exclusion, deprivation and discrimination. This can be called a gift of representative democracy that socially excluded, poverty-stricken, illiterate masses could mobilise people by forming their own political party. But soon, Dalit Panthers Party got fragmented because of both internal and external pressure (Kumar 2006).

In the 1970s there emerged a parallel phenomenon which may again be called as the product of democratic development in India. However, it escaped the eyes of social scientists or they deliberately did not capture it. This phenomenon was mobilisation of employees of exuntouchable *'jatis'*, especially government employees who had benefitted from the policy of reservations. Kanshi Ram, an employee of the Explosive Research and Development Laboratory at Kirki started mobilising the *'jatis'* in the name of 'Bahujans'. 'Bahujans'in English means majority. He called them victims of the Brahminical social order *(Manuvad)*. The Bahujans included members of Scheduled Castes, Scheduled Tribes, Other Backward Classes (OBCs) and converted minorities (Dalit Muslim, Sikhs and Christians). Again, a question emerges: which identity was Kanshi Ram referring to-caste, religion or class. No clear answer has come from the social scientists who have analysed Kanshi Ram's movement. BAMCEF, an employees' federation, became so powerful that it produced a political party the Bahujan Samaj Party, in 1984 (Kumar, Forthcoming). The formation and development of the party was blacked out by the mainstream social scientists. That is why someone from abroad had to call this phenomenon as 'Silent Revolution'. But as an insider, I call it 'India's Roaring Revolution' and India's First Democratic Revolution' (Kumar 2006).

It is also true that this is the period during which India's Shudra castes had also independently asserted by floating their own political parties in Tamil Nadu, Bihar, Uttar Pradesh, Andhra Pradesh and Punjab (Mukherji and Ganguli 2011: 109-140). The whole process of emergence of BSP and other regional forces had broken the monopoly of the so-called Savarna *'jati'* domination in the Hindi heartland politics. This can be called as the beginning of the. new democratic politics in India.

In his BAMCEF and BSP movement, Kanshi Ram was again, like Oalit Panthers Party, trying to mobilise people based on their exclusion, deprivation, discrimination and denial of social justice. He was not telling Oh Chamars! Oh Mahars! or Oh Malas!or Oh Pulayas! or Oh Holiyars! to name a few, to corne and unite. In fact, he created a very different narrative of mobilisation. The slogans of his party speak for themselves. Each slogan proves the deep commitment of his movement to democracy and belief in constitutional provisions. The slogans reflect the numerical strength of a population, value of a political vote and representation of people in the democratic process according to their proportion of population. That is why we have devoted a whole section in this book to explain how BSP's movement is not an identity politics (Chapters 7-11). It is my contention that social scientists have called it identity politics because they have a wrong notion of democratic mobilisation of the victims of the *'jati'* exclusion and deprivation. The BSP movement has not created division in the society; rather, it has strengthened the Indian democracy by bringing the most excluded individuals in its fold. Further, its movement has created consciousness among Shudra, exuntouchable and Muslim Pasmanda *'jatis'* for their self-representation not only in the sphere of politics but also in other spheres of social and educational life. The exuntouchable *'jatis'* have again taken the lead with their literature (see Chapters 20-21).

Three Developments in Indian Democracy

As the time has gone by, three very significant developments have taken place in Indian democracy as far as victim *'jatis'* are concerned.

One, most of the SC and OBC *'jatis'* have established their own political parties to participate in the democratic institutions. That is why we have witnessed a number of regional parties emerging on the basis of one dominant caste. However, all of them put together have not been able to form an All India political organization. OMK, AIAOMK, TOP, MOMK, PMK, Shiv Sena, Samjwadi Party, Rl0, lD(U), Lok lanashakti Party, NCP, Trinamool Congress, Akali Oal and Haryana Vikas Party are a few regional political parties who wish to have some say at the Centre and thereby keep themselves going in their states. The Bahujan Samaj Party has shown an aspiration to go all-India, but it has not been very successful beyond Uttar Pradesh.

The second phenomenon in Indian democracy is the phenomenal rise in the number of cases of atrocities against the ex-untouchable *'jatis'* all over India. The National Crime Bureau data hold testimony to this fact. I treat this rise in atrocities on the ex-untouchable 'jatis' as a result of the assertion of these *'jatis'* in every walk of life. The process has challenged the hegemony of the Savarna *'jatis'*. However, there have been atrocities on Dalits by the so-called Shudra *'jatis'*. On the basis of the nature of these atrocities, I call them as secular atrocities, more related to the day-to-day affairs of the relationship. Of late, in South India, especially the upper echelons of the Shudra *'jatis'* have perpetrated traditional types of *'jati'* atrocities. These include killings in the name of honour when a love marriage takes place between a Dalit boy and a Vanniar girl. But that has not dampened the assertion of the ex-untouchable youth who argue 'if this is a mistake, we will keep on repeating this mistake'. In sum, we will have to take a holistic picture of such assertion at pan-India level in different spheres of society. This gives a positive image of their assertion.

The third significant development in Indian democracy is the maintenance of monopoly of certain *'jatis'* over the institutions of governance, production and education. For a real analysis of the role of *'jati'* in Indian democracy, therefore, we will have to analyse the social composition of the aforesaid institutions. These institutions were supposed to be established on the basis of universalistic principles, devoid of any primordial material of *'jati'*, religion, language or region. These institutions are polity, judiciary, bureaucracy, industry, university, civil society and the media. Each of these institutions has further vertical and horizontal linkages. It was envisaged that as time goes by, there will be more democratization of these institutions. However, the present data of the composition of these institutions does not indicate that these institutions are democratizing. Further, on the one hand, state is criticized for granting exuntouchable and OBC *'jatis'* more and more benefits. On the other hand, there has not been any significant change in the composition of these aforesaid institutions. It is this monopolization of these institutions that may be regarded as the real impediment to the distributive justice to the erstwhile victim *'jatis'* and for emergence of a truly democratic society.

That is why in the wake of emerging democracy in a hierarchically arranged society; Ambedkar discussed the operationalization of equality, liberty and fraternity, considered to be cardinal principles of any democracy. He argued that 'we must ... not. .. be content with mere political democracy ... we must make our political democracy a social democracy as well' (Ambedkar 1994:1216). Ambedkar went on to define social democracy in these words, 'What does social democracy mean? It means a way of life which recognises liberty, equality and fraternity as the principles of life. These ... are not to be treated as separate items of trinity' (Ambedkar 1994: 1216). He further explained the nature of three cardinal principles of social democracy, that is, liberty, quality and fraternity. He opined:

> They form a union of trinity in the sense that to divorce one from the other is to defeat the very purpose of democracy. Liberty cannot be divorced from equality; equality cannot be divorced from liberty. Nor can liberty and equality be divorced from fraternity. Without equality liberty would produce the supremacy of the few over many. Equality without liberty would kill individual initiative. Without fraternity, liberty and equality could not become a natural course of things ... We must begin by acknowledging the fact that there is complete absence of two things in Indian society. One of these is equality. On the social plane, we have in India a society based on the principle of graded inequality which means elevation of some and degradation of others. On the economic plane, we have society in which there are some who have immense wealth as against many who live in abject poverty. (Ambedkar 1994: 1216)

Finally he cautioned the Indians to eradicate the conditions of persisting inequality and support emerging equality for strengthening the parliamentary democracy. In his own words:

> On the 26th of January ·1950, we are going to enter into a life of contradictions. In politics we will have equality and in social economic life we will have inequality. In Politics we will be recognizing the principle of one man one vote and one vote one value. In our social and economic life, we shall, by reason of our social and economic structure, continue to live this life of contradiction? How long shell we continue to live this life of contradictions? If we continue to deny it for long, we will do so only by putting our political democracy in peril. We must remove this contradiction at the earliest possible moment ... The second thing we are wanting in is recognition of the principle of fraternity. What does fraternity mean? Fraternity means a sense of common brotherhood of Indians-If Indians being one people. It is the principle which gives unity and solidarity to social life. It is difficult thing to achieve (Ambedkar 1994: 1216-1217).

References

Anderson, Perry, 2012, The Indian Ideology, The Three Essay Collective, Haryana, Haryana.

Ambedkar, B.R, 1979, Dr. Babasaheb Ambedkar Writing and Speeches Vol. 1, Education Department, Government of Maharashtra, Mumbai.

_____, 1982, Dr. Babasaheb Ambedkar Writing and Speeches Vol. 2, Education Department, Government of Maharashtra, Mumbai.

_____, 1991 "What Congress and Gandhi have done to the Untouchables", in Dr. Babasaheb Ambedkar Writings and Speeches Vol. 9, Education Department, Government of Maharashtra, Mumabi.

_____, 1994, Dr. Babasaheb Ambedkar Writings and Speeches Vol. 13, Education Department, Government of Maharashtra Mumbai.

_____, 1995, Dr. Babasaheb Ambedkar Writings and Speeches Vol. 14 (Part I), Education Department, Government of Maharashtra, Mumabi.

Bourdieu, P. 1973, Cultural Reproduction and Social Reproduction in R. Brown (ed.) Knowledge, Education, and Cultural Change, Tavistock, London.

Bougie, Celestin, 1971, Essays on the Caste System: The European Understanding of India, Cambridge University Press, New York.

Dumont, Louis, 1999, Homo Hierarchicus: The *Caste* System and *its Implications*, Oxford University press, New Delhi.

Dirks, Nicholas, B., 2004, Caste of Mind: Colonialism and the Making of Modern India, Permanent Black, New Delhi.

Green, Philippe (ed.), 1993, Key Concepts in Critical Theory: Democracy, Humanities Press, New Jersey.

Hasan, Zoya, 1998, Quest for Power: Oppositional Movements and Post-Congress Politics in Uttar Pradesh, Oxford University Press, New Delhi.

Jaffrelot, Christophe, 2003, India's Silent Revolution: The Rise of the low Castes in North Indian Politics, Permanent Black, New Delhi.

Kaviraj, Sudipto (ed.), 1999, Politics in India, Oxford University Press, Delhi.

______, 2011, The Enhancement of Democracy and India: Politics and Ideas, Permanent Black, New Delhi.

Keer, Dhananjay, 1964, Mahatma Jotirao Phooley: Father of Indian Social Revolution, Popular Prakshan, Bombay.

Kenneth, Minogue, 1985, Democracy in Adam Kuper and Jessica Kuper (eds.), The Social Science Encyclopaedia, Rutledge and Kegan Paul, London.

Kumar, Vivek, 2010, Different Shades of Dalit Mobilizations, in T.K. Oommen (ed.), Social Movements 1: Issues of Identity, Oxford University Press, New Delhi.

______, 2006, India's Roaring Revolution: Dalit Assertion and New Horizons, Gagandeep Publications, New Delhi.

______, 2003, Dalit Leadership in India, Kalpaz Publications, New Delhi.

Kumar, Vivek, Forthcoming, Saheb To Manyavar: Biograpghy of Kanshi Ram, Palm Leaf Publication, New Delhi.

Mukherji, Rahul and Ganguly, Sumit (ed.), 2011, India Since 1980, Cambridge University Press, New Delhi.

Ohanlon, Rosalind, 1985, Caste, Conflict and Ideology: Mahatma Jotirao Phule and Low Caste Protest in Nineteenth-Century Western India, Orient Longman, Delhi.

Oomrnen, T.K., 2005, Crisis and Contention in Indian Society, Sage Publications, New Delhi.

Rudolph, Susanne Hober& Rudolph, Lloyd, I., 1987, The Modernity of Tradition: Political Develop in India, Orient Longman, Delhi.

Singh, Y, 1994, Modernization oflndian Tradition, Rawat Publications, Jaipur.

Smith, Vincent A., 1958 (1919), The Oxford History of India (Percival Spear ed.), Oxford University Press, London.

Veermani, K, Dr., 2005, Rationalist Thought, in Collected Works of Periyar E.V.R., The Periyar Self-Respect Propagation Institution, Chennai.

Zelliot, Eleanor, 2004, Dr. Babasheb Ambedkar and The Untouchable Movement, Blumoon Books, New Delhi.

PART–I: UNDERSTANDING CASTE

1

Caste and Hindu Social Order: Some Pedagogic Issues

The practice of sociology in India has been marked by the world view and vocabulary of the so-called upper-caste male. In this context, T.K. Oommen has rightly argued, "All available evidence suggests that the Indian sociologists and social anthropologists were predominantly drawn from the twice-born Hindu castes" (2001: 16). They therefore preferred a particular type of literature for establishing the subject matter of sociology. Adherence to *Sanskritic* texts for carving out the subject matter of Indian sociology was advocated by the first generation of Indian sociologists, most notable of them being G.S. Ghurye, often said to be the father of Indian sociology (Upadhya, 2002: 28-57). Likewise, D.P. Mukherjee, as a first president of the Indian Sociological Society, argued in 1955 that all our *Shastras* are sociological and Indian sociologists can acquire 'Indianity' by taking sociological training in Sanskrit language in which traditions have been embodied (Oommen, 2001: 17). Although Mukherjee also stated that Indian sociologists ought to be familiar with Indian lores both high and low, rarely have they used sources other than Sanskritic texts for teaching caste and Hindu social order. If this was the source for the book view of so-called 'upper caste' sociologists, their field view was not very different. For instance, while doing field work in the village of Sripuram in Tamil Nadu, Andre Beteille wrote:

> I did my field work in Sripuram while living with the people as one among them. I was permitted to live in the *agraharam,* in a Brahmin house-a privilege ...I dined with the Brahmins and had access to most of their houses ...I was identified with the Brahmins by my dress, my appearance, and the fact that

> I lived in on their houses...I soon discovered that it made me suspect in the eyes of the non-Brahmins and Adi-Dravidas... (Beteille 1971: 9-10).

The passage is self-explanatory. It is in this context that one interrogates the manner that the Hindu social order is presented as a given in mainstream sociology. This paper attempts to highlight how this domination unfolds in Indian sociology. This chapter takes the specific case of the dalits and contends that sociologists have not seriously included dalits in the curriculum of sociology.

I

The Dominant Theory of Hindu Social Order

Hindu social order as taught in the sociology classrooms is a construct, a handy work of certain sociologists and anthropologists. Some will argue that it is the handy work of 'Orientalists' (Thapar, 2002) and others that of 'Nationalists'. I am not going to enter that debate. The point I seek to make is that this construct is presented as the given reality in classrooms of sociology throughout the country.

According to a dominant theory, Hindu society can be divided into two races-Aryans who came from elsewhere and Dasas who were indigenous to present day India. The Aryans were fair in colour while the indigenous *Dasas* were dark (Ghurye, 1979: 46). The Aryan included only the twice-born castes. Yet there is little in common between the dalits of South India and Punjab. There are perhaps more similarities between the dalits and Brahmins of South India. Ambedkar had argued on similar lines:

> What racial affinity is there between the Brahmin of the Punjab and the Brahmin of Madras? What racial affinity is there between the untouchable of Bengal and the untouchable of Madras? What racial difference are there between the Brahmin of the Punjab and the Chamar of the Punjab? What racial differences are there between the Brahmin of Madras and the Paraiah of Madras? The Brahmin of Punjab is racially of the same stock as the Chamar of the Punjab and the Brahmin of Madras is of the same race as the Pariah of Madras...Caste system is a social division of people of the same race (Ambedkar 1979: 48-49).

Romila Thapar too argues that the racial construction of Hinduism is only a nineteenth century construction:

> ...Its roots were provided by yet another nineteenth-century obsession, that the theory of Aryan race... concern with European origins was transferred to India... The notion of an Aryan race has now been generally discarded in scholarship and what we are left with is essentially a linguistic category: the Indo-Aryan speaking people (Thapar 2002: 81-82).

In the same vein, Trautmann has also questioned the validity of racial theory of *varna.* He argues:

> The racial theory of Indian civilisation was constructed by narrativising the encounter of the polar opposites of Victorian racial thought, the fair-skinned Aryan and the dark-skinned savage, and by finding evidence for their encounter in the Vedic texts. It was the work of Sanskritists who were at the forefront in its construction. The leading texts were those of Max Muller...and John Muir's original Sanskrit texts on the origin and history of the people of India (1874: 84) (Trautmann, 1997: 206).

Sociologists routinely teach that the Hindu social order comprises four *varnas* and thousands of castes. However, the *Rig Veda,* which is the basis for this four-fold so-called Hindu social order, mentions many other groups like Dasas, Dasyus, Rakshas, Panis, Nishads etc. Mukherjee, 1988). Mukherjee himself argues that "from the evidence *Rig Veda* we find that besides the *Rig Veda* people there were other autochthonous groups in society ..." But nobody knows why the details of these groups are missing from the sociology curriculum. The question that arises is, "What would have been the nature of the Indian society had the groups Dasas, Dasyus, Rakshas, Panis, Nishads, etc. been included along with Brahmins, Kshatriyas, Vaishyas and Shudras?" The process of reducing the other groups into a blanket category Shudras has hidden a vast body of knowledge about society.

Hindu Social Order: Pan-Indian or Restricted to Indo-Gangetic Plains

The other fact about this construction of the four-fold social structure of Hindu social order is that it is found in its purest form only in the Indo-Gangetic plains. We can find the presence of Brahmins and ex-untouchables in every geographical area in the country but we will not find the equivalent of the Kshatriya and Vaishya of north India in other regions. Vincent Smith thus argues: "The Hindu theory that mankind is divided into four *varna,* ... was wholly foreign to the southerners. To this day Kshatriyas and Vaisyas do not exist among them". (Smith 1986: 42-42).

Hindu Social Order: Carving out a Majority Community Identity

This construction of Hindu social order has serious implications for the structure and processes of the Indian society. At the outset, this has produced the identity of a majority community, i.e., Hindus. Second, this identity of Hindus subsumed other groups which had different belief, knowledge system, customs and culture. In this manner the Brahmanical culture, world view etc. got universalised and it became the hegemonic reference point for all others. It assumed an all-India character and therefore even where the Brahmins were not present their hegemony worked. In the words of Thapar, "The need for postulating a Hindu community became a requirement for political mobilisation in the nineteenth century when representation by religious community became a key to power and where such representation gave access to economic resources...A Hindu community with common identity would be politically powerful" (Thapar 2002: 86).

When caste is recognised, and when denied

Caste has been for long understood in terms of purity and pollution. The dalits are called impure on the basis of their defiling occupation. But dalits argue that it is the dalits who keep the whole society clean then how is it then that it is they who become impure? Second, it is ironical that it is the caste of people who defecate and are unable to clean their own excreta, remove their dead animals, are unable to help their women to deliver their babies, cannot clean their clothes soiled by blood of menstruation, cannot dig graves for their dead who are deemed clean and pure? The very language of analysis is such that it articulates the domination of twice-born castes and negates the creativity and contribution of the dalits in the Hindu social order.

A number of sociologists have made their career by writing on caste. When they write and teach about caste in the academic world, they readily accept its presence in Indian society. They discuss at length about the nature of caste, its characteristics, adaptability, its role in politics and even mobility in the structure of caste. Shiv Vishvanathan

(1990: 31-36) argues that based on the studies of many Indian sociologists a number of policies on caste have been formulated and many of them have themselves been members of the committees and commissions. Yet when it comes to the issue of policy formulation for the upliftment of the dalits or other backward castes (OBCs) the same sociologists virtually deny the existence of caste in public life.

II

Erroneous Conceptual Categories to Understand Indian Society

If Indian sociologists have constructed an imagined Hindu social order, they have also carved out other theoretical frameworks and conceptual categories to understand the Indian society. One attempts to look at some of these.

Hindu Social Order: The Ambiguous Position of Dalits

The Brahmanical hegemony is visible in the manner that the dalits are accorded an ambiguous position in the Hindu social order. No teacher ever explains how the metaphor fifth *varna* arose. It is very clear from the *Rig Veda's* 'Purush Sukta' theory that there are four *varnas* in the Hindu social order (Ghurye, 1979: 44, Srinivas, 1985: 150-51). *Manu Smriti* which codified Hindu society, has also argued that there is no fifth *varna* (Dumont, 1999: 66-67). Why then do sociologists argue in the classrooms that "there are four *varnas* and there is a fifth also". For instance, Ghurye indirectly includes them in the four-fold *varna* hierarchy and argues that they are part of the Hindu social order. According to him, "The Scheduled Castes, formerly known as depressed classes, ... the fifth order of the four-fold society of Hindu theory" (Ghurye, 1979: 307). In this regard, Dumont has remarked "First and foremost, these texts were to mask the emergence, the factual accretion of a fifth category, the untouchables, each emulating the others in proclaiming that there is no fifth..." (1999: 68).

The existence of fifth *varna* - 'the dalits' - is further denied in the Hindu social order by its sacred texts in the way the functions and stages in the life of a Hindus are prescribed in them. Everyone is aware that the four *varnas* mentioned in the sacred texts have been assigned their duties or jobs (*dharma*) by these texts. For example, in the hymns of the *Rigveda,* the job of the Brahmin *varna* was to read and write, teach and preach, offer and officiate sacrifices. The Brahmins were obliged by this tradition to undergo a life of study, mediation, and penetration into the mysteries of God and *dharma.* Ghurye argues that the occupation of Kshatriyas, "must have consisted in administrative and military duties...In the prayer for the prosperity of Kshatriya, he is said to be an archer and good chariot-fighter " (Ghurye, 1979: 48). The Vaishyas formed the third order and were supposed to be traders. Further, Ghurye argues, "The name of the fourth class, the Shudra...It seems ...represented domestic servants, approximating very nearly to the position of slaves. The Shudra is described as 'the servant of another', 'to be expelled at will', and 'to be slain at will'. The *Panchvimsha Brahmana* defines this position still more precisely when it declares that the Shudra, even if he is prosperous, cannot be but a servant of another, washing his superior's feet being his main business... The Shatapatha Brahmana goes to the length of declaring that the Shudra is untruth itself'(*ibid.* 50-51).

Apart from the aforesaid duties assigned to various *varnas*, the book view of caste system also prescribed an elaborate arrangement for various socio-economic, political and religious activities to be performed by an individual in various stages of his/her life. The dalits are completely excluded from this. These stages are termed as *ashrams*, which are four in number, namely, *brahmacharya*, *grihastha*, *vanaprastha* and *sanyasa.* The male members of Brahmin, Kshatriya and Vaishya *varnas* pass through these four stages in their life. The first *ashram* is called *brahmacharya ashram* from which the fourth *varna*, viz., Shudra and the women of the first three *varnas* were barred.

A number of questions emerge. First, even if we believe the sacred texts on the origin of caste/*varna*, where does the metaphor of the fifth *varna* originate? Second, accepting that there is a fifth *varna*, the natural corollary is what will be its *dharma* and which *ashrama* can its members follow? No convincing explanation is given by Indian sociologists, yet they treat dalits as part and parcel of the Hindu social order.

Dalit Movements : Refutations of being Part of Hindu Social Order

The Dalits have contested their inclusion in the Hindu social order. In the past they have launched a number of movements highlighting their independent identity and their status as the original inhabitant of this land. These movements included the Adi Hindu, Adi Dravida, Adi Andhra, Adi Karnataka and Ad Dharma movements. Through these movements they tried to moot a racial theory in which Aryans were depicted as outsiders who have subjugated the indigenous dalits who were the original inhabitants of this land. The term 'Adi Hindu' spread along a sizeable number of north Indian dalits during the 19th century. In Uttar Pradesh, Swami Acchutananda (1879-1933) launched the Adi Hindu movement.

The Adi Hindu movement with vision of a separate identity of the Dalits got strengthened with four Adi Hindu conferences organised in Hyderabad between 1912 and 1924. The main organisers began to use Adi Hindu nomenclature (Omvedt, 1994: 122). Radicalisation among Dalits throughout South India resulted in the emergence of 'Adi ideology'. In Hyderabad Adi-Hindu movement emerged among Malas (an untouchable caste) who were led by Bhagyareddy Verma (1888-1939), a steward from a Catholic family which educated him.

The Dalit assertion in South India was also evident in Kerala where Pulayas - the untouchables - had organised socio-cultural revolts since the beginning of the 20th century under the able leadership of Ayyankali and Vellikkara Choti. The aim of such revolts initially was not economic gain but entry into educational institutions and other public places (Mathew, 1986: 102). Dalit organisations also came into existence in the erstwhile Mysore state where Murgesh Pillai led the Adi Dravida Abhi-Vrudhi Sangh, which was mainly supported by Tamils although it did include the Kannadigas in its fold and programmes. An organisation called Adi Jambava Sangha was exclusively formed and supported by the Madigas - now a major Scheduled Caste (SC) group in Andhra Pradesh. Although mainly a social organisation, its leader convened a 'political conference' of the Panchamas in 1920 to which Ambedkar was also invited, although he could not attend due to a ban on his entry into the state. It is not known if the conference had adopted any political resolution. Other conferences were organised in 1923 and 1925 under the presidentship of M.C. Rajah. These conferences passed resolutions on various issues concerning the untouchables using the Adi Karnataka and Adi Dravida terminology. Their basic demands were admission of dalit students to educational institutions, access to water tanks, temple entry, etc. From the 1920s, dalits also asked the government for allotment of waste and other fallow lands for cultivation and also for land to be allotted/leased/sold to them at reduced/concessional prices in the newly irrigated tracts around Irwin canal. In addition, demands were made that dalits be relieved from traditional caste duties. It was also argued that, if they were not relieved, the government should directly pay to them for their duties out of the cess collected from the peasants.

The Adi Dharama movement emerged in 1926 as an organised movement of dalits in Punjab, with Mangoo Ram as the President of the Executive Committee. Mangoo Ram was a folk hero and had lived with the activists of the Gadar Party. The main plea of the Adi Dharama movement was that the untouchables (dalits) constituted a *quam,* a distinct religious community similar to the Muslim, Hindu and Sikh communities, and that their *quam* had existed in India from time immemorial.

Their ancient civilisation was destroyed by the Aryans and they were subjugated to the point where they forgot their own identity. In restoring that lost identity Ad Dharmis held to a non-theistic view of divinity, worshipped low caste saints like Kabir, and especially their fellow Chamar Ravidas, collected their writings, and read them in their *Satsangs,* which resembled Sikh worship...A high point came early in Ad Dharm history when they gained recognition-as a separate *quam* in the religion chapter of the 1931 census and recorded 418,789 Ad Dharmis (Webster, 2002: 27).

In the later stages, the leaders of the Adi Dharma movement were drawn two models of social organisations and political influence. One was the example set by Muslim nationalists, who had demanded a separate territory of their own. The other was provided by political parties and religious-communal supports for electoral candidates. "Members of Dalit community in the Punjab adopted the first model along the lines of Muslim separatism and came up with the notion of Achutistan, a geographically distinct, "land of the untouchables". The idea was never worked out in any systematic way nor was there even a suggestion as to which area of India might be incorporated into such a nation.

In the end, we can argue that the 'Adi' movements through which dalits asserted that they have their own identity, separate from the Hindus, and the critique of Aryans who were responsible for their wretched condition in contemporary Indian society, could not emancipate dalits from their stigmatised identity and accord them a dignified position in the society. Therefore, these movements lost their influence among dalits in different parts of the country. Moreover, many alternative movements like those led by Ambedkar, Indian National Congress and Hindu Mahasabha also emerged during this period, which attracted dalits towards their ideology and subsumed them and their leaders.

Assertion for Exclusive Existence from Hinduism

In modem times the assertion of the dalits can be seen in the following slogans which assert their brotherhood and proximity with the Muslims rather than Hindus, although it is in the realm of politics and movement. The first instance is of Agra in Uttar Pradesh where Republican Party of India contested election in alliance with Muslims in 1962 and coined the slogan:

> Jatav Muslim Bhai-Bhai, Hindu Kaum Kahan se Ai *(Lynch, 1969: 102)*.

Similarly, in central Uttar Pradesh, Rajendra Singh highlighted the proximity of dalits and Muslims in the land-grab movement of 1970. The slogan states:

> Muslim Harijan Bhai-Bhai, Hindu Jati Khan se Ai *(Singh, 2000: 137)*

Ambedkar's critique of the Hindu social order and a possible Hindu nation is instructive.

> There is utter lack of what the sociologists call "consciousness of kind". There is no consciousness of kind.... That is the reason why Hindus cannot be said to form a society or nation... Men do not become a society by living in physical proximity... Secondly, similarity in habits and customs, beliefs and thoughts is not enough to constitute men into society. Things may be passed physically from one to another like bricks...Culture spreads by diffusion and that is why one finds similarity between various primitive tribes in the matter of their habits and customs, beliefs and thoughts although they do not live in proximity. But no one could say that because there was similarity the primitive tribes constituted one society. This is because similarity in certain things is not enough to constitute a society. Men constitute a society because they have things which they possess in common. To have similar things is totally different from possessing things in common. And the only way by which men can come to possess things in common with one another is by being in communication with one another... Parallel activity, even if similar, is not sufficient to bind men into a society. This is proved by the fact that the festivals observed by the different castes amongst the Hindus are the same. Yet these parallel performances of similar festivals by the different castes have not bound them into one integral whole. For that purpose what is necessary is for a man to share and participate in a common activity so that the same emotions are aroused in him that animate the others. Make the individual a sharer or partner in the

associated activity so that he feels its success as his success, its failure as his failure is the real thing that binds men and makes a society of them. The caste system prevents common activity and by preventing common activity it has prevented the Hindus from becoming a society with a unified life and a consciousness of its own being (Ambedkar 1979: 50-51).

In a similar view Kancha Ilaiah emphasises that dalits and backward castes (Shudras) are not Hindus. He also raises the issue of exclusion of dalits from the day-to-day life of the Hindu social order. In his own words, "I was not born a Hindu for the simple reason that my parents did not know that they were Hindus. This does not mean that I was not born as a Muslim, a Christian, a Buddhist, a Sikh or a Parsee" (Ilaiah, 1996: 1). Ilaiah further elaborates this by arguing that, "People belong to a religion only-when they know that they are part of the people who worship that God, when they go to those temples and take part in the rituals and festivals of that region" (*ibid.*). Justifying the structural location of Shudras independent of Hinduism, Ilaiah remarks, "My parents had only one identity and that was their caste ...Their festivals were local, their Gods and Goddesses were local (the Hindu patriarchal Gods do not exist there) and sometimes these were even specific to one village. No centralised religious symbols existed for them* (Ilaiah, 1991: 1).

Village as a Functional Category

Village community is the most celebrated category of Indian society. It has been regarded as an ideal form of social organisation to which there is no parallel anywhere in the world. Within it the unity of village is further magnified by Indian sociologists. While editing a volume of the studies conducted in the 1950s M.N. Srinivas (1978: 6-8) depicted this unity in Indian villages as a central theme in his works. Would the same unity be perceived by all castes? Ambedkar's observes:

The Hindu village is a working plant of the Hindu social order. One can see there the Hindu social order in full swing...The Indian village is not a single unit. It consists of castes. But for our purpose, it is enough to say ...The population in the village is divided into two sections...Touchables and Untouchables...What are the terms of associated life on which the Touchables and Untouchables live in an Indian village? In every village the Touchables have a code which the Untouchables are required to follow. This code lays down the acts of omission and commissions which the Touchables treat as offences...

> Another important thing to note is that the punishment for these offenses is always collective. The whole community of untouchables is liable for punishment though the offence have been committed by an individual...The right to beg for food from the Touchable is now the principal means of livelihood for ...Untouchables in India... Such is the picture of the inside life of an Indian village. In this Republic there is no place for democracy. There is no room for quality. There is no room for liberty and there is no room for fraternity. The Indian village is the very negation of a republic. If it is republic, it is republic of the Touchables, by the Touchables, and the Touchables. The Untouchables have no rights...They have no rights because they are outside the village republic and because they are out side the so-called republic they are outside the Hindu fold. (Ambedkar 1989: 19-26)

The Process of Dalitisation or 'Hygienicaisation'

According to the theory of sanskritisation, caste is far from a rigid system in which the position of each component caste is fixed for all time. In this context, it would be worth mentioning Romila Thapar:

> In the process of articulation the perspective is generally limited to lat of the *sanskritisation* of the latter. It might be historically more accurate on occasion to view it as the reverse, as for example, in the lit of Viththala at Pandharpur or that of Jagannatha at Puri. In such cases the deities of tribals and low caste groups become for reasons other than the purely religious, centrally significant and Brahmanism has to adapt itself to the concept of such deities... (Thapar 2002: 65-66).

The concept 'sanskritisation' ignores the fact that dalits too may hold negative views about the 'upper castes' - a fact eloquently brought out by Ambedkar, quoting Abbe Dubois:

> Even to this day a Pariah is not allowed to pass a Brahmin street in a village, though nobody can prevent or prevent his approaching or passing by a Brahmin's house in town.

Furthermore, quoting the editor of the gazetteer of the Tanjore district, he argues:

> These castes (Paraayan and Pallans or Chakkiliyan castes of Tanjore district) strongly object to the entrance of a Brahmin

into their quarters believing that harm will result to them therefrom (*ibid.*).

Although the propounder of the theory of sanskritisation delineates the cultural traits of the Brahmins and other twice-born castes he is not bothered to shed any light on the cultural traits of the dalits and Shudras. Is this a lapse on the part of researcher who hails from a particular social background or is it a deliberate attempt on his part to misrepresent. The second problem with this concept is, can we say that drinking alcohol, eating carrion, sacrificing animals etc. were prescribed and codified cultural traits of dalits and Shudras. Or put it differently, on what basis can we argue that living without non-vegetarian food, not drinking alcohol, not sacrificing animals to their deities becomes imitation of Sanskritic values.

The third problem with this conceptualisation is that the researcher is concerned only with the upward movement of the lower castes in the caste hierarchy in the Hindu social order by imitating the Brahmins and other twice-born castes on the basis of very few case studies. But why did he remain silent or why could he not see so many Brahmins and other twice-born castes taking non-vegetarian food or not performing the rituals in day-to-day life etc. Therefore, logically, can we argue that at cultural level it is process of downward mobility for the twice-born castes, i.e., it is a process of *dalitisation* though structurally the so-called twice-born castes maintain their higher status in the caste hierarchy?

The fourth problem in this concept is that the imitation of Sanskritic values is nothing but the imitation of values of Brahmins. And, the mobility can occur only in the Brahmanical framework, because only Brahmins were and still are the custodians of the so-called Hindu religion and culture.

Further sanskritisation raises the question whether the dalits are part of a Hindu social order? Because had they been part of the same social order then there would have been similarities between them and the twice-born castes and hence there would have been no scope for imitation of the cultural traits of the so-called upper castes by the so-called lower castes. Last but not the least, the problem with the formulation of the concept is that while we do not see any such processes in contemporary times this process of sanskritisation is still being taught in the classes as if it is still taking place.

Analysing the Concept of Class in the Hindu Social Order

Sociologists have applied the concept of 'class' to measure the economic status of the people in general. In most cases the concept of class is exclusively identified with the economic status of individuals without any attention to the social aspects such as caste and religion which also play a dominant role in deciding the economic status of individuals and groups in India. As religion and caste play a dominant role in the social status of an individual or group, it is difficult to analyse the real social status of poor Brahmin and poor dalit through the concept of 'class' alone. Though there is a general understanding that the poor are all equal it can be easily argued that the poor of the so-called upper castes and lower castes are not similarly placed because of the contribution made by religion and caste in the formation of a class. Hence, we can objectively argue that the causes of poverty of dalits and upper castes are different and depend on their structural location in the social structure. For instance, a penury-stricken Brahmin who comes and begs is blessed by the donor. On the contrary, a cobbler who polishes shoes with his labour or a sweeper who cleans excreta is treated with contempt and usually people throw the money at them from a distance lest their touch defile them. Likewise, the richest industrialist goes and bows at the feet of a Brahmin in Kasi or Haridwar. Similarly, a Rajput or Kshatriya landowner will never plough his land even though he is economically in a desperate situation because he will lose his caste. Likewise a hardworking dalit will not be allowed to open an eatery shop in the countryside even today.

III

The Construction of the Hindu Social Order and its Consequences

At the societal level dalits face an extreme form of exclusion and deprivation in society. They are not given any rights. This happens I agree on account of their forced co-option in the Hindu social order. Otherwise, how does one explain that a collectivity, which forms a part of the social order, is forced to live in isolation?

At another level the dalits have been excluded from the curriculum in social sciences in general and sociology in particular. And when represented, there is a serious misrepresentation of dalits. This happens because neither have they been able to justify their exclusion from the Hindu social order nor their inclusion in the Hindu social order in the academic literature. As far as their exclusion is concerned, they are totally excluded from the Hindu social order. One can infer even from the book view of the Hindu social order as taught in the class rooms, that there is denial of every right whatsoever to the dalits - no place in *varna* hierarchy, non-existence of any *Ashrama Dharma* to follow for them, denial of *Purusharthas*, or any *Rinas,* denial of access to the gods pantheon of denial to perform a clean occupation and the oppressive existence of caste endogamy.

I therefore agree strongly that the sociologists have tried unsuccessfully to include the dalits in the Hindu social order. Usually, they are treated as a fifth *varna* although they are a conglomeration of number of a hierarchically arranged castes. Usually, in the *varna* hierarchy, there are sub-castes, having at least a number of social ties with touchability. But dalits do not have any avenue of interaction with other castes as well as castes which are considered as untouchables. Then, how can one contend that they are a part of the *varna* system in the scheme of Hindu social order?

On the other hand, the sociologists have again unsuccessfully tried to hide the exclusion of the dalits from the Hindu social order by not discussing the real nature and scope of exclusion in the curriculum sociology. The aforesaid phenomenon has brought to fore the real of Hindu social order in which dalits occupy a status "excluded but included in the collectivity". This unique status of dalits has never recorded by the Indian sociologists earlier. A combination of developments has forced Indian sociology to grapple with this. One is cess of democratisation of the society on the basis of constitutional rights. Then, equipped with these constitutional rights, there has been dalit assertion in every realm of Indian society whether religion, politics, culture, etc. More recently the market has played a role in marketing the dalit literature written both by the dalits and non-dalits.

This exclusion of the dalits from the curriculum of sociology in India can be captured through five simultaneous processes which are deployed by the Indian sociologists to analyse the dalits by placing the imagined Hindu social order. These five processes are:

- Cognitive blackout
- Forced availability
- Chequered accessibility
- Pseudo inclusivity
- Lack of reflexivity

Cognitive Blackout

At the outset the exclusion of dalits in the subject matter in sociology takes the shape of a 'cognitive blackout'. It is a well-known fact that the description of dalit's society, their icons, their movement, world view or contribution of their labour in the annals of Indian sociology is rare. Dalits have their own vibrant culture and literature. They have their songs and dance and art forms but all has been blacked out in the annals of sociological discussions and literature. This has been eloquently portrayed by Oommen. He writes:

> There has been a cognitive black-out in Indian social science, until recently, as far as knowledge regarding the life - world of Dalitbahujans. The fact the life-styles of upper castes and *Dalitbahujans vary* dramatically in terms of food habits, worship patterns or gender relations is tacitly acknowledged. But instead of squarely recognising these variations and explaining why they exist, the dominant tendency in Indian Sociology, at least until recently, has been to suggest that the *Dalitbahujans* are abandoning their way of life in favour of the life-styles of caste Hindus. This is what *sanskritisation* is all about. In this perspective, not only the norms and values of caste Hindus are privileged but they are also christened as norm-setters and value-givers for the society as a whole. Conversely, the norms and values of *Dalitbahujans* are knocked out, ignored, stigmatised and delegitimised" (Oommen, 2001: 21).

In this context, Gough had argued that there is (1956: 846) a difference between the cultures of untouchables and Brahmins. According to her, there is a tacit opposition between the inhibiting 'culture' of the Brahmins and the free 'nature' of the untouchables. Both differ in their attitudes towards sexuality, and aggression towards elders and peers. Engaged in the practical business of earning a living through manual labour, the low castes care more for health and prosperity in this life. Indian sociologists have failed to record this.

Forced Availability

Forced availability means that the availability of dalits as subject matter in sociology has been forced by an external agency and it has not emerged out of conscious effort made by the Indian sociologists. In this regard, we have to observe the fact that till yesterday the Indian sociologists never bothered to study the dalit society. If we take 1914 as the starting point when the first department of sociology was established in India at Bombay University, we find that it was only in 1970s that few studies on dalits were taken up by the sociologists of Indian origin and that too at the behest of Indian Council of Social Science Research (ICSSR). That means, it took 56 years before 'dalits' could become a worthy category and also a subject of enquiry for the Indian sociologists although many of the anthropologists or sociologists from Europe and America had already done some very fine work on dalits. Another aspect of this forced availability is that by 1970 dalit society, its movements, its icons, its production of knowledge etc. had become so visible that it was not possible for the mainstream sociologists of Indian origin to not to consider dalits as the subjectmatter of their study. Yet they did succeed in not including the dalits in mainstream sociology curriculum.

It is astonishing to note that till late 1995 or so the dalits could not become the part of curriculum of sociology in most of the universities both at the graduate and postgraduate levels. The teaching community argued that there is dearth of quality material on the topic which can be taught in the classroom. But as time passed the abundance of literature related to the dalits forced the sociologists to take cognizance of the alit society. This material on dalit society belongs to the three streams one stream included the material written by the foreign authors like) M. Lynch, Robert Hardgrave, Michael Moffat, Eleanor Zelliot, Mark Gallentar etc., the second stream included material written by the socalled the upper caste Indian writers like G.S. Ghurye, Sachidanand Sinha etc. and the third one by the dalit themselves like Ambedkar, C. Parvathamma, Nandu Ram etc. to name a few. Therefore, the state agency, the dalit assertion and abundance of dalit literature forced Indian sociologists to include the topics related to the dalits in the curriculum. The forced nature of the inclusion of dalit study in the curriculum is evident in the manner that a topic on the dalits in a book is usually given a place in the end of the book. In all probability the write-up will be by a dalit scholar.

Chequered Accessibility

This brings to the next point of chequered accessibility of the subject matter of dalits. Even if the subject matter related to dalits is available in the curriculum, it is quite common to find that teachers and students have no access to the relevant material. The nature of accessibility is also very different. The Indian sociologists would like to access relevant material written either by the so-called upper castes or by foreign authors. The indexes and bibliographies of books and references of different articles would also suggest that the works of dalits by dalits are seldom referred.

Pseudo-inclusivity

If the subject matter related to dalits is available and is also accessible, then, we have to analyse the nature and manner in which it has been included in the curriculum taught in the classrooms. A key question that needs to be asked is: Does the teacher have a reductionist attitude towards the dalits as the subject matter? A look at how dalits are placed in the curriculum would be instructive. They have been understood through the vantage point of reservation, atrocities, educational status, poverty etc. Seldom has their contribution in running the economy and polity of this country been understood. They have been reduced to the status of dirty drunkards, devoid of any merit, *sarkari* Brahmins, burden on this earth, etc. The process of reductionism of the dalit society has been noted by Viswanathan, who writes: "The privileging of Gandhi as an emblem of non-partisan feeling has, as its inverse, the demonisation of Ambedkar as a purveyor of sectarian politics. The view that 'the national hagiography in India has rarely conceded a space for Ambedkar alongside Gandhi' is borne out by amasing exclusion of Ambedkar from several well known literary works about untouchability" (Vishwanathan, 2001: 220).

Lack of Reflexivity

There is also a lack of reflexivity on the dalits as a subject matter in sociology because the subject matter has not been treated seriously. From the definition of the term 'dalit', the language used to describe them (Kumar, 2005: 520-521), is all tentative. We have yet to find a concrete definition of the term 'dalit' to be sure which collectivity we are talking about. Some sociologists usually define dalits without taking any difference of caste, gender or class into account. Therefore, their definition of dalit includes all the economically poor persons. Most of the times they include scheduled castes, scheduled tribes, other backward castes, and also women of both general and dalit groups. I have read research proposals without any concrete definition of the collectivity called dalits. The whole approach towards evolving a clear-cut definition of dalit is very casual. Whosoever wants can explain the term 'dalit' in whatever manner he/she deems it fit to define. It is interesting also to note the student's response to the teaching on dalits. It has been observed that the students are not particularly interested in the topics related to dalits. They do not actively participate in the discussions on the topic and remain more or less passive or indifferent in the classroom. Further, they do not attempt the questions given on the topic in the examinations unless they are compulsory.

IV

Conclusion

The central argument of this chapter is that the Hindu social order as taught in sociology classes by Indian sociologists is a mere social construct. Through this construction a majority community, namely, 'the Hindus' has been carved out. This has led to the marginalisation of dalits not only in the society but also in the sociology curriculum. This is the basic reasons for the alienation of dalits from the curriculum of Indian sociology. They have been raising a number of perplexing questions whether they meet you as students or as the conscious member of society. They ask why one should study sociology when we do not teach about the life and world views of a majority of the population? Why should one study 'Indian' culture and society, which is about the so-called castes that have always discriminated the lower strata and dominated the Hindu social order? Why should we not study the cultural traits and elements of the dominated and discriminated groups? The dalits ask why one should study India's social reform movements led by Raja Ram Mohan Roy, Dayanand Saraswati, or Mohandas Karamchand Gandhi only? Why can't we also include social reform movements led by a number of dalit and backward caste social reformers like Jotiba Phule, Narayana Guru, Achutanand, Ambedkar, or Periyar E.V. Ramaswamy, Uda Devi? Similarly, why does one have to study social thought of icons like Gandhi, Aurobindo, Tagore, only? Why has the social thought of aforesaid social reformers belonging to the dalits and backward castes not been included in the sociology curriculum? Why should we study origin and development of Indian National Congress party only, why not the history and development of Bahujan Samaj Party also?

Therefore, the chapter humbly submits that if the practice of sociology in India has to reflect and project a total picture of Indian society, and if it has to remain relevant for Indian society, then its subject matter and teaching has to become more inclusive. It has to be more representative of the cultural traits of the discriminated dalit group. Sociology curriculum as taught at the various levels should include studies related to the life of dalits, their culture, world view, sufferings, discriminations and humiliation. The sociology curriculum has to move beyond tokenism and symbolic representation of the dalits with concrete studies on their achievements, their contribution in running the economy, polity and society of the country. We have to question the existing concepts and theories through which Indian society and structures are understood. We have to also ask questions about the existing concepts and theories regarding the basic structures and processes as propounded by Indian sociologists in India. For instance, we have to question basic institutions like village, evaluate the feasibility of concepts like class in Indian society and analyse the process of sanskritisation to name just a few. We have to analyse the lopsidedness and limitations of the tools and methods of data collection with which sociological data about Indian society has been collected. It is on the basis of such data that generalisations on India has been made and the same is being taught in classrooms. This has to change, if sociology in India has to have rigour and relevance.

References

Ambedkar, B.R. 1979. "Annihilation of Caste", in *Dr Babasaheb Ambedkar Writings and Speeches*, Vol. 1, Education Department, Government of Maharashtra, Mumbai.

—. 1989. "The Indian Ghetto-The Centre of Untouchability", in *Dr Babasaheb Ambedkar Writings and Speeches*, Vol. 5, Education Department, Government of Maharashtra, Mumbai.

—. 1990. "The Untouchables: Who Were They and Why They Became Untouchables", in *Dr Babasaheb Ambedkar Writings and Speeches*, Vol. 7, Education Department, Government of Maharashtra, Mumbai.

Beteille, Andre. *1971*. Caste, Class and Power: Changing Patterns of Stratification in a Tanjore Village. Berkeley: University of California Press.

Dirks, B. Nicholas. 2004. Castes of Mind: Colonialism and the Making of Modern India. New Delhi: Permanent Black.

Dumont, Louis. 1999. Homo Hierarchicus: The Caste System and Its Implications. New Delhi: Oxford University Press.

Ghurye, G.S. 1979. *Caste and Race in India.* Bombay: Popular Prakashan.

Gooptu, Nandni. 1993. "Caste and Labour: Untouchable Social Movements in Urban Uttar Pradesh in the Early Twentieth Century", in Peter Robb (ed.), *Dalit Movements and the Meanings of Labour in India.* New Delhi: Oxford University Press.

Gough, Kathleen. 1956. "Brahmin Kinship in Tamil Village", *American Anthropologist,* 58: 826-53.

Ilaiah, Kancha. 1996. *Why I am Not a Hindu.* Delhi: Samaya.

Lynch, Oven M. 1969. *The Politics of Untouchability.* New Delhi: Oxford University Press.

Kakar, Sudhir. 1982. "Setting the Stage: the Traditional Hindu View and the Psychology of Erik H. Erikson". in Sudhir Kakar (ed.), *Identity and Adulthood.* Delhi: Oxford University Press.

Kumar, Vivek. 2003. *Dalit Leadership India.* New Delhi: Kalpaz Publications.

—. 2005. "Locating Dalits in Indian Sociology", *Sociological Bulletin.*

—. 2005. "Situating Dalits in Indian Sociology", *Sociological Bulletin* Special Issue on South Asia, Vol. 54, No. 3, September-December 2005, New Delhi.

—. 2006. India's Roaring Revolution: Dalit Assertion and New Horizons. New Delhi: Gagandeep Publications.

Lorenzen, David N. (ed.), 1996. *Bhakti Religion in North India.* New Delhi: Manohar Publishers and Distributors.

Mathew, Joseph. 1986. Ideology, Protest and Social Mobility: Case Study of Mahars and Pulayas. New Delhi: Inter-India Publications.

Mukherjee, Prabhati. 1988. *Beyond the Four Varnas: The Untouchables in India.* Delhi: Motilal Banarsidass.

Oommen, T.K. 1990. *Protest and Change: Studies in Social Movements.* New Delhi: Sage Publications.

—. 2001. Understanding the Indian Society: The Relevance of Perspective from Below. Department of Sociology, University of Pune, Pune.

Omvedt, Gail. 1994. Dalit and the Democratic Revolution: Dr Ambedkar and the Dalit Movement in Colonial India. New Delhi: Sage Publications.

Singh, Rajendra. 2000. "Peasant Movements in Uttar Pradesh", in M.S.A. Rao (ed.), *Social Movements in India.* Delhi: Manohar.

Singh, Y. 1986. Indian Sociology: Social Conditioning and Emerging Concerns. New Delhi: Vistaar Publications.

Smith, Vincent A. 1986. *The Oxford History of India,* edited by Percival Spear, New Delhi: Oxford University Press.

Srinivas, M.N. 1978. *India's Villages.* Bombay: Media Promoters and Publishers Pvt. Ltd.

—. 1985. *Caste in Modern India and Other Essays.* Bombay: Media Promoters and Publishers Pvt. Ltd.

Thapar, Romila. 2002. *Interpreting Early India.* New Delhi: Oxford University Press.

Trautmann, R. Thomas. 1997. *Aryans and British India.* New Delhi: Vistaar Publications.

Upadhya, Carol. 2002. "The Hindu Nationalist Sociology of G.S. Ghurye", *Sociological Bulletin,* Vol. 51, No. 1, March, New Delhi.

Vishwanathan, Gauri. 1998. *Outside the Fold: Conversion, Modernity, and Belief.* Delhi: Oxford University Press.

Wankhade, M.N. 1992. "Friends, The Day of Irresponsible Writers is Over", in Arjun Dangle (ed.), *Poisoned Bread (translated from the Modern Marathi Dalit Literature).* New Delhi: Orient Longman.

Webster, John C.B. 2002. Religion and Dalit Liberation: An Examination of Perspectives. New Delhi: Manohar.

2

Caste: Views from the Field

Introduction

Field-view or the view from the field refers to an orientation to the experiences of people, with their inner tensions and contradictions which one seeks to understand and interpret (Beteille, 1997). In fact, Srinivas proposed the distinction between the 'book-view' and the 'field-view' of Indian society. He maintained that there is a book-view of every major institution: of castes, of joint family, and of village community. Accounts based on fieldwork reveal a distinct departure from accounts drawn from the texts. The book-view of the caste system upholds the superior position of Brahmins in the social hierarchy while the untouchables occupy the lowest rungs. There is strict restriction on commensality and mobility. More importantly, the book-view is projected as uncontestable and immutable. View from the field particularly in the context of caste situation, brings out lived reality of the people, the articulation of what is contained in the scriptural texts in real life situations. Here, social mobility assumes importance. Further, accounts based on fieldwork reveal a distinct departure from accounts drawn from texts in the sense that the latter bring out the actual working of the caste system at the grassroots.

This chapter focuses on the operation of caste at the grass roots. In doing this it takes a departure from the earlier chapter on the Brahminical perspective on caste that dealt with ideas about caste contained in the sacred texts and the Hiundu social order as given. Here we will explore how caste system works in different societies by reviewing some field based studies.

An Overview of Caste Situation in Different Societies

Many sociologists and anthropologists have tried to analyse the basic tenets of caste system on the basis of their experience in the field. All of them have found new dimensions of caste that were either not present in the book-view of the caste system or was not specifically highlighted by the authors.

Srinivas adds a significant dimension to field-based studies of caste system in proposing the concepts of sanskritisation and dominant caste. Sanskritisation is the, "process by which a low caste or tribe or other group takes over the customs, rituals beliefs, ideology, and style of life of a high and in particular 'twice-born' (dwija) caste. The Sanskritisation of a group has usually the effect of improving its position in the caste hierarchy" (Srinivas, 1989:56). The other concept that assumes importance in the field-view of caste is that of dominant caste which he explains is one which is numerically preponderant and wields economic and political power. What is important to note is that ritual status does not necessarily determine dominance of a caste group over others.

Sanskritisation and Westernisation

The idea of hierarchy is central to caste. The customs, rites and way of life were different among the higher and lower castes. The dominant caste punished those who encroached on forbidden ground, but the process could not be stopped. This adoption of the symbols of higher status has been called Sanskritisation. The Lingayats of Mysore Sanskritised their way of life over eight centuries ago. In recent times, Sanskritisation has been widespread both spatially as well as structurally. The Ilavans of Kerala, the Smiths of South India, the Ramgharias of Punjab, the Chamars of Uttar Pradesh and many other castes have all tried to sanskritise their way of life. Liquor and forbidden meals are given up. Sanskritic ritual is increasingly adopted and there is an increasing demand for the services of a Brahmin priest at wedding, birth, funeral rites and *sraddha.*

On the other hand, the higher castes, especially those living in the bigger cities, are undergoing a process of Westernisation. Westernisation, like Sanskritisation, is a blanket term: it includes Western education as well as the adoption of Western ways of life and outlook. It also implies a degree of secularisation and rationalism, and in these two respects it stands opposed to Sanskritisation. In certain other respects, Westernisation helps to spread sanskritisation through the products of its technology—newspapers, radios and films.

In some exceptional cases, the lower castes and tribes are being Westernised without undergoing a prior process of Sanskritisation. Again, Sanskritisation occurs generally as part of the process of the upward movement of castes while Westernisation has no such association. In fact, unlike Sanskritisation, Westernisation is more commonly an individual or family phenomenon and not a caste phenomenon, though some groups (Kodagus) and some areas (Punjab) may be said to be more Westernised than the others. Again, some groups may be more Westernised in the sense that they are highly educated, whereas some others may be Westernised in their dress, food habits and recreation" (Srinivas, 1980:77-78).

Mencher analyses the caste system from bottom-up approach on the basis of fieldwork among 'untouchables' in Tamil Nadu. She argues that the functionality of the caste system is only for those castes that enjoy the privileges. On the other hand, the caste located at the lowest rung of the caste hierarchy suffers from economic and social exploitation. She reveals that there has been a protest from the castes located at the lowest rung of the hierarchy, sometimes explicitly other times tacitly. But the fact of the matter is that these protests were not recorded so they do not constitute significant part of historical evidence. One of the reasons why this happened was because the untouchables could never gather enough courage to lodge their complaint against the so-called upper castes, as they were economically dependent on them.

In a study of Jatavs of Agra, Lynch (1974) has highlighted the fact that the Jatavs who once wanted to sanskritise, rejected the complete process of sanskritisation when they got other avenues of mobility. These avenues, he argues, have been thrown open by the process of parliamentary democracy, and possibilities of political participation of the Jatavs. In this context the Jatavs, hitherto untouchables, with stigmatised identity have taken refuge in the democratic constitution of the social fabric in independent India. They assert their right on the basis of equality and argue for provision of equality of opportunity. The Jatavs formed secular association instead of traditional panchayats. They also contested elections by forming political parties and thereby tried to enhance their social status. They also attained political and economic powers that were denied to them in the traditional caste system.

In another case, Singh (1994:55) discussing patterns of sanskritisation reveals another fact about the rejection of traditional caste hierarchy by the hitherto untouchables. In his words, "The third pattern in Sanskritisation is even more important from a sociological point of view. Sanskritisation in such cases takes place through increased Puritanism and traditionalism in a caste along with rejection of the superiority of the 'twice-born' castes." Certain castes of eastern Uttar Pradesh refused to accept water even from the Brahmins, considering them less pure than themselves. Similarly, in many other untouchable castes, the process of Sanskritisation includes the rejection of some models of book-view of caste system'. In this regard Cohn (1955:215) writes:

> "Literacy has enabled the Chamars to relate to aspects of the Hindu Great tradition, through reading stories available in vernacular books. Urban employment has enabled Chamars to participate in rituals, derived from the Hindu Great tradition, at low caste temple in the cities. Simultaneously, there continues an earlier movement, the Siva Narayan sect, whose goal was Sanskritisation. Another strand is represented by the celebration of Rai Das birthday, which now is in hands of Chamar college students, who are, among other things, using political action. Their stories about Rai Das have an anti-Brahmin tint to them and they stress right action and right principles rather than the more orthodox activities, worship and rituals". Another aspect that deserves mention is the protest of the non-Brahmin communities against the domination of Brahmins in different parts of the country. The apical position accorded to the Brahmins in the sacred texts was challenged.

Further, we have noted that the caste system has often been considered a system which is maintained rigidly through the practice of endogamy and the ideology of purity-pollution ignoring conflict of power and privileges. The field-view of caste has, however, revealed that the caste system was (and is in the present day too) much influenced by political and economic factors. The study of Nadars of Tamil Nadu is a case in point. Defining the importance of caste in Indian politics, Rudolph and Rudolph (1987) reveal that political clout can be used to change even the status in the caste hierarchy and many rights can bc acquired which were once denied to a caste. They took the case of an untouchable community i.e. Shanans of Tamil Nadu and explained how it could change the social status with the help of political mobilisation and association. In their words, "In 1921, the Shanans succeeded in officially changing their name. Their metamorphosis was wrought neither by the institutions of traditional society nor by findings of the legal system, of the British State customs or the sacred texts of traditional society justified Shanan claims. It was government of Madras that wrought this important symbolic change, and its reasons for doing so were in considerable measure political. Nadars (as they were later on called) had brought increasing political pressure to bear on government to recognise the changes in self and social esteem resulting from a century of social change and mobility." (Rudolph and Rudolph, 1987:45).

Pollution Rules

Pollution rules are much less strictly observed in cities than in villages. In fact in certain areas of urban life pollution has ceased to have any application. People mix freely in factories and schools, and very few bother about the caste of fellow-passengers in train and buses. In cities pollution is being increasingly confined to the house, to women and to ritual occasions. In older days the higher castes regarded contact with the lower castes as polluting, and the latter were also subjected to some disabilities. For instance, the lower castes were not allowed to build tiled houses, wear the clothes that the upper castes wore or take out wedding processions in streets inhabited by high castes. Punishment for an offence varied according to the caste of the persons who committed it and against whom it was committed. Mahatma Gandhi roused the conscience of educated Indians about the practice of untouchability. Apart from the injustice, educated Indians realised the political dangers of trying to deny basic conditions of decent living to large numbers of people on the ground of birth in a particular caste. It is this awareness that has led to the adoption of various measures in independent India to put an end to untouchability and to enable the scheduled castes and tribes to advance to the level of the high castes. The grosser expression of untouchability has disappeared in the cities, but in rural areas it still holds sway. The economic emancipation of the Harijans and their increased migration to urban areas are necessary for the complete eradication of untouchability" (Srinivas, 1980:78-79).

The caste system in its traditional form has undergone tremendous change because of politicisation. In the domain of politics, both caste and kin seek to establish new identities and strive for enviable positions. Politicians find caste groupings readily available for political mobilisation. Kothari (1970) explains that, traditionally, there were two aspects of the secular organisation of caste: the governmental aspect which included caste councils, village arbitration procedures and so on; and the political aspect which included the intra-caste and inter-caste authority and status alignments and cleavages. These were dispensed through authority relationships of the local elites and the central political system(s). In the present day, electoral and party politics assume tremendous importance. There is continuous co-option of more and more strata in political-decision making processes. In some regions the Brahmins got involved readily, in others particularly where the Brahmins were not dominant, certain agricultural upper castes got involved.

According to the dalits, the caste system was framed by the Aryans to subjugate them. They say that since the Aryans were few in number and needed to control the indigenous people i.e., the dalits who were egalitarian, they devised the caste system. Various caste movements as the Adi-Dravida, were led by this ideology (Omvet, 1994). Dalits assert that their conversion to different religions–Islam, Sikhism and Christianity introduced the element of caste in them too. Later the dalit leaders mobilised the untouchables and Shudras (who constitute the Dalit and other backward classes category in contemporary times) under the banner of majority-minority communities. They argue that the Brahmins, Kshatriyas, and Vaisyas constitute only 15 per cent of the population, hence they are in minority to Dalits who constitute the remaining population.

Field Based Studies

The field-view of caste comes out most clearly from studies at the grass roots by sociologists and social anthropologists. Further, in specific terms the field view localises our understanding of caste and makes the researcher aware about the historical forces operating in the particular village or region down the ages. The field view also equips the researcher to take into account the internal factions within the caste. A researcher can observe everyday interaction between various castes in a village in economic, political and socio-religious spheres in a field situation and then develop a holistic framework for exploring the social status and mobility of different castes.

What follows now are specific, field based studies that bring to light the working of the caste system in the lives of people. Let us turn to a detailed study of some important aspects of field-view with specific examples. Here we have tried to evaluate the analysis of caste undertaken F. G. Bailey, Adrian C. Mayer, McKim Marriott, and O.M. Lynch. The contribution made by these authors is significant because their understanding of caste is based on field view. This means they have tried to look at the caste system in India in operational terms. All the scholars have closely observed and recorded the intra/inter-caste interactions in the villages/regions of their studies and have discussed the implications of such an inter-caste interaction for the ranking of castes in the hierarchy. Nevertheless, they vary in their emphasis and focus of study.

(a) Kishangarhi Village in Aligarh

In the village of Kishangarhi located in Aligarh district, Uttar Pradesh, McKim Marriott set out to study the nature of social hierarchy. The village was one with people belonging to different castes, practicing different occupations. Interestingly, all the people did not give the same rank order to castes. Again, there was disparity between the rank ascribed to a caste in the scriptures and that ascribed to it by the people. What this means is that, the castes did not seem to derive their position in the social hierarchy from the highness or lowness of their attributes. In Met some of the attributes such as diet and occupational restrictions were not determinate in ascription of rank to a caste. This stood out in contrast to the emphasis on the two attributes in the texts. He found that the categorisation of food into *pucca* and *kuchha* and its acceptance from those equal in caste rank or refusal from those lower in caste rank was not a sufficient criterion of determining the position of a caste in the hierarchy. In the Kishangarhi village itself the vegetarian castes (as the washerman i.e., Dhobi) and the non-vegetarian caste (as the leather workers i.e., Chamar) occupied the same position in the caste hierarchy.

Marriott found that in relation to the occupational hierarchy or ranking of castes on the basis of purity of occupations, the placement of castes did not follow from the highness or lowness of occupation, Thus, those castes that followed clean occupations were ranked differently; the carpenter was higher than the gardener who was considered higher than the cultivator and so on. The barber, shepherd and several others were, however, placed on the same level of the local hierarchy.

Other scholars note that, castes following clean and pure occupations and food habits are often ranked below those castes that follow the less pure or more polluting occupations. In a Mysore village studied by Srinivas, for example, there were both vegetarian and non-vegetarian castes, and castes following both clean and unclean occupations. The trader's caste is both a vegetarian and follows a clean occupation as compared to other castes such as the peasants. But castes such as the peasants rank above the traders. This shows a discrepancy between the attributes of the caste and its rank.

It is found that a caste may follow a pure occupation and be non-vegetarian or an impure occupation and be vegetarian. Thus both the castes combine the pure and impure attributes. In such a caste, determination of rank is not easy. A caste often consists of an admixture of attributes that are treated as pure and those that are treated as impure. Often, a caste cannot be said to be completely pure or completely impure. Take for instance the case of Brahmins in different parts of the Indian subcontinent. According to the book-view of the caste system, the Brahmins practice pure occupations, such as priesthood, observe purity of diet i.e. strict vegetarianism and teetotalism (i.e., avoidance of alcohol) and, among other reasons, because of these attributes they occupy the highest rank in the hierarchy. But, when we take the example of the Brahmins of Kashmir, Bengal and several other regions we find that they are non-vegetarians and in spite of such dietary habits they continue to occupy important social position in the caste hierarchy. The book-view remains silent on the question of vegetarianism and nature of occupation as being sufficient criteria for determining the position of a caste in social hierarchy neither does it take note of the different permutations in which the attributes combine and recombine in actual lives.

Just as Marriott (1955) found in his village study that castes having the same attributes of diet and occupation, often get ranked differently, F.G. Bailey (1957) in his study of village Bisipara in Orissa, points out how there are many castes in the village each of which is non-vegetarian yet they are ranked differently by the villagers.

(b) Caste in Bisipara Village of Orissa

Bailey studied the Bisipara village of Orissa which had several caste groups represented by different population size that varied from one person to 150 people said that caste groups are united into a system through two principles, namely, segregation and hierarchy. "Castes", according to Bailey (1963:123), "stand in a ritual and secular (political, economic) hierarchy expressed in rules of interaction." Here Bailey sees the caste system as a dynamic one in which different castes are held together by the power of dominant caste. According to him, the component of ritual status of a caste group goes hand-in-hand with the political and economic status. The relationship between castes is simply based on practice of rituals. The concern is with power because, many castes are subordinate to the dominant caste. In fact, the caste system is held together because of the concentration of power (and force) in the hands of the dominant caste. Since ritual rank is always consistent with political and economic status, once a caste becomes wealthy it changes its pattern of interaction with other castes so that it may claim a higher rank in hierarchy. In other words, a caste's rank in the hierarchy is expressed through its pattern of interaction with the other castes. Here, the pattern of interaction becomes an indicator of its ritual status in the hierarchy. The pattern of interaction includes the acceptance and distribution of food; acceptance of water; willingness to smoke together and/ or to sit together may also be treated as an indicator of pattern of interaction. Exchange of gift is included in the list. Bailey also talks about the interaction between people of same caste spread over different villages in the region. A caste spread over a particular region may come together and strengthen ties through marriage. When this region-wide relationship matures, the caste may strive for power in the political sphere, Bailey explains the aforesaid issue by looking at inter-caste interaction in Bisipara.

> "Dr. Bailey's study, *Caste and The Economic Frontier* (1958), provides a good example of kind of changes which came in the wake of British rule. In Bisipara, a village in Khondmals in Orissa, two non-landowning castes made money because they could get a monopoly of the profitable trade in hides and liquor. It would have been polluting for the higher castes to handle liquor or hides. Of the two castes one was able to raise itself up in the hierarchy by Sanskritising its ritual and way of life; the other, found that untouchability came in the way of its mobility" (Srinivas, 1986:76).

According to Bailey, generally speaking, in the upper and lower extremes of the hierarchy, one can find perfect correspondence between ritual, political and economic status. In Bisipara, the warriors stood at the top of the caste ritual hierarchy next only to a sole Brahmin family in the village. But in the secular hierarchy consisting of political and economic statuses, warriors were the dominant caste. They owned a large part of the land and dominated the village council. But what happened after the change that swept Bisipara in the post-independence period is more important to note from the vantage point of field-view of caste system. After experiencing the winds of change, the warriors' position came to be ambiguous in the ritual hierarchy because they lost much of their land. Moreover, the merchant caste as well as the distiller caste people came to claim a position next to that of Brahmins. None of these castes would accept food or water from one another anymore. Thus, conflict developed between the distillers and the warriors regarding their position in the ritual hierarchy.

Warriors like the Brahmins, accepted water from the herdsmen caste but not from the distillers. Thus implicitly, the warriors placed the distillers below herdsmen in the ritual hierarchy. The herdsmen, accepted food and water from warriors but refused it from the distillers. The distillers now reacted by accepting food and water only from the Brahmins and no one else. Thus, distillers of Bisipara claimed for themselves a position next to the Brahmins, after attaining wealth and weakening of the economic status of warriors. The Bisipara case of distillers reveals that whenever there is an improvement in political and economic status, castes tend to change their pattern of interaction only to claim a higher rank in the ritual hierarchy. This is contrary to the book-view that assigns a fixed ritual hierarchy for all the times with Brahmins at the top and the Shudras at the bottom.

(c) Caste in Ramkheri Village in Madhya Pradesh

Ramkheri village is situated near a small town by the name of Dewas in Madhya Pradesh. Ramkheri had twenty-five Hindu and two Muslim castes. Commensal relations were strictly regulated, though flexibility was possible occasionally. To understand the hierarchy of commensal relations, Mayer observed the following:

(i) Types of activities: Eating, drinking water, smoking

(ii) Types of food: *Pakka* food, *kachha* food

(iii) The place and context of eating: Wedding or mourning

(iv) Who is seated next to whom while eating?

(v) Who provides the food? Who cooks the food?

(vi) In what vessel is water given, brass or earthen pot?

Mayer projects the village as a concrete reality affecting human relationships. It is from the interaction between the various castes in a village that a hierarchy of caste emerges. (See unit of ESO-12 of B.A. Programme) Mayer analyses inter-caste relations and their relation with the unity of the village. Mayer identifies economic and political interaction and more importantly, commensality (interdining) as the factors, which determine caste hierarch in the village.

According to Mayer (1970), it is difficult to measure the ranks on the economic and political basis of caste ranking. The problem with economic and political factors is that, all members may not come together or have interaction in the economic and political sphere. It is also a fact that economic wealth may cut across caste divisions. In other words, a person of a 'high' caste may have a poor economic status and vice versa. These problems are resolved in the context of ritual status. Ritual status in the caste hierarchy uniformly applies to everyone in the caste. Even in the patterns of interaction, it is only the 'commensal hierarchy' that can give an intricate system of relations between castes. In the words of Mayer (1970:59), "The ranking of castes is nowhere more clearly seen than in the commensal rules of eating, drinking and smoking". Caste hierarchy is not determined solely by economic and political factors, although these are important. For him, the single most important factor is commensality, which clearly indicates the hierarchy prevalent in the village.

It is a fact that, "The commensal hierarchy is based on the theory that each caste has certain quality of ritual purity which is lessened, or polluted by certain commensal contacts with castes having inferior quality" (Mayer, 1970: 33). Hence, a superior caste does not eat from the cooking vessels or the hands of a caste that it regards as inferior, nor wilt its members sit next to the inferior people in the same unbroken line (*pangat*) when eating. Drinking and smoking follow similar rules of exclusion. According to Mayer, "The position of a caste on the commensal hierarchy can be assessed on the principle that eating the food cooked or served by another caste denotes equality with or inferiority and that not to eat denotes equality and superiority... To put it another way, those from whom all will eat are higher than those from whom none will eat" (Mayer, 1970:34).

Mayer explains that the Brahmins come first in the undisputed position. The Brahmins of Ramkheri village eat *kachha* food cooked only by members of their own caste or sub-caste. All the other castes accept the food cooked by the Brahmins and drink freely from their earthen pots. Moreover, according to Mayer, next to the Brahmin in the hierarchy are two groups of castes, one group is vegetarian while the other is non-vegetarian. Rajputs eat non-vegetarian food, but consider barbers and the potters as inferior because they accept *kachha* food from the inferior carpenter or farmer. The dairymen of Ramkheri accept *kachha* food only from the Brahmins but from no other caste. Only some most inferior castes (weaver, tanner, sweeper) accept food from them. In a similar way, oil-pressers of Ramkheri are ranked slightly above the dairymen, because at least a fey/ castes above them eat from them. Carpenter, gardener, smith, farmer and tailor castes accept *kachha* food only from the Brahmins. Carpenter is placed high because he eats only from the Brahmins and the farmer is placed lower than carpenter because he accepts food from Rajputs and potters as well.

Still lower in the hierarchy are the bhilala, mina, nath and drummer. None of these castes accept *kachha* food from each other. Weavers, tanners and sweepers are at the lowest order of the hierarchy. Sweeper is considered to be the lowliest of all castes in Ramkheri village because he alone eats the left-over from the plates of other castes. Now from the above description of caste hierarchies, it becomes clear that the commensal relations in Ramkheri village indicate and express the ritual status of various caste groups. The other indicators of hierarchy as emphasised in the sacred scriptures have been rendered inconsequential.

Conclusion

We have come to realise that the caste situation at the grass roots presents several dimensions that are not contained in the sacred scriptures. The view from the field lays emphasis on the secular, day-to-day interactions between people belonging to different castes and among people belonging to the same caste. Now, while the texts classify people into four *varnas* (Brahmin, Kshatriya, Vaishya, and Shudra) based on a theory of their origin from different parts of the body of the creator (later the fifth varna comprising those presently known as 'untouchables', harijans' was added) at ground-reality, there are several jatis or castes based on occupation. The book-view of caste was a rigid and closed system with negligible scope for social mobility. The thrust was on rituals, hierarchy based on purity-impurity. Surely, then caste emerged as a static entity. It may be safely concluded that the 'book-view' of caste gives us only partial reality of the structure and functioning of the caste system in India. It gives a normative and prescriptive order that does not work in all situations. It can also be ascertained from the above that the normative principles enshrined in the sacred texts on the basis of which most of the notions of book view of caste are carved for individuals and groups are governed by different principles in a given geographical and socio-political situation. The field situation is plagued with social change and conflict. It also points to the possibility of an alternate way of explaining caste.

The field view brings to light the dynamics of caste relations in which the element of ritual does not remain excessively significant. Wealth and power rather ritual assume greater importance and determine and social hierarchy. Dominant caste (defined by Srinivas as one which preponderates numerically over the other castes, and wields preponderant economic and political power) governs inter-caste relations. Education and constitutional provisions for the backward caste have had a profound impact on the operative aspect of the caste system. There is fuzziness of hierarchy in the caste occupying the middle rungs.

Further Reading

Lynch, Owen, M., 1974. *The Politics of Untouchability:* National Publishing House, Delhi.

Mayer, Adrian, C., 1970. *Caste and Kinship in Central India: A Village and its Region,* University of California Press. Berkeley and Los Angeles.

Rudolph, I., L. Rudolph, Susanne, Hoeber, 1987, *The Modernity of Tradition: Political Development in India.* Orient Longman.

3

Caste: Views of Ambedkar and Lohia

Introduction

Babasaheb Ambedkar (1891- 1956) was a Dalit who assumed the role of social, political, and spiritual leader first for the Dalits and subsequently for the whole nation. He gave the country a democratic constitution; as a spiritual leader he revived the legacy of Buddha. On the other hand, Ram Manohar Lohia (1910-1967) - a socialist by ideology championed the cause of the disadvantaged of India including minorities and women. Ambedkar and Lohia identified the caste system as degenerate in Indian society and wanted to annihilate it. That is why towards the fag end of his life Ambedkar was in touch with Lohia exchanging views through letters. In fact both of them wanted to launch a political party with scheduled castes, scheduled tribes, women and minorities at their base constituency.

This chapter consists of views of Babasaheb Bhimrao Ambedkar and Ram Manohar Lohia on the caste system in Indian society. It starts with a brief introduction to Ambedkar's interpretation of Hindu social order based on the varna theory and goes on to explore his vision on genesis, and spread of caste system. The unit presents the views of Ambedkar on caste consciousness and its dysfunctional aspect. It also deals with the ideas of Ram Manohar Lohia on the dysfunctional aspects of the caste system and his vision to annihilate it.

Ambedkar on Caste

Ambedkar drew attention to the rigidity of the caste system and its essential features. He argued that the principle of graded inequality as a fundamental principle is beyond controversy. The four classes are not only different but also unequal in status, one stands above the other. In the scheme of Manu, the Brahmin occupies at the uppermost rank followed by the Kshatriya, Vaishya and Shudra. Below the Shudra is the Untouchable. This principle regulates many spheres of life. An officer distributing money and/or other relief material to famine-stricken people, for example, would give a larger share to a person of high birth than he would to a person of low birth. The Hindu social order does not recognise equal need, equal work or equal ability as the basis of reward for labour. It favours the distribution of the good things of life among those who are reckoned as the highest in the social hierarchy. The second principle on which the Hindu social order is founded is that of prescribed graded occupations that are inherited from father to son for each class. The third feature of the Hindu social order according to Ambedkar is the confinement of interaction of people to their respective classes. In the Hindu social order there is restriction on interdining and inter-marriages between people of different classes. According to Ambedkar there is nothing strange or peculiar that the Hindu social order recognises classes. There are classes everywhere and no society exists without them even a free social order will not be able to get rid of the classes completely. A free social order, however, aims to prevent isolation and exclusiveness because both make the members of the class inimical towards one another (Ambedkar, 1987: 113).

(a) Interpretation of Varna Theory

Ambedkar recognised the existence of four varnas in the Hindu social order. He emphasised that the Hindu social order is primarily based on the class or varna and not on individuals. He opined that the unit of Hindu society is not the individual Brahmin, or the individual, Kshatriya, Vaishya, Shudra, or the 'Untouchables'. Even the family is not regarded in the Hindu social order as a unit of society except for the purposes of marriage and inheritance. The unit of Hindu society is the class or varna. In the Hindu social order, there is no room for individual merit and no consideration of individual justice. If a person has a privilege it is not because it is due to him/her as an individual. The privilege goes with the class, and if he/she is found to cnjoy it, it is because he/she belongs to that class. Conversely, an individual suffers not because he/she deserves it by virtue of his/her conduct; rather it is because he/she belongs to that class.

Ambedkar analysed the impact of the division of the society into varnas on the Hindu social order. He argued that because of this division the Hindu social order has failed to uphold liberty, equality and fraternity — the three essentials of a free social order. The Hindus do believe that god created different classes of people from different parts of his divine body. According to Ambedkar, (1987:100) "The doctrine that the different classes were created from different parts of the divine body has generated the belief that it must be divine will that they should remain separate and distinct. It is this belief which has created in the Hindu an instinct to be different, to be separate and to be distinct from the rest of his fellow Hindus". In the same vein Ambedkar adds, "The most extensive and wild manifestation of this spirit of isolation and separation is of course of the caste-system... Originally, there were four only. Today, how many are there? It is estimated that the total is not less than 2000. It must be 3000... Castes are divided into sub-castes." (Ambedkar, 1987: 102)." The question that Ambedkar raised is, "What fraternity can there be in a social order based upon such sentiments?"

Ambedkar asks, 'Does the Hindu Social Order recognise equality?' He says that while the Hindu social order accepts that men have come from the body of the Creator of the Universe, it does not treat them as equal because they were created from the different parts of his body that are themselves graded in terms of perceived importance and location. The Brahmins were created from the mouth, the Kshatriyas from the arms, the Vaishyas from his thighs and the Shudras from the feet. Ambedkar agrees that it is a fact that men were not equal in their character and natural endowments, he opined that the Hindu social order, "refuses to recognise that men no matter how profoundly they differ as individuals in capacity and character, are equally entitled as human beings to consideration and respect and that the well-being of a society is likely to be increased if it plans its organisation that, whether their powers are great or small, all its members may be equally enabled to make the best of such powers as they possess" (Ambedkar, 1987:106). It is for this reason that he feels that the Hindu social order is against the "equalitarian temper" and does not allow equality of circumstances, institutions and lifestyle to develop.

In the same context, Ambedkar upholds that there is absence of liberty specifically 'liberty of action' in the Hindu social order because the occupation and status of the individuals are all fixed on the basis of their birth in a particular family. The same is true for political liberty too. The Hindu social order does not recognise the necessity of a representative government chosen by the people. According to him, though the Hindu social order does recognise that laws must govern the people, it negates the idea that the laws can be made by the representatives chosen by the people. Ambedkar submits that, the Hindus are of the opinion that the law by which people are to be governed already exist in the Vedas and no human being is empowered to bring about a change in the existing laws (Ambedkar: 1987:114).

(b) Genesis of Caste System in India

Ambedkar studied the definitions of caste proposed by Senart, Nesfield, Risley, and Ketkar closely. According to Senart, "a caste is a close corporation, in theory at any rate rigorously hereditary; equipped with a certain traditional and independent organisation, including a chief and a council, meeting on occasion in assemblies of more or less plenary authority and joining together at certain festival: Bound together by common occupation, which relate more particularly to marriage and food and to questions of ceremonial pollution, and ruling its members by the exercise of jurisdiction, the extent of which varies, but which succeeds in making the authority of the community more felt by the sanction of a certain penalties and above all by final irrevocable exclusion from the group". Nesfield defines a caste as, "a class of the community which disowns any connection with any other class and can neither intermarry nor eat nor drink with any but persons of their own community". Ambedkar quotes Risley, according to whom, "a caste may be defined as a collection of families or groups of families bearing a common name which usually denotes or is associated with specific occupation, claiming common descent from a mythical ancestor, human or divine, professing to follow the same professional callings and are regarded by those who are competent to give an opinion as forming a single homogenous Community". Finally, Ambedkar took note of Ketkar's definition of caste. According to Ketkar caste is, "a social group having two characteristics— (I) membership is confined to those who are born of members and includes all persons so born. (II) the members are forbidden by an inexorable social law to marry outside the group". Reviewing the aforesaid definitions of castes given by different social scientists, Ambedkar emphasises that most scholars have defined caste as an isolated unit.

Ambedkar analyses only those elements from the definitions of castes which he regards peculiar and of universal occurrence. For Senart, the "idea of pollution" was characteristic of caste. Ambedkar refutes this by arguing that by no means it is peculiar to caste. It usually originates in priestly ceremonialism and in the general belief in purity. Its connection with caste as an essential element may be ruled out because even without it the caste system operates. He concludes that the idea of pollution is associated with caste only because priesthood and purity are old associates and it is the priestly-caste, which enjoys the highest rank in the caste hierarchy. Ambedkar identifies the absence of dining with those outside one's own caste as one of the characteristics in Nesfield's definition of caste. He points out that Nesfield had mistaken the effect for the cause. Absence of inter-dining is effect of the caste system and not its cause. Further, Ketkar defines a caste in its relation to a system of castes. Ketkar identified two characteristics of caste, (a) prohibition of inter-marriage and (b) membership by autogeny. Ambedkar argues that these two aspects are not different because if inter-marriage is prohibited, the result is that membership is limited to those born within the group. After critical evaluation of the various characteristics of caste, Ambedkar infers that prohibition or rather the absence of inter-marriage between people of different castes is the only element that can be considered as the critical element of caste. Among the Hindus, castes are endogamous while gotras within a particular caste are exogamous. In spite of the endogamy of the castes, exogamy at the level of gotra is strictly observed. There are more rigorous penalties for those who break the laws of exogamy than those who break the laws of endogamy. It is understandable that exogamy cannot be prescribed at the level of caste, for them caste, as a definite, identifiable unit would cease to exist.

Ambedkar further says that, preventing marriages out of the group creates a problem from within the group, which is not easy to solve. The problem is that the number of individuals of either sex is more or less evenly distributed in a normal group and they are of similar age. If a group desires to consolidate its identity as a caste then it has to maintain a strict balance in the number of persons belonging to either sex. Maintenance of numbers becomes the primary goal because, if a group wants to preserve the practice of endogamy, it is absolutely necessary to maintain a numerical equality between marriageable individuals of the two sexes within the group. Ambedkar (1978: 10) concludes, "The problem of caste, then, ultimately resolves itself into one of repairing disparity between the marriageable units of the two sexes within it." What naturally happens is that there is a 'surplus' of either sex in the society. If a man dies his wife is 'surplus' and if a woman dies her husband is 'surplus'. If the group does not take care of this surplus population, it can easily break the law of endogamy. Ambedkar argues that there are two ways in which the problem of 'surplus women' is resolved in society. 'Surplus women' may either be burnt on the funeral pyre of their husbands or strict rules of endogamy may be imposed on them. Since burning of women cannot be encouraged in society, widowhood bringing with it prohibition of re-marriage is imposed on them.

As far as the problem of 'surplus men' is concerned, Ambedkar says that men have dominated the society since centuries and have enjoyed greater prestige than women. The same treatment, therefore, cannot be accorded to them. A widower can remain so for the rest of his life; but given the sexual desire that is natural, he is a threat to the morals of the group particularly if he leads an active social life and not as a recluse. He has to be, therefore, allowed to marry second time with a woman who is not previously married. This is, however, a difficult preposition. If a widower is provided a second woman, then an imbalance in the number women of marriageable age is created. A 'surplus man' can therefore, be provided wife who has not yet reached marriageable age i.e. a minor girl. Ambedkar identified four means by which numerical disparity between two sexes can be dealt with, burning of widow with her deceased husband; compulsory widowhood; imposition of celibacy on the widower; and wedding of the widower to a girl who has not yet attained marriageable age. In Hindu society, the customs of sati, prohibition of widow remarriage, and marriage of minor girls are practiced. A widower may also observe *sanyasa* (i.e. renounce the world). These practices take care of the maintenance of numerical balance between both the sexes, born out of endogamy.

For Ambedkar, the question of spread and origin of caste are not separated. According to Ambedkar the caste system has either been imposed upon the docile population of India by a lawgiver as a divine dispensation or it has developed according to some law of social growth peculiar to the Indian people. Ambedkar refutes the notion that the law of caste was given by some lawgiver. Manu is considered to be the law-giver of Hindus; but at the outset there is doubt whether he ever existed. Even if he existed, the caste system predates Manu. No doubt Manu upheld it and philosophised about it, but he certainly did not and could not ordain the present order of Hindu society. His work ended with the confiscation of existing caste rules and the preaching of caste *dharma* or duties obligations and conduct associated with each caste. Ambedkar rejects the argument that the Brahmin created the caste. He maintains that it was necessary to dismantle this belief because still there is a strong belief in the minds of orthodox Hindus that the Hindu society was moulded into the framework of the caste system and that it is consciously crafted in the shastras. It may be noted that the teaching and preaching of shastras or the sacred texts is the prerogative of the Brahmins.

Ambedkar agrees with the second argument, i.e., of some law of social growth peculiar to Indian people about the spread of caste system. According to western scholars, the bases of origin of various castes in India are occupation, survival of tribal organisations, the rise of new belief system, crossbreeding and migration (Ambedkar, 1978:17). The problem, according to Ambedkar, is that the aforesaid nuclei also exist in other societies and are not peculiar to India. Ambedkar asked, "why they did not 'form' caste in other parts of this planet?" At some stage, the priestly class detached itself from rest of the body of people and emerged as a caste by itself. The other classes that were subject to the law of social division of labour underwent differentiation. Some of these classes got divided into bigger groups and some into smaller ones.

According to Ambedkar, "This sub-division of a society is quite natural. But the unnatural thing about these sub-divisions is that they have lost the open-door character of the class system and have become self-enclosed units called castes. The question is: were they compelled to close their doors and become endogamous, or did they close them of their accord? I submit that there is a double line of answer: Some closed their door: Others found it closed against them. The one is a psychological interpretation and the other is mechanistic, but they are complementary" (Ambedkar, 1978: 18). Explaining the psychological interpretation of endogamy, Ambedkar opined that endogamy was popular in the Hindu society. Since it had originated from the Brahmin caste it was whole-heartedly imitated by all the non-Brahmin sub-divisions or classes, who in their turn, became endogamous castes. Ambedkar quotes Gabriel Tarde's law of imitation in this context. According to Tarde, "imitation flows from higher to lower". Secondly, "the intensity of imitation varies inversely in proportion to distance... Distance is understood here in its sociological meaning" (Ambedkar, 1978: 19).

Ambedkar points out that some castes were formed by imitating others because crucial conditions for the formation of castes by imitation existed in the Hindu society. He feels, (i) that the source of imitation must enjoy prestige in the group; and (ii) that there must be "numerous and daily relations" among members of the group. Ambedkar opined that the Brahmin is treated as next to God in Indian society. His prestige is unquestionable and he is the fountainhead of all that is good. He is idolised by scriptures therefore, "Such a creature is worthy of more than mere imitation, but at least of imitation; and if he lives in an endogamous enclosure should not the rest follow his example?" (Ambedkar, 1978:19).

He argues that the imitation of non-Brahmin of those customs which supported the structure of caste in its nascent days until it became embedded in the Hindu mind and persists even today, is testimony to fact that imitation is the cause of formation of caste. The customs of sati, enforced widowhood, and girl marriage are followed in one way or the other by different castes. Ambedkar opines, "Those castes that are nearest to the Brahmin have imitated all the three customs and insist on the strict observance thereof. Those that are less near have imitated enforced widowhood and girl marriage; others, a little further off, have only girl marriage and those furthest of have imitated only the belief in the case principle" (Ambedkar, 1978: 20).

(c) Caste and the Division of Labour

Ambedkar says that the caste system assigns tasks to individuals on the basis of the social status of the parents. Looked at it from another point of view, this stratification of occupations that is the result of the caste system is positively pernicious. Industry is never static. It undergoes rapid and abrupt change. With such changes an individual must be free to change his occupation. Without such freedom to adjust to changing circumstances, it would be impossible for a person to earn a livelihood. Now, the caste system does not allow Hindus to adopt occupations that do not belong to them by heredity. By not permitting readjustment of occupations, caste becomes a cause of much of the unemployment in the country. Furthermore, the caste system is based on the dogma of predestination. Considerations of social efficiency would compel us to recognise that the greatest evil in the industrial system is not so much poverty and the suffering that it involves as the fact that so many people have callings that hold no appeal to them. Such callings constantly evoke aversion, ill will and the desire to evade. The occupations that are regarded as degraded by the Hindus such as scavenging evoke aversion for those who are engaged in them. Given the fact that people pursuing such occupations out of some compulsion want to give them up, what efficiency can there be in a system under which neither people's hearts nor their minds are in their work?

(d) Socialists and the Caste System

Ambedkar further analyses the steps taken by the socialists to annihilate the caste system through economic development and reforms. Ambedkar questions the wisdom of socialists who professed that acquiring economic power is the only motive by which man is actuated and economic power is the only kind of power that one can exercise effectively over others. He opined that social status of an individual by itself often becomes a source of power. He suggests that religion, social status, and property are all sources of power and authority that come into play in different situations. Ambedkar feels that without bringing reform in social order one cannot bring about economic change. He also cautioned the socialists that the proletariat or the poor do not constitute a homogeneous category. They are divided not only on the basis of their economic situation but also on the basis of caste and creed. They cannot, therefore, unite against those who exploit them. According to Ambedkar (1978:48), "It seems to me that other things being equal the only thing that will move one man to take such an action is the feeling that other men with whom he is acting are actuated by feeling of equality and fraternity and above all of justice. Men will not join in a revolution for the equalisation of property unless they know that after the revolution is achieved they will be treated equally and that there will be no discrimination of caste and creed. The assurance must be the assurance proceeding from much deeper foundation, namely, the mental attitude of the compatriots towards one another in their spirit of personal equality and fraternity". The elimination of caste through economic reform is not tenable hence socialists would have to deal with hierarchy in a caste first before effecting economic change.

(e) Annihilation of Caste

Ambedkar explains that caste is not a physical object like a wall of bricks or a line of barbed wire that prevents the Hindus from free social interaction. Caste is a notion; it is a state of the mind. If someone wants to break the caste system, he/she has to attack the sacredness and divinity of the caste. Ambedkar believed that the real way to annihilate the caste system is "to destroy the belief in the sanctity of the shastras. How do you expect to succeed, if you allow the Shastras to continue to mould the beliefs and opinions of the people? Not to question the authority of the Shastras, to permit the people to believe in their sanctity and their sanctions and to blame them and to criticise them for their acts as being irrational and inhuman is an incongruous way of carrying on social reform. Reformers working for the removal of untouchability including Mahatma Gandhi, do not seem to realise that the acts of the people are merely the results of their beliefs inculcated upon their minds by the Shastras and that people will not change their conduct until they cease to believe in the sanctity of the Shastras on which their conduct is founded" (Ambedkar, 1978: 68).

Ambedkar further added that the caste system has two aspects, it divides men into separate communities; and it places the communities in a graded order one above the other as discussed earlier. The higher the grade of a caste, the greater is the number of religious and social rights. Now, this gradation makes it impossible to organise a common front against the caste system. Castes form a graded system of sovereignties, high and low, which are jealous of their status and which know that if a general dissolution happened, some of them would lose more prestige and power than others. It is, therefore, not possible to organise a mobilisation of the Hindus.

Can you appeal to reason and ask the Hindus to discard caste as being contrary to reason? Here, Ambedkar quotes Manu "So far as caste and varna are concerned, not only the Shastras do not permit the Hindu to use his reason in the decision of the question, but they have taken care to see that a rational way the foundations of his belief in caste and varna" (Ambedkar, 1978: 72). Ambedkar argues that if one wanted to dismantle the caste system then one would have to implement law(s) to change the caste system. He proposes the following reforms within the Hindu religion in order to dismantle the caste system, (i) There should be one and only one standard book of Hindu Religion, acceptable to all Hindus and recognised by all Hindus; (ii) it would be appropriate if priesthood among Hindus was abolished, failing which the priesthood should at least cease to be hereditary. Every person who professes to be a Hindu must be eligible for the position of a priest. Law should ensure that no Hindu performs rituals as a priest unless he has passed an examination prescribed by the state and holds a permission from the state to practice; (iii) no ceremony performed by a priest who does not hold the permission would be deemed to be valid in law, and a person who officiates as priest without the permission should be personalised; (iv) a priest should be the servant of the state and should be subject to the disciplinary action by the state in the matter of his morals, beliefs; and (v) the number of priests should be limited by law according to the requirements of the state. These, according to Ambedkar, would provide the basis for the establishment of a new social order based on liberty, equality and fraternity, in short, with democracy.

Having analysed the exploitative nature of Hindu social order born out of varnas, castes and sub-castes, Ambedkar gives his own vision of an ideal social order. He looked forward to a society based on liberty, equality and fraternity. Fraternity creates more channels for association and sharing experiences. This helps in establishing an attitude of respect and reverence among the individuals towards fellowmen. For Ambedkar, liberty benefits the people by giving them freedom of choice of occupation. Lastly, it is a fact that all men are not equal in terms of their physical and economic endowment people alike these elements were absent in a caste-ridden society.

Ram Manohar Lohia on Caste

Ram Manohar Lohia believed that caste system is directly related with the division of labour. According to him caste system will exist in one form or the other wherever there is hereditary production though on a small-scale. Further, he said that whenever there is centralisation of land or when landowning classes hold power, there would be Kshatriya varna. Wherever there is priestly class for the assistance of Kshatriya, there will be Brahmin varna. Wherever there is agriculture, and exchange, there will be Vaishya varna, and wherever the branches of production are developed in special form of branches of artisans, there will exist a Shudra varna.

The development of caste system is related with the development of craft knowledge. Brahman is a varna, but the varna in itself does not connote an occupation. This is also true of the Kshatriya and Vaishya varna. Vaishyas, for example, can be traders, agriculturists and/or pastoralists. They do not follow only one occupation. Reference to Kumhar, Lohar, Sunar, and Chamar is, however, accompanied with connotation of occupation. Hence according to Lohia castes are, in reality, found in the Shudra varna only. With the development of one kind of craft, a group of peoples get associated with it. All the kinds of crafts are collectively put together.

The Jat, Gujar, Ahir are groups, which are treated as jats. We don't come to know about any occupation just by reference to a jati. The trade of milk is now associated with Ahirs. Traditionally, the Ahirs were not traders of milk. According to Lohia they were a republic society, which settled in India and then merged with the federal system. This merger gave them the identity of a caste. Further, according to him, endogamy is the second characteristic of the caste system. There are number of gotras in a particular caste. Individuals of a given gotra believe that that they have descended from a common ancestor and are of common blood. It is for this reason that people of a gotra do not marry among themselves. They marry outside their gotra but within the caste.

Caste Restricts Opportunity

"Unlike the Marxist theories which became fashionable in the world in the 50's and 60's, Lohia recognised that caste, more than class, was the huge stumbling block to India's progress. Then as today, caste was politically incorrect to mention in public, but most people practiced it in all aspects of life - birth, marriage, association and death. It was Lohia's thesis that India had suffered reverses throughout her history because people viewed themselves as members of a caste rather than citizens of a country. Caste, as Lohia put it, was congealed class. Class was mobile caste. As such, the country was deprived of fresh ideas because of the narrowness and stultification of thought at the top, which was comprised mainly of the upper castes, Brahmin and Baniyas, and tight compartmentalisation even there, the former dominant in the intellectual arena and the latter in the business. A proponent of affirmative action, he compared it to turning the earth to foster a better crop, urging the upper caste as he put it, "to voluntarily serve as the soil for lower castes to flourish and grow", so that the country would profit from a broader spectrum of talent and ideas. In Lohia's words, "Caste restricts opportunity. Restricted opportunity constricts ability. Constricted ability further restricts opportunity. Where caste prevails, opportunity and ability are restricted to ever-narrowing circles of the people". In his own party, the Samyukta (united) Socialist Party, Lohia promoted lower castc candidates both by giving electoral tickets and high party positions. Though he talked about caste incessantly, he was not a casteist - his aim was to make sure people voted for the Socialist Party candidate, no matter what his or her caste. His point was that in order to make the country strong, everyone needed to have a stake in it. To eliminate caste, his aphoristic prescription was, "Roti and Beti", that is, people would have to break caste barriers to eat together (Roti) and be willing to give their girls in marriage to boys from other castes (Beti)," (cited from Ramakrishnan, 2005: 2-3).

Quoting Marx, Lohia writes that there is division of labour in the society and people get associated with an occupation. Division of labour leads to specialisation in labour. Large number of branches of production also emerges. People, therefore enter in exchange relationship with other societies (Marx, 1867: 353). According to Lohia the important aspect in Marx's writing is that the exchange takes place not only at individual level, but also at the level of family and tribe. Production takes place at the family level too. Marx believed that the exchange does not take place at individual level. From this we should understand that one or two people do not participate in production, trade and exchange. The whole family takes part in these processes.

Lohia believes that - the caste system is restricted to the Shudra varna. He said that the leaders of the society always want to preserve the varna system (Sharma, 2000). He argues that the custodians of society are not bothered if the individuals from the lower varna change their occupation and status but if they try to take up the occupation of the higher varna people and aspire to acquire their status then it is dysfunctional for the society and is strongly resisted by the elite groups (Plato quoted in Sharma, 2000).

(a) Dysfunction and Annihilation of Caste

Lohia was of the opinion that caste system in India is the largest single cause of the present material and spiritual degeneration of the country. People often equally the prosperity of their own caste with the country's progress. This is detrimental to the nation's progress. Several political parties talk about abolition of the caste system. Lohia pointed out that while women, harijans, shudras, depressed Muslims and Christians, and Adivasis constitute more than 85 per cent of the total population, their representation in the domains of politics, army, trade, and highly paid government jobs is dismal. Caste system can be abolished only when this imbalance is corrected. He strongly felt that the backward castes should get the opportunity to lead. They should get at least 60 per cent of the key posts in public life. This change should be effected through legal protection. Lohia was optimistic about the preferential opportunity extended to the backward classes. He thought this way India would emerge as a powerful nation.

Preferential Opportunities

"Lohia identified the prevalent caste system to be the main cause of India's degeneration in all respects including economic and spiritual. According to him, the caste system crushes the human spirit and individual freedom of low castes. For this reason, he suggested special opportunity to be provided to the backward classes. He argued that preferential opportunities should be provided to scheduled caste and other backward sections of the society. Lohia pointed out that backward class consists of women, Harijans, Shudras, Adivasis, depressed Muslims, High caste, English education and wealth are the main criteria of India's ruling class therefore, Lohia suggested that preference should be given to these backward classes in the matters of land distribution, employment, and educational opportunities" (Nath, 2002: 216).

Lohia also wanted that the backward castes should understand their own shortcomings. He opined that a lower stratum of society instinctively imitates the elite groups. The backward castes should refrain from imitating the vices of the twice-born castes. Those of the low-caste who hold the positions of leadership must get rid of jealousy and should endeavour to acquire a strong character, because jealousy would throw leadership into the hands of people with evil intentions. Another obstacle in the way of progress of the backward castes is the consolidation of power in the hands of few. Hundreds of 'backward castes' that constitute two-thirds of India's population continue to aspire for access to resources. For parliamentary elections, such backward castes should get our attention. Leaders should be created from their ranks, so that their voices and actions may infuse and inspire satisfaction, self-respect and fearlessness among them.

To make a backward caste prosperous in its collectivity, self-respect and fearlessness are important. A political programme to attack the caste system must be coupled with social activities such as collective feasting. Lohia was convinced that literature, participation dramas, fairs, and games might serve, as media of cultural interaction, exchange, and diffusion. Arguing against the case that by the destruction of capitalist system through class struggle caste will automatically wither away, Lohia, said, "In the first place, in a country cursed with the caste system, it is not possible to end the feudal and capitalist inequalities through class struggle alone. Moreover, why are those, who view class struggle as inevitable for the establishment of a classless society, so much averse towards caste struggle for creation of a casteless society?"

One must strive for destroying class and caste through non-violent and peaceful means of propaganda, organisation and struggle.

(b) Lohia's End Caste Conference

Lohia organised a conference "End Caste Conference" in Patna, on March 31- April 2, 1961 and passed the following resolution for the annihilation of caste in India:

(1) Mixed Dinner: The Conference appealed to the people of India and its units to organise mixed dinner parties everywhere in the country especially in the village.

(2) Marriage: The Conference was of the opinion that the caste system can be destroyed only when inter-caste marriages became common. To propagate these ideas discussions, plays and fairs should be organised. The enforcement of inter-caste marriages by government would not suffice. The Conference was clear that here inter-caste marriage would mean the marriage between Dvija and Shudras or Syeds and Julahas, and not between different sub-castes among high-castes.

(3) The Conference suggested opined that titles affixed to names should be evolved in such a way that it does not indicate the caste of a person.

(4) The Conference also passed a resolution for granting special opportunities to those who have been oppressed for thousands of years so as to bring about a positive change, in the traditional set up in society because the caste system results in erosion of strength and ability of these. Keeping in mind the question of merit the Conference resolved, "Whether able or not, Women, Shudras, Harijans, Backward Castes, Adivasis, and Muslims like weavers will have to be given 60 per cent reservation" (Lohia, 1964: 141).

The Conference agreed that religious, social, and economic programmes would have to be carried out along with a political programme to eradicate the caste system. Landless lower castes will have to be provided of land for cultivation and housing by way of re-division of land or through land army. Further, "Religion will also have to be cleared of its rubbish about castes" (Lohia, 1964: 141).

Conclusion

As you would have realised, the ideas of Ambedkar and Lohia converge on many counts. Both of them regarded caste as an oppressive, exploitative system which restricts opportunities and create imbalances and inequalities should be annihilated through they differed in the basic approach and the means to annihilate it. While Ambedkar talked about one, common book of Hindu religion and abolition of the institution of traditional priesthood, Lohia focused attention on creating situations of common, feasting cultural interactions and cultural exchange. It also favoured implementation of preferential polities for the weak and the downtrodden.

Further Reading

Ambedkar B.R., 1978, *Dr. Babasaheb Ambedkar's Writings and Speeches,* Vol. 1, Education Department, Government of Maharashtra, Bombay.

Lohia, Rammanohar, 1964, *The Caste System,* Rammanohar Lohia Samta Vidyalaya Nyas Nyas, Hyderabad.

Nath, J.P., 2002, *Socialist Leadership in India,* Kanishka Publishers, New Delhi.

4

Epistemology of Caste Based Social Exclusion

Introduction

Social exclusion is a contested concept as there is no universal definition of this term. However, if we take dictionary meaning, of the term 'exclusion' we come to know that the term emerges from the English word 'Exclude', which means to refuse to admit or consider (Webster's New World Dictionary). Keeping in view the etymological usage of the word 'exclusion', one assumes it as a process in sociological parlance. As this process unfolds in the society the term 'social' is pre-fixed to 'exclusion' giving birth to the term 'Social Exclusion'. Hence the term 'Social exclusion' can be defined as a process by which, certain collectivity or group or individuals are denied access to social, economic and political rights by a dominant group or groups. By doing so the dominant group keeps out the other groups from being part of their own. This process of 'exclusion' can be observed in both 'socio-religious' and 'secular' domain of life. Further, social exclusion can take place on ascribed statuses like- caste, race, gender, etc. or achieved statuses like- class, occupation, education etc. Moreover, there can be inter-sections within each group. An excluded individual or group or groups may be excluded on multiple pretexts like religion, gender, regional, linguistic identity etc.

Locating Social Exclusion in Indian Society

Social exclusion is a socio-psychological fact which exists in every known society in one form or the other. However, its nature and degree differs from society to society. Within a society it differs from strata to strata. Hence Indian society has its own specificities with regard to presence of process of 'social exclusion' and thereby inclusion. If we analyse the nature of Indian society then we find that it is four into one society. According to Oommen, "Like all societies, Indian society's stratification is based on age, gender, rural-urban and class...(secondly) Indian society is marked by ...cultural heterogeneity...(thirdly it has) religious plurality...(fourthly is has) pervasive caste hierarchy" (Oommen 2007: 94). Hence we can easily locate social exclusion of individuals and groups in India on the following bases:

(a) Social Stratification (on the bases of age, gender, class, rural and urban, literate and illiterate).

(b) Cultural heterogeneity (on large number of speech communities counting more than 1500 including 460 tribal communities).

(c) Religious plurality (all the world's major religion are found in India-Hinduism, Islam, Christianity, Sikhism, Jainism, Buddhism, Zoroastrianism, Bahai).

(d) Caste Hierarchy (There are 1038 Scheduled Castes and Mandal Commission identified 3743 castes as socially and educationally backward caste).

There may be number of other basis of social exclusion but I think the aforesaid characteristics of Indian society present an exhaustive list of bases of exclusion in Indian society. These elements produce different structures in the Indian society through which the process of exclusion is actualised. These categories are not mutually exclusively rather they may be interconnected and interrelated forming different permutation and combinations for giving birth to exclusion. Thus, having discussed the different bases of social exclusion existing in Indian Society let us see how social exclusion can be defined on the basis of caste.

Understanding 'Caste' as the Basis of 'Exclusion'

When we conceptualise the process of exclusion with specific reference to caste, exclusion is predominantly based on ascribed features. The critical ascribed features are carried through caste i.e., birth in a particular 'jati' because of deeds of the past incarnation. These ascribed features are justified on religious grounds through sacred texts and religious philosophy. A point should be noted here that although all the differences (social and economic) between groups and individuals are artificially created by human beings yet it is professed that some human qualities are inferior therefore stigmatised and those who perform them are looked down upon. On the other hand there are some qualities which are superior and pure, it is popularised that one needs special acumen or qualities to perform them. That is why those who perform them are given higher status and enjoy charisma. People look towards them with awe. People perusing the stigmatised jobs are excluded from different spheres of life and are denied their basic human rights to lead a dignified life. Therefore we can argue that if we want to observe the process of 'exclusion' in any meaningful manner then it has to be located in a particular frame of reference or paradigm. It is important to do so because 'exclusion' in Hindu social order is governed by different paradigms. Here paradigm means "practice which include law, theory, application and instrumentation" in caste social order to exclude Dalits. Hence we can argue that the paradigm of social exclusion of Dalits emanates from social structure justified by religion in which historicity plays a dominant role.

Relationship between Exclusion, Deprivation and Discrimination

Researchers use the terms like exclusion, deprivation and discrimination interchangeably as if they mean same thing. However, from the caste perspective, if we analyse the nature and scope of the processes like exclusion, deprivation, and discrimination then we will come to know that these three processes means different things although they are interrelated and interconnected. Now let us distinctively understand what the terms exclusion, deprivation and discrimination mean in the sphere of caste.

Social Exclusion: Indian Perspective

As far as the exclusion of '*shudra*' and '*adivasi*' (Dalits and Tribes) in the caste system of Hindu social order is concerned, it is obvious that they both were totally excluded from the normative pattern of society prescribed by the sacred texts of the Hindu society. For instance, the '*Purush Sukta*' theory of 10th *Mandal* in *Rig Veda* does not mention both '*shudra*' and '*adivasi*'. This means they are totally excluded from the normative and prescriptive Hindu Social Order. Once they are denied a place in the *Rig Veda* they were/are also denied a reference in the *varna* scheme and have/had no right to wear sacred thread. They were also excluded from Ashrams which give meaning to the life of a Hindu. They also do not know which *Dharma* to follow in others they were not assigned any duties in the society. Dalits and Tribes in turn are excluded from *Purushartha* and their by predestination also. They cannot get rid from the cycle of death and birth. In one word there is total blackout of their existence according to the book view of the Hindu Social Order. However, it is a fact that both Dalits and Tribes are living physical and social entity existing in the society that cannot be ignored. One can argue that in this modern age exclusion from the *Varna* social order, should not affect Dalits and Tribes in any way. But, if exclusion from this *Varna-Ashrma-Dharma* based social order is analysed a little bit objectively then we can observe that it has had a significant impact on the psyche of both those who enjoyed the fruits of the systems (*Brahmins, Kshtriyas* and *Vaishyas*) and those who suffered from the systems ('*shudra*' and '*adivasi*'). This social order closed virtually all the channels of mobility for Dalits and Tribes. And later on even Hindu women also suffered. It has a stigmatising impact on Dalits. There was loss of cultural capital which could be utilised in the contemporary times for gaining social mobility. For thousands of years they were denied opportunities to have access to different institutions of governance, production, education, religion etc. This had crippled them of their capacities which forced them to lag behind even today. Hence we can argue exclusion in Indian society means total negation of existence of the groups in the society.

Deprivation

Deprivation means a process by which the dominant group deprives another group which is subordinated because of the ideological and religious reasons. They are also deprived from their human and social rights which are essential for human being to survive and lead a dignified life. Seen in this context, we can observe that Dalits and Tribals who were totally excluded from the normative and prescriptive Hindu social order, based on sacred texts of Hindus were deprived the right to free interaction, occupation, access to available resources, etc. although, they existed in the society, like any other group. They were deprived of the right to live in the same vicinity as others lived and were forced to live outside the main village. Further, they were deprived of freedom of occupation although they were forced to perform certain very essential duties which were necessary for the survival of the society and which non-Dalits and non-Tribals never wanted to perform. They were deprived of the right to property although they contributed their labour in running the economy of the society. The water resources and other available spaces were kept out of the bounds of Dalits and Tribals. This list of deprivation can be long one. But, for emphasising the issue and meaning of deprivation these examples will suffice. Hence, we see that the process of deprivation in the name of caste is cumulative in nature and if violated, Dalits had to face penal actions. Either they faced violent action or excommunication, boycott, or even death penalty.

Social Discrimination

However with the development of constitutional rights in India, Dalits and Tribals who were totally excluded from the normative and prescriptive Hindu Social Order and were deprived of human and fundamental rights were accorded similar rights like any other citizen. With the commencement of Indian Constitutions Dalits and Tribals were to be administered democratic and equal rights through different institutions. They both were supposed to be treated like any other social and religious groups. However this arrangement made by the framers of the Constitution has not been implemented in letter and spirit by the implementers of the Constitution. And hence they started erecting new hurdles for the Dalits when it came to deliver the equal rights for the Dalits, the rights which were enshrined in the Constitution. This process of denial of legitimate rights guaranteed by the constitution of India can be termed as discrimination. This discrimination was/is based on caste ideology and assumes the pan-Indian character. There is contempt and prejudice for the Dalits in the system of delivery and the functionaries of delivery system. That is why they use stigmatised euphemism for the Dalits. This euphemism has emerged since the reservation policy has started. They call Dalits as '*Sarkari Damad*' (government son-in-law), dirty, drunkard and devoid of merit etc. In this manner we see the dominant section discriminate against Dalit while delivering political, economic, educational, and other rights which are enshrined for them in the Indian Constitution.

Sequencing of Exclusion, Deprivation and Discrimination

We can observe that, in Hindu social order which is anchored in the caste system, processes of exclusion, deprivation and discrimination forms a sequence which gives birth to a situation in which groups move from the position of absolute exclusion to be included yet discriminated. This sequence can be understood in following manner-first certain groups are completely excluded from the normative pattern of the Hindu Social order. However in practical sense of the term the groups are physically present in the society but they are deprived of various rights and sometimes they were deprived of their human rights also on the basis of religious sanctions. However, because of their assertion when they were recognised as citizens and were granted equal rights specially with commencement of Indian Constitution but the dominant sections of the society do not administer the legitimate constitutional rights to them as they feel threatened to lose their privilege position and hence they discriminate. The excluded groups were granted rights so that they can have access to modern democratic institutions like– Judiciary, Bureaucracy, Polity, University, Media and Market, to name just a few. However they have not been welcomed in these institutions which were supposed to function on the universalistic principles. That is why the Dalits and Tribes have a negligible presence in them. The irony is that the discrimination is so subtle that it is very difficult to measure unless there is some very glaring violation of rights takes place. And their meager presence is justified on number of constructed ideas like lack of merit, lack of capacity etc.

Exclusion and Inclusion: A Dichotomy or Continuum?

Exclusion and inclusion can be defined both as a dichotomy and continuum. If we take both the processes as dichotomous then exclusion can be defined as means to refuse to admit or consider inclusion means to accept and consider. For instance, if social exclusion means denial of existence of a group and thereby their rights and privileges as we have discussed its mechanism earlier. Then inclusion means accepting the existence of the group or individual and thereby their legitimate rights and privileges. The groups and individual is treated as equals and the rights are legitimately granted as matter of design and not by accident. In this context social exclusion and inclusion as dichotomy then it can be argued that if one will exists then other will not. However this is an ideal type of situation which does not exist in reality hence we can also argue that the dichotomy of social exclusion and inclusion is only a heuristic tool for measuring both the processes.

If that is the dichotomy of exclusion and inclusion then let us observe both as continuum. In this context social exclusion and inclusion are held at two opposite poles or ends. Continuum then means that exclusion is already given and inclusion is to be attained. Inclusion is a journey which is slow, gradual and deliberate by design. If we accept this position, then the society make efforts to include the excluded categories. In this process of inclusion by design excluded groups or individuals may be included in one or the other spheres of social and secular life. But it is not necessary that groups of individuals who were deliberately and absolutely excluded may be included in every spheres of life. There may be many reasons of the same. One of the important reason of lack of inclusion in every spheres of life is temporal discontinuity between exclusion and inclusion. The process of inclusion started very late and has a very short duration.

The second reason why people may not get included in every spheres of life is because the paradigm of exclusion and inclusion has been different. The paradigm of exclusion is social and informal in nature and paradigm of inclusion is constitutional and formal in nature. That is why groups and individuals may feel included and yet excluded. There is bound to be gap in the process of exclusion and inclusion if we take them as continuum. This gap may give rise to more and more policies and programmes of inclusion. Or it may give rise to social movements and mobilisation demanding their inclusion. Having defined adequately the exclusion and the relationship between exclusion, deprivation and discrimination let us understand the Epistemology of Caste.

Epistemology of 'Social Exclusion'

The principal questions of epistemology are questions as to the nature and scope of human knowledge: what can be known with certainty and what must be left to faith or opinion? What is the proper source or foundation of knowledge? A central pre-conception in epistemology is search for criteria by which to distinguish scientific knowledge from non-scientific (Berton 1977: 18-19). Going by the first question which epistemology asks is the question of the nature and scope of the human knowledge about 'social exclusion'. Here we have to accept social exclusion as a process. Its nature is dynamic. It takes shape in time and context and hence has to be located in proper socio-political contact. This will give us the location, contours and characteristics of the groups and individuals which we want to study. We should be methodologically clear about the size of the social group, historicity of its exclusion, whether exclusion is in multi-sphere or in single sphere.

The second aspect of epistemology of exclusion is how to identify sources of exclusion. How to objectively measure social exclusion? This can be done by listing the sources of social exclusion. We can draw a table of units of social exclusion. The list may include different sources of social exclusion belonging to both secular and social spheres. To make this list objective and meaningful we can put units of social

Table I: Representation of Social Exclusion of Dalits

	Types of Exclusion		*Nature of Exclusion*
1.	**Social Exclusion**		
		1. a	Absence from *Rigveda*
		2. b	Absence from the *varna* scheme
		3. c	No right to sacred thread
		4. d	Exclusion from *Ashrmas*
		5. e	No prescription of *Dharma*
		6. f	Exclusion from *Purushartha*
		7. g	Exclusion predestination or *Moksha*
	Practice of Untouchability		
		8. a	Residential exclusion (in the south of the village)
		9. b	Denial of accepting water
		10.c	Denial of access to water resources
		11. d	Denial of accepting of food
		12. e	Restriction on sitting together
		13. f	Restriction on celebrating together
		14. g	Denial of entry into house
		15. h	Denial of entry into kitchen
		16. i	Denial of entry into temples
		17. j	Denial of wearing of clothes/shoes/ turbans etc. similar to upper castes
		18. k	Denial of right to wear clothes/ ornaments/shoes/*chapals*/ they like and carrying of umbrella
		19. l	Denial of access to burial and funeral grounds
	Atrocities		
		20. a	Rape of Dalit Women (a caste act)
		21. b	Murder of a Dalit
		22. c	Grievous Hurt
		23. d	Arson/loot
		24. e	Ridicules in society and sacred tests

	Types of Exclusion		*Nature of Exclusion*
	Hazardous and Stigmatized Occupation		
		25. a	Cleaning Human excreta
		26. b	Scavenging /cleaning manholes
		27. c	Midwifery role by Dalit Woman
		28. d	Removing Carcasses
		29. e	Grave digging/Burning dead/Drum beating at the time of death
		30. f	Piggery/Butchery/toddy tapping
		31. g	Cleaning of soiled clothes
2.	**Political Exclusion**	32. a	Denial of participation in electioneering process
		33. b	Denial of participation in the decision making processes
3.	**Religious Exclusion**	34. a	Religious legitimacy to Exclusion from
		35. b	and the legitimacy of religion for exclusion
4.	**Economic Exclusion**	36. a	Denial of freedom of occupation
		37. b	Denial of access to resources
		38. c	Denial of rights of keeping pets other than donkeys and pigs
5.	**Educational Exclusion**	40. a	Exclusion from the ownership of educational centres
		41. b	Exclusion from becoming Knowledge seekers
		42. c	Exclusion from becoming Knowledge givers
		43. d	Exclusion from curriculum
6.	**Enemy within**	44. a	Oppressors of the same colour
		45. b	Oppressors of the same religion

Source: Kumar, Vivek (2007: 73-75).

exclusion depending on their temporal existence in a chronological order. For instance, we would put the sources of exclusion first which existed in the time and space. If we take the case of Dalits and want to make a table of the sources of exclusion then chronologically we will put the religious and social units of exclusion first. The economic, political, educational etc sources of exclusion will follow next (see table I). Each unit of social exclusion can be given a numerical value which can be added up to measure the indices of social exclusion of a particular group.

One can ask a question that why is necessary to know the sources of social exclusion. The answer is that once we know the sources of exclusion then it becomes easy to engage with and eradicate the sources of exclusion. The second benefit of knowing the sources of exclusion is that we come to know that whether there is a singular source of exclusion in the society or there are multiple sources of exclusion. If we come to know that there are multiple sources of exclusion then we can identify them easily as well. If we come to know that there are multiple sources of exclusion and different groups suffer from different sources then we can have different programmes and policies for their inclusion also. Otherwise we see that although the nature and sources of exclusion are different yet we apply the similar method and policies of inclusion.

Further, the epistemology of exclusion will help us to identify agency of social exclusion. Social exclusion in not a natural process, which occurs on its own rather it, occurs because of systems and structures. The structures and systems are artificial creations which are erected by individuals or groups which can be called as agency of social exclusion. Once we come to know the agency we can also try to find whether there is one agency of social exclusion or there are multiple agencies of social exclusion. If there is an agency of exclusion and people come to know it then there are a possibility people can be mobilised support against that agency. If there are multiple agencies there will be multiple mobilisations simultaneously. People can launch multiple movements against the multiple agencies. It is in this context necessary to note that if we know the sources of social exclusion and agency of social exclusion then we can also understand the nature and path of assertion of the excluded. By knowing the path of the assertion we can try to easily evolve the strategy to control the situation before they go out of control.

Last but not the least; epistemology helps us to understand the paradigm of social exclusion and inclusion. It will be easy to understand whether the paradigm of the two processes is same or different. For instance, when we observe the social exclusion of Dalits and Tribals in Indian society we find that the paradigm of exclusion is social and informal. That is based on ascriptive and religious principles which are particularistic in nature. However, the paradigm of their inclusion is constitutional and secular. These are based on universalistic principles enshrined in the Indian Constitution and have to be administered by bureaucratic institutions.

Now we will try to locate and understand the process of exclusion with reference to caste and Dalits in Indian society.

Pioneering Voices Against Exclusion in Indian Society

Exclusion in India is an age old problem. However, it has not been articulated in these specific terms. The groups and individuals have highlighted the issue of exclusion both by their words and action. The voices of the saint poets belonging to stigmatised identities of caste seem to be first voices against the exclusion of certain categories of people. That is why they started propagating a separate branch of religion of 'formless God' (*Nirgun Shakha*) which became so powerful that it came to be known as 'Bhakti Movement'. Names of Bhakti saints like *Ravi Das* or *Raidas*, *Kabir* and *Chokha Mela* to name just a few are prominent in this regard. Conversion to different religions like-Buddhism, Islam, Sikhism and Christianity for a dignified existence, by the ex-untouchable castes and tribes proves the point that they were excluded from day-to-day affairs of social interactions. Similarly, Dalits launched many movements to have a separate identity from Hinduism and claiming an independent status as 'original inhabitants of this land'. The name of movements like Adi-Hindu, Adi-Dravida, Adi-Karnataka, Adi-Andhra, Ad-Dharm are few such movements through which Dalits wanted to gain an independent and autonomous identity away from Hinduism.

In the modern times, according to historical sources a number of social reformers and leaders belonging to *Shudra* and ex-Untouchable castes raised the issue of exclusion of *Shudras* and ex-untouchables. Jotiba Phule, Narayan Guru, Chhtrapati Sahuji, B.R. Ambedkar, E.V. Ramaswamy Nicker (Periyar), Ayyankalli, Gopal Baba Walankar, Swami Acchutanand, Mangoo Ram etc. to name just a few, highlighted the issue of social exclusion of Dalits and Other Backward classes. *Birsa Munda* and others led the issue of exclusion of Tribals in the Indian Society. However it is a fact that Ambedkar was possibly the first person to use the term 'exclusion' in India while defining the oppression and exploitation of Dalits in Indian society. Ambedkar raised the issue of exclusion of Dalits systematically using modern weapons like-educational, political, constitutional means along with different types of socio-political movements. Of course, he first used the term 'Bahishkrit' a Sanskrit / Hindi word meaning exclusion for defining the exclusion of Dalits and their wretched condition in the Indian society. He used this term for the first time in 1924 when he established the organisation '*Bahiskrit Hitkarini Sabha*' (Society for serving the Interests of Excluded). Then he used the term again when he launched the fortnightly '*Bahiskrit Bharat*' (Excluded India) in 1927. Later Ambedkar used the exact term 'Exclusion' in 1930s while highlighting the exclusion of Dalits, OBC's and minorities by Brahmins from Indian Civil Services.

Ambedkar and the Usage of the term Exclusion

Ambedkar used this term responding to Gokhale who was pleading against the exclusion of Indians from the British Civil Services in India. Ambedkar argued that Dalits, Backward Castes and minorities can make similar types of allegation against Brahmins as Gokhale was making against British. In his own words, "Is it not open to the Depressed Classes, the non-Brahmins and the Mohammedans to say that by their exclusion from the Public Service a kind of dwarfing or stunting of their communities is going on? Can they not complain that as a result of their exclusion they are obliged to live all the days of their lives in an atmosphere of inferiority, and the tallest of them has to bend in order that the exigencies of the existing system may be satisfied" (Ambedkar 1982: 395)? That means Ambedkar was not only highlighting the exclusion of the Dalits and other marginalised communities he was also highlighting the impact of exclusion of them from the Indian bureaucracy. He decried the exclusion of the Dalits and argued that If to exclude the advanced communities from entering into public service of the country was a moral wrong, the exclusion of the backward communities from the same field must be a moral wrong and if it is a moral wrong it must be righted. Later on Ambedkar launched number of socio-religious and political movements to highlight the prevailing exclusion of the Dalits in different spheres of Indian society and demanded their inclusion in them.

Social Exclusion in Indian Society and Hindu Social Order: A Book-view

As soon as we try to understand and analyse the process of 'exclusion' within Indian society in general and in Hindu society in particular we get a very specific picture of exclusion. To observe 'exclusion on' the basis of Caste we have first observed the anchorage of caste which lies in the Hindu Social Order. Hindu Social Order as defined by the sociological texts (Ghurey 1979, Dumont 1999, Srinivas 1985), which have taken clue from the sacred texts of Hindu social order like Vedas and *Smritis*, is based on *Varnas* (social Classes) arranged in a hierarchal manner. This hierarchical arrangement automatically excludes different *Varnas* (social Classes) from each other on different accounts viz. occupation, marriage, commensality, governance etc. It is in this context we will borrow from Ambedkar (1979, 1987, and 1989) and his perspective about exclusion which according to him produces exclusion. The real basis of processes of social exclusion is the philosophy of Hinduism. According to him Hindu Philosophy produced *Varna* which he considers as parent of caste. That means Ambedkar has understood 'Philosophy of Hinduism' (Ambedkar 1987: 3-94) which in turn has given birth of caste system that acts as an 'Institution of exclusion' since time immemorial. Ambedkar has argued that in particular 'Philosophy of Hinduism' denies justice to the people of different castes. For him, "...Justice is simply another name for liberty, equality, and fraternity" (*ibid*: 25). According to Ambedkar because Hindu social order is based on 'rank and gradation' it does not recognise equality. However Ambedkar is perturbed about, "how in every phase of life Manu has introduced and made inequality the vital force of the life...by taking a few examples such as slavery, marriage and Rule of Law" (*ibid*: 25-26). Hence, it becomes clear that denial of equality, liberty, and fraternity of groups and individuals because of the caste system is the main reason of exclusion.

Endogamy as the Real Basis of 'Exclusion'

As we all know that for Ambedkar, "...the absence of intermarriage-endogamy...the only one that can be called the essence of the caste when rightly understood...Caste in India means an artificial chopping off of the population into fixed and definite units, each one prevented from fusing into another through the custom of endogamy" (Ambedkar 1979: 8-9). However to make his definition even anthropologically sound Ambedkar added another element of exogamy in defining caste. That is why he argued, "...in the final analysis creation of castes, so far as India is concerned, means the superimposition of endogamy on exogamy" (*ibid*). In todays context marriage is important aspect of exclusion of different groups located at the different levels in Hindu social order. The young Indian males and females argue that caste curtails their choices of spouses and excludes a whole group as far as interaction between to groups is concerned.

Exclusion of Dalits in Hindu social Order

This book view of exclusion because of Institution of caste can be extended to ex-untouchables of the Indian society. The ex-untouchables now Dalits have not been included in the book view of the Hindu social order although they have existed physically side by side in the society. For instance it is very clear from *Rig Veda* tenth *Mandal Purushsukta* theory that there are four Varnas in the Hindu Social Order (Ghurey 1979: 44, Srinivas 1985: 150-51). Later on *Manu Smriti*, which codified the Hindu Society, has also argued that there is no fifth Varna (Dumont 1999: 66-67). It is not only the Dalits have been excluded from the Varna scheme they have been excluded for the rights and privileges of the society. Therefore we can logically evaluate the absolute exclusion of the Dalits in the Hindu social order and based on this exclusion we can differentiate their exclusion with the exclusion faced by tribals, and religious minorities, and women in the Indian society. Two important elements which we have observed in the process of exclusion of the Dalits is that their exclusion is absolute. Second their enemy belongs to same religion and therefore it is within.

Hinduism as religious ideology has been a source for producing exclusion for different groups within the Hindu society. Apart from Hindus in general it has specifically laid the foundation of exclusion for Dalits as well.

Social Exclusion of Dalit in Hindu Social Order: Views from the Field

Now we will try to record and analyse the process of social exclusion of Dalits in the day today interaction. That can be called as field view of exclusion on the basis of caste. According to this view the social exclusion of Dalits emerges precisely because of prescriptions in the religious texts about the different castes were implemented in letter and spirit in the society. Here again it was most significant with regard to *Shudra* and Dalits. For instance Ambedkar wrote, "Under the rule of the

Peshwas in Maratha country the untouchable was not allowed to use the public streets if a Hindu was coming along lest he should pollute the Hindu by his shadow. The untouchable was required to have a black thread either on his wrist or in his neck as a sign or a mark to prevent the Hindus from getting them polluted by his touch through mistake. In Poona, the capital of the *Peshwa*, the untouchable was required to carry, strung from his waist, a broom to sweep away from behind the dust he treaded on lest a Hindu walking on the same should be polluted. In Poona, the untouchable was required to carry an earthen pot, hung in his neck whenever he went, for holding his spit lest his spit falling on earth should pollute a Hindu" (Ambedkar 1979: 39).

Similarly Ambedkar argued that *Balais,* an untouchable community in Central India (now Madhya Pradesh) were told as late as in 1928 that if they want to live in the village then they have conform to certain rules like-*Balais* must not wear gold-lace-bordered turban. They must convey intimation of the death of any Hindu to relatives of the deceased-no matter how far away these relatives may be living. In all Hindu marriages, *Balais* must play music before the processions and during the marriage, *Balai* women must not wear gold or silver ornaments, *Balai* women must attend all cases of confinement of Hindu women, *Balai* must render service without demanding remuneration and must accept whatever a Hindu is pleased to give, If the *Balais* do not agree to abide by these terms they must clear out of village (Ambedkar 1979:39-40). Describing the exclusion of the *Shanans*-a lower caste of Tamil Nadu in south India Rudolph & Rudolph (987:38) argued, "*Shanans* were not allowed to enter the compounds of temples consecrated to Brahmanical deities such as Shiva or to use wells of higher castes. At least in Travancore, they were expected to maintain a prescribed physical distance between themselves and Brahmans. In multi-caste villages, barbers and washer-men would not ordinarily serve them".

Social Exclusion and Dalit Women: A Field-view

Apart from community as a whole the exclusion and exploitation of the Dalit women at different point in time assumes notion of social fact in the Indian society. In this context taking specific example Omvedt argues that, "the Dalit girls were dedicated to the goddess Yellama/ Renuka...Following this 'marriage to the god' most of the girls remained in their own village; they were considered accessible to any men but at the same time not bound to or polluted by sexual relations...These girls were known as '*Murali*' among *Mahars*, '*Matangi*' among the *Madigas* and '*Basavi*' among *Holeyas*...whatever the 'matriarchal' or 'matrilineal' remnants that can be seen in the custom, by late feudal times it also helped to institutionalise the sexual accessibility of the Dalit women for higher caste men (Omvedt 1994:72).

On the other hand Briggs has highlighted the vulnerable condition of Dalit women in his study of *Chamars*- an untouchable caste of North India. He wrote in 1920s that, "There are other social customs, more or less objected to but often allowed and not considered wrong, which are gradually disappearing under modern conditions. Such are the *just prima noctics* of landlords and gurus. The *Zamindar* often has liberties with Chamar's wife in consideration of his payments to the Chamar. The *Sais*'s wife gives immoral services where her husband is employed in the towns or cities" (Briggs 1920:43). Further in Tamil Nadu Rudolph & Rudolph (1987:39) have also revealed the pathetic condition of *Shanan* women in the area. They argued that a riot broke out in 1858 when *Shanan* women emulated to cover their breasts like locally dominant Nair caste. The next year, Sir Charles Terevelyan, the governor of Madras, granted them permission to wear a cloth over their breasts and shoulders. Hence, we can observe that Dalit women were exploited in every direction of India and they could not stop such exploitation forcing them to lead a subjugated life which can be regarded as exclusion.

Social Exclusion and its Impact on Indian Society

Having defined exclusion, its basis, epistemology, the voices of descent, and agency of the existing phenomena of social exclusion both in theory and practice let us now understand the impact of social exclusion on Indian society in general and Dalits in particular. We have seen earlier how 'philosophy of Hinduism' based on sacred text have produced a social structure that is *Varna* and caste. These structures have denied equality, liberty and fraternity to different groups. Because of *Varna* groups were excluded from institution of occupation, governance, production, education, day-to-day life interaction. Caste system further created divide among people by forcing them to marry within their own caste. This was artificial chopping of people. Above all the emergence of institution of untouchability further created a wedge among people excluding a vast majority from different spheres of life (see Table 1). Hence, social exclusion in Indian Society, special because of caste/Varna hierarchy has had profound impact on the one hand on the nature and development of Indian society as a whole and on the other hand the status of Dalits. Accordingly social exclusion has produced following impact in Indian society:

1. Hindrance in making of a society
2. Hindrance in the process of nation building
3. Hindrance in effective governance
4. Committed a moral wrong on excluded
5. Demands for self-representation

Hindrance in Making of a Society

At the outset the process of exclusion in Indian Society has created a hindrance in making India a unified society. Some ask why and answer is not for to seek. Ambedkar has rightly highlighted that, "There is an utter lack among the Hindus of what the sociologists call "consciousness of kind". There is no Hindu consciousness of kind. In every Hindu the consciousness that exists is the consciousness of his caste. That is the reason why the Hindus cannot be said to form a society or a nation… The Caste System prevents common activity and by preventing common activity it has prevented Hindus from becoming a society with a unified life and a consciousness of its own being" (Ambedkar 1979: 50-51). He further has also argued that Indian society also lack equality, liberty and fraternity (Ambedkar 1987). That is why as the Chairman of the Drafting Committee of the Constitution he enshrined equality, liberty and fraternity in the preamble of the Constitution of India.

Hindrance in the Process of Nation Building

Ambedkar had pointed the danger of caste exclusion in the path of nation building also. He wondered that, "How can people divided into several thousands of castes be a nation? ... The castes are anti-national in the first place because they bring about separation in social life. They are anti-national also because they generate jealousy and antipathy between caste and caste… (Therefore)… we must overcome all these difficulties if we wish to become a nation in reality. For fraternity can be a fact only when there is a nation" (Ambedkar 1994: 1216-7). That is why he had mooted the idea and mechanism of annihilation of caste. His ways of annihilation of caste included inter-caste marriage and questioning of the scared text of Hindus because caste system draws legitimacy from these books (Ambedkar 1979).

Hindrance in Effective Governance

Exclusion in governance is harmful for every member of the society. However it is most harmful to Dalits because they are the most disadvantaged in the society and need maximum support. But prevalent caste prejudices in institutions of governance never allow the implementation of policies effectively. It is so because the whole bureaucracy is dominated by the so-called upper-castes (Fourth Report of Scheduled Caste and Scheduled Tribe Commission: 1996-97: 22). Ambedkar had highlighted the dangers of domination of so-called upper –castes in the institutions of governance. According to him, "It must be accepted as beyond dispute that such wide powers of rule-making affecting the welfare of large classes of people cannot be safely left into the hands of the administrators drawn from particular class which as a matter of fact is opposed to the rest of the population in its motives and interests, (which) does not sympathise with the living forces operating in them, is not charged with their wants, pains, cravings and desires and is inimical to their aspirations" (Ambedkar 1979: 50-51). This story still continues and we find delivery of government services hampered because of caste identities of recipients.

A Moral Wrong Towards Excluded

Further, social exclusion has committed a moral wrong towards the members of caste located lower in caste hierarchy. As discussed earlier, historically Ambedkar highlighted the moral evils arising out of the exclusion of a person from the public service by quoting Gopal Krishna Gokhale. Drawing an analogy between the Brahmins and allied castes with the foreign agency, i.e., the British, Ambedkar argued that, "Is it not open to the Depressed Classes, the non-Brahmins and the Mohammedans to say that by their exclusion from the Public Service a kind of dwarfing or stunting of their communities is going on? Can they not complain that as a result of their exclusion they are obliged to live all the days of their lives in an atmosphere of inferiority, and the tallest of them has to bend in order that the exigencies of the existing system may be satisfied? ...If to exclude the advanced communities from entering into public service of the country was a moral wrong, the exclusion of the backward communities from the same field must be a moral wrong and if it is a moral wrong it must be righted" (Ambedkar 1982: 395-6). This moral wrong still continues as has been argued earlier that the Indian bureaucracy is still dominated by the so-called upper castes.

Demand for Self-representation

Social exclusion forced Dalits and other deprived sections to demand self-representation. Why was self-representation necessary? Ambedkar explained the reasons for self-representation of the Dalits by the Dalits themselves. In his own words, "as can be easily seen they can be represented by the untouchables alone. They know distinctively their own interests and none can truly voice them...Untouchability constitutes a definite set of interests which the untouchables alone can speak for (Ambedkar 1982: 256)". Secondly, the personal representation for the Dalits is also important because, Ambedkar opined in his written statement given to the Southborough Committee on franchise in 1919 that, "As the government is the most important field for the exercise of individual capacities, it is in the interest of the people that no person as such should be denied the opportunity of actively participating in the process of government. That is to say popular government is not only government for the people but by the people. To express the same in a different way, representation of opinions by itself is not sufficient to constitute popular government. To cover its true meaning, it requires personal representation as well" (Ambedkar 1979: 247). Thirdly, self-representation of Dalits and other marginalised section of the society is necessary because, "A Government for the people, but not by the people, is sure to educate some into masters and others into subjects...To be specific, it is not enough to be electors only. It is necessary to be law-makers; otherwise who can be law-makers will be masters of those who can only be electors" (Ambedkar 1982: 251). That is why; Ambedkar not only demanded separate electorate but also reservation in the cabinet as well. According to him, "Just as it is necessary that the Depressed Classes should have the power to influence governmental action by seats in the Legislature so also it is desirable that the Depressed Classes should have the opportunity to frame the general policy of the Government. This they can do only if they can find a seat in the cabinet. The Depressed Classes therefore claim that in common with other minorities, their rights to be represented in the Cabinet should be recognised. With this purpose in view the Depressed Classes propose: that in the Instrument of Instructions an obligation shall be placed upon the Governor and the Governor-General to endeavour to secure the representation of the Depressed Classes in the Cabinet" (Ambedkar 1991: 52).

Conclusion

To conclude, the paper argues the need of an indigenous definition of the term 'exclusion' which can take care of peculiarities of Indian society which is caste ridden. Secondly, in this context we need to look relationship between already existing terms like deprivation, and discrimination and exclusion. From the above analysis we have found that they are different yet interrelated and inter-connected. Further, we have seen that these three terms form a sequence or linearity that is one comes after the other. Thirdly, we have also tried to understand social exclusion and inclusion as dichotomy and continuum. In this context it is interesting to note that although there is a tendency to analyse these two processes as dichotomies but in real sense of the term what exists in society is the continuum. That means groups may be included in some aspects and excluded in other. Hence people may be included yet excluded or there is exclusion in inclusion. This article also tries to record the epistemology of social exclusion. Accordingly we have tried to record the nature and scope of social exclusion. For this we have seen sources of social exclusion specifically in the Indian society. After identifying the sources of exclusion we have also discussed the necessity of understanding the sources of social exclusion. In the epistemology we have also analysed the agency of social exclusion. The third aspect of epistemology of social exclusion is the paradigm of exclusion which helped us to ascertain the paradigm of inclusion. We found them different - one is social and informal and the other is constitutional and formal. The pioneering voices against social exclusion in India have also been probed in this paper. Saint poets belonging to the *Shudra* and Dalits castes were the first to raise the voice against social exclusion of their own community. In modern times, Ambedkar was the first educated leader to counter the social exclusion through modern Institutions. The discrimination in Hindu social order, thereby of Dalits and Dalit women has also been analysed in the article. For doing the same we have used both book view and field view. Hence the paper is an attempt to understand social exclusion specifically related to Indian society and within that on the basis of caste system and conclude social exclusion in this context is a group phenomenon. Secondly the paradigm of exclusion and inclusion is different and hence there will always a gap between exclusion and inclusion in the society which will give rise to different social policies and movements.

References

Ambedkar, B.R. 1979. *Annihilation of Caste, in Dr. Babasaheb Ambedkar Writings and Speeches,* Vol. 1, Education Department, Mumbai: Government of Maharashtra.

———. 1982. *Dr. Babasaheb Ambedkar Writings and Speeches,* Vol. 2, Education Department, Mumbai: Government of Maharashtra.

———. 1987. *Philosophy of Hinduism in Dr. Babasaheb Ambedkar Writings and Speeches,* Vol. 3, Education Department, Mumbai: Government of Maharashtra.

———. 1989. *The Indian Ghetto-The Centre of Untouchability, in Dr. Babasaheb Ambedkar Writings and Speeches,* Vol. 5, Education Department, Mumbai: Government of Maharashtra.

Berton, Ted, 1977, Philosophical Foundation of the Three Sociologies, London: Routledge & Kegan Paul.

Briggs, G.W. 1920. *The Chamars*, re-published in 1990, Delhi: Low Price Publications.

Ghurey, G.S. 1979. *Caste and Race in India*, Bombay: Popular Prakashan.

Dumont, Louis. 1999. *Homo Hierarchicus: The Caste System and its Implications*, New Delhi: Oxford University Press.

Kumar, Vivek, 2007, Social Exclusion and Different Shades of Dalit Movements, Department of Sociology, Pune: University of Pune.

Oommen, T.K., 2007, Knowledge and Society: Situating Sociology of Social Anthropology, New Delhi: Oxford University Press.

Omvedt, Gail. 1994. *Dalit and the Democratic Revolution: Dr. Ambedkar and the Dalit Movement in Colonial India*, New Delhi: Sage Publications.

Rudloph, Lloyd and Susanne Rudolph. 1987. The *Modernity of Tradition: Political Development in India*, New Delhi: Orient Longman.

Srinivas, M.N. 1985. *Caste in Modern India and other Essays*, Bombay: Media Promoters & Publishers Pvt. Ltd.

5

Caste and Politics of Reservation

The Congress-led UPA government has started a dialogue on affirmative action including reservation in the private sector for dalits. The Congress-led government in Maharashtra had even introduced a bill in this regard before the 2004 assembly polls. It is interesting to note that the Congress government in Madhya Pradesh had implemented a supplier and dealership diversity for dalits in January 2002.

A question is why at all are Congress-led governments so eager to provide reservation to dalits in the private sector? This question is significant because there has not been any genuine demand by the dalits for reservation in the private sector. There have been no movements worth mentioning for reservations. Even the Backward and Minorities Communities Employees' Federation (BAMCEF), the biggest employee group of dalit employees, has not made this demand. Yet the Congress is thinking along these lines. In the past too it was the Congress, the then Indian National Congress led by Mahatma Gandhi, which forced Babasaheb Ambedkar to accept reservations under the Poona Pact, though Babasaheb had asked for separate electorates for dalits and had achieved that as well. But he had to sacrifice those achievements to save Gandhiji's life. Since then it is an established fact that the Congress has benefited from the reservation under Poona Pact by getting elected only those dalits who speak its language [Ambedkar 1991: 88-102, Ram 1982].

Therefore, notwithstanding the importance of dialogue for reservation in the private sector, because of shrinking job opportunities in the government/public sector and the spread of the private sector in the wake of liberalisation. The dalits have their own doubts about the policy. Is it only a political gimmick or is the government serious, they wonder.

This scepticism is easy to understand. The various governments, in which the Congress has been most prominent, have not been able to fulfil the allotted quota of reservation of 15 per cent for scheduled castes and 7.5 per cent for scheduled tribes enshrined in the Constitution under Article 335 even after 57 years of commencement of this policy. Similarly, the governments at the centre took 44 years to identify OBCs and implement reservations for them. So the logical question is that if the governments have not been able to implement the reservation policy for so long, how long will they take to implement a policy which has not yet born? Can any one specify the time which the legislature, judiciary, and bureaucracy will take to dovetail the policy so that it can be implemented smoothly?

Need for a White Paper

If the government is truly sincere about opening up employment opportunities to the socially oppressed, it must first come out with a white paper on the present status of reservations. Such a document must detail how many jobs have been identified for reservation in all the sectors, how many jobs have been filled and how many vacancies have remained vacant. It should look into the causes of omission and commission, and help plug the gaps as well. If there are problems at the government end it should specify them, and if at the dalit community's end then some immediate measures should be taken.

Further, if the government is convinced that reservations can uplift dalits, it should outline the time table in the paper to fulfil the backlog of vacancies within the government and public sector. In the same vein, the government of the day should extend reservations to dalits and OBCs in the key offices of the country like the judiciary, army, vidhan parishads, Rajya Sabha and various regulatory bodies in different sectors which are still under the government's control. Instead of taking these aforesaid steps the government is having a dialogue with the private sector and that too without any concrete preparedness. The government should have prepared itself on certain issues, which would help it in negotiating with the private sector.

How Private is the Private Sector?

For instance, the government should reveal what is so private about the private sector. The government has not analysed whether this sector should be called a private sector at all, especially in the light of the types of concessions given to it by the government - like land and registration charges at concessional rates, tax holidays, bank loans, besides the indirect contribution made by government in their development in the form of maintaining law and order, development of technology, research and development, trained human resources, road, rail and air and communication facilities, etc. Has the government documented the total cost of these subsidies? Had it done so, it would have been easier for it to show the real worth of the private sector. There is also a need to tell the masses how government money was provided as doles during the private sector's infancy. The Tatas and Birlas have thrived only on public money of the past and enjoyed government the patronage. Under these circumstances, can we call the private sector really private?

Evaluating Merit and Efficiency

Similarly, the government should have prepared a concept paper on the issue of 'merit' in general and 'merit and efficiency' in the private sector in particular. This is necessary because whenever the issue of reservation crops up, it is certain that the whole dalit community is portrayed as devoid of any merit. Nobody even cares to note that there are millions of dalits who survive without availing of reservation. In this evaluation the rest of society is depicted as meritorious while the merit of the other side has never been assessed. The government should critically evaluate the performance of the private sector in terms of its inefficiency, and uncompetitiveness. For instance, by telling the citizens the amount of money lost by the public sector banks because of the 'Non-Performing Assets' of the private sector and the large tax evasion. The government should also reveal the number of private industries which die every year or which declare themselves bankrupt. It must declare the number of fraudulent non-banking financial companies, which have duped the public of their money. In this regard, "The Ministry of Company Affairs (MCA) has released a concept paper on the Companies Act. In this lengthy document, the MCA has dealt with the concept of 'vanishing companies' ... The concept paper has identified 122 such companies (which raised public money to the tune of Rs 838 crore)" [Bhutani 2004]. The government can draw on such material.

The merit and efficiency of the private sector can be easily assessed by the contribution it makes to the world export market; it is a meagre 0.7 per cent only. Similarly, the same private sector has been demanding a level playing field for itself with the onset of the process of liberalisation. How can the private sector yet boast of its efficiency and merit? If Indian industry was so meritocratic why is it that it has not produced a single brand or item, which can be called an international commodity? Above all, what right do the industrialists of today have to call themselves as meritorious when most owners of established business houses have inherited the companies. None of the top industrialists is a first generation industrialist. They might have expanded the business but they could do so only because they belong to a certain pedigree. That is why a number of social scientists have rejected the view of 'merit'. They have argued that the rewards in the educational and economic system are not based on merit. The educational and occupational attainments are related to the family background rather than talent and ability. Thus, the children of the wealthy and powerful tend to obtain high qualifications and then highly rewarded jobs irrespective of their ability. It is this that the educational system disguises with the myth of meritocracy [Bowles and Gintis 1976]. In the same vein the social scientists have also rejected the narrow definition of merit in terms of intelligence, which is a measure of just one portion of the total spectrum of human mental abilities associated with knowledge and memory rather than the ability of reason [Jensen 1973].

Therefore, the government should, in fact, seek responses from the intelligentsia - particularly the dalit intelligentsia - to explode the myth of merit once for all. Theories to defend the dalits on the issue of merit are needed. Starting from the contribution made by dalits' labour in running the economy and polity of the nation to the role of mid-wives played by the dalit women, should be evaluated and highlighted. Who decides which occupa¬tion is of a 'functional importance' and therefore accorded higher prestige [Tumin 1967]? And why should merit only be evaluated in terms of performance of these 'functionally important' occupations? Why cannot the labour of the dal its be a commodity worthy enough to be called creative, artistic, and hence prestigious? Secondly, to detonate the myth of merit the government should use its own data to show that enough trained and qualified dalits students are available for jobs in the private sector (see the Table). This can negate the argument put forward by the private sector that the dalit candidates are not available or suitable from the available data. Further, the government should also start collecting data on other streams of professional education gained by dalits to show the true size of the pool of talent among the dalits. Until now the data published by the SC/ST

Commission includes only the traditional educational degrees like the BA, MA and BE, which does not indicate the real potential of the dalits.

Evaluating Merit

Are the communities who do not avail of constitutional reservation necessarily meritorious, dalits wonder. They evaluate the Indian performance on the basis of the traditional social structure to assesses the 'merit' of the aforesaid groups. There were varnas - brahman, kshatriya and vaishya assigned with particular functions, which were initially open but became closed later. The brahman had the privilege of teaching, the kshatriya of protecting all creatures, and vaishya living by commerce [Dumont 1970:69]. Today dalits ask if the brahmans were so meritorious then why is it that half of the country's population is still illiterate? If the kshatriyas were so meritorious why then could they not defend our borders? The Tartars, Mughals, British, etc., all defeated them and subjugated us. Similarly, if the vaishyas were so meritorious then why is the trade and commerce of India in a shambles?

In contemporary times as well, look at the low Human Develop Index (HDI) of India. In terms of HDI, India is placed at the 124th position in the group of 174 countries. Similarly in the 'Corruption Perception Index' for the year 2004 India ranks 90th in the group of 146 countries (Transparency International India Report 2004). Above all the external debt of India is a whopping Rs 5,11,861 crore [Economic Survey 2003-04:128]. All the meritorious economists and administrators are managing the affairs of the country without any reservation, even then why is the situation so bad? The situation in science and technology which is considered the realm of high specialty and hence kept out of bounds of reservation is also not very encouraging. In this regard, "Professor Nian Chai Liu and his colleagues at the Shanghai Jio Tong University in China spent two years collating and analysing the output of 2,000 universities worldwide and ...published their results by ranking 500 universities. Only three universities/institutions from India figure in the top 500 - the Indian Institute of Science (260) and 'the Indian Institutes of Technology at Kharagpur and Delhi (459) and (460)" [Mohan 2004]. In this context it will be worth mentioning to look at the merit of the doctors working in the most prestigious hospital of the country. If the Indian doctors and medical specialists are so meritorious then why is it that most of the VVIPs run away to foreign countries for treatment of the simplest of their illnesses. Even the former prime minister Atal Behari Vajpayee, an ardent supporter of 'Swadeshi', had to call in an NRI orthopaedic surgeon for his knee operation. Last but not the least, is it really logical and possible to measure the merit of the professionals passing out from the various private engineering, medical, management, etc., colleges where a seat can be bought for few lakhs of rupees.

Private Sector: Discrimination

It is a fact that there exists discrimination in the private sector. Beteille (1997: 203) accepts that "Although the new occupations in the office and factory are in principle caste free, the 'association between caste and occupation is carried over from the traditional to the modern occupational settings. The various castes are not represented in the occupations according to their proportions in the population. The inferior castes in general, and the scheduled castes in particular, are very thinly represented in the superior administrative and managerial occupations. In a society which has adopted the principle of equality of opportunity but whose members remain acutely conscious of caste distinctions, these disparities are now a source of anxiety and concern." Further, he argues that, "There are several reasons why the untouchables and other inferior castes are so thinly represented in the higher occupations. While Article 15 prohibits discrimination on the grounds of caste and Article 16 guarantees equality of opportunity in public employment, there is, in fact widespread prejudice against the inferior castes in general and the untouchables in particular. This prejudice is not easy to measure and by its nature it is difficult to establish in the individual case. It operates more actively at the lower levels of employment where recruitment, tenure and promotion are to a large extent personalised than perhaps at the higher levels where these processes are organised in a more impersonal way. But there is reason to believe that some candidates are at every level rejected on account of prejudice even when they have the necessary qualification" (*ibid*: 203-04).

Similarly, the discrimination exists in the private sector of account of denial of equal employment opportunities especially because of an informal and opaque medium of recruitment. In the name of cost-effective choices of the most suitable person, these private sector industries make appointments of personal choices without adverting the jobs. Vernacular newspapers and backward areas are deliberately blacked out to reduce the pool of talent; a foreign degree and high pedigree become the basis of evaluating merit. This recruitment pattern is increasing day by day. Human Resource Head of the software company,

Adobe India, says, "Employee referrals are a major source of recruitment for us. Our employees understand our requirements very well and have friends with a similar academic background and skills." In the same vein, the director of MAQ Software argues, "we reach candidates with better profiles who cannot be reached otherwise through other channels like online sites or placement agencies". Apart from Abode and MAQ Software, there are a few more in the same league like Infosys and Wipro who have internal employee's referral schemes for employment. Not only that, if they hire an employee on the basis of referrals then the employee who has referred the new recruit is paid an increment as well [Singh 2004]. This is discriminatory practice, which has gone on for long in the private sector in India.

Though there is no research on the demerits of this system of recruitment in India, studies abroad suggest that the discrimination does exist. Commenting on the demerits of the informal system of recruitment in UK, the Commission for Racial Equality once observed, "As far as informal recruitment methods in many industries are concerned, ethnic minorities never come to know of vacancies because they have never worked in those industries. They are unable to pass on to their friends and children the information on vacancies. Therefore such establishments will always remain all white" [Anwar 1990: 58]. Further, "The commission's investigations have shown that the word of mouth recruitment is unlawful as it discriminates indirectly against particular racial groups. However, even when these methods of recruitment are corrected to remove their unlawful effect, it can take many years before an impact is made on the opportunities for ethnic minority people." Though the aforesaid fact is from abroad they can just as well be relevant for the Indian industrial system and the plight of the dalits who are under-represented in the private sector.

Therefore, unless the government debates, highlights and discusses the aforesaid issues, the general masses and dalits will not be aware about the myths of reservation. If they fail to do so, then the dialogue on reservation in private sector will be considered only a political gimmick on more than one account. One, a ploy to garner dalit votes. Two, to grant legitimacy to the private sector and that too by using the most deprived section of society. And last, but not the least, to thwart the development of the emerging independent dalit assertion and thereby the independent dalit movement.

References

Ambedkar, B.R. (1991): 'What Congress and Gandhi Have Done to the Untouchables, *Dr Babasaheb Ambedkar Writings and Speeches,* Vol. 9, Education Department, Government of Maharashtra, Mumbai.

Anwar, Muhammad (1990): *Redressive Action Policies in the United Kingdom*, Popular Prakashan, Mumbai.

Beteille, Andre (1997): *Society and Politics in India,* Oxford University Press, New Delhi.

Bhutani, Mukesh (2004): 'Keeping Company with Phantoms', *The Indian Express,* September 25, New Delhi.

Bowles, Samuel and Herbet Gintis (1976): *Schooling in Capitalist America,* Routledge and Kegan Paul, US.

Dumont, Louis (1970): *Home Hierarchicus: The Caste System and its Implications,* Oxford University Press, New Delhi.

Jensen, A.R. (1973): *Educational Differences,* Methuen, London.

Mohan, Dinesh (2004): 'The Science of Dumbing Down', *The Indian Express,* July 16, New Delhi.

Ram, Kanshi (1982): *The Chmcha Age (An Era of the Stooges),* Vedic Mudranalaya, Delhi.

Singh, Rupashree (2004): 'Refer to Win', *Hindustan Times,* New Delhi.

Tumin, Melvin, M. (1967): *Social Stratification: The Forms and Functions of Social Inequality,* Englewood Cliffs, Princeton Hall.

6

Untouchability in Uttarakhand: Views from the Field

Untouchability exists even among the docile people of the hills of Uttaranchal, the new state carved out of Uttar Pradesh. Even after attaining political separation there has been no social movement in the state to dismantle this evil. Though we still do not have, new census data of 2001 we have to rely on the 1991 Census data of undivided Uttar Pradesh for this analysis, it is necessary to know the contextual reality of Uttaranchal at this point in time because the state is going to announce number of policies like domicile policy, reservation policy, identification of minorities for the dispensation of justice.

The nine districts of Uttaranchal of undivided Uttar Pradesh, viz. Uttarkashi, Chamoli, Tehri Garhwal, Dehradun, Garhwal, Pithoragarh, Almora, Haridwar, Nainital accounted for 4.21 per cent of total dalit population of Uttar Pradesh. Out of these districts both Uttarkashi and Almora have similar 22 per cent of dalit population, which is the highest amongst the districts. There were about 15 scheduled castes in the hills according to the undivided schedule of castes of UP. The dalits like aujis, darjis, lohar, koli, teli, tamta, dhunar, badi, kolta, mistri, roria, kevat, dom, hyrakia, od, etc., are the original inhabitants of the hills. On the other hand the dalit castes like valmikis and mochis (chamars) have migrated from nearby planes of Uttar Pradesh.

A visit to Malaitha village of Chakrata block just 60 km from the capital (according to the local people it should have been in the centre of the state) Dehradun will provide us evidence to prove the fact that untouchability exists and is still thriving. Malaitha village, according to 1991 Census, is inhabited about 819 individuals out of which nearly 66

Table 1: Distribution of Dalit Population in Hill Districts

Districts	*Total Population*	*Scheduled Castes Population*	*Percentage of Scheduled Caste Population*
Uttarkashi	239709	54594	22.78
Chamoli	454S71	79572	17.49
Tehri Garhwal	580153	82394	14.20
Dehradun	1025679	137464	13.40
Garhwal	682535	92251	13.52
Pithoragarh	566408	115832	20.45
Almora	836617	184237	22.02
Haridwar	1124488	242658	21.58
Nainital	1540174	243314	15.80
Total	7050634	1232316	17.48 *

Source: Census of India 1991. Senes-25, ran 11-0(1), p. 90.

percent, 530 are dalits. The dalits, popularly referred to as shilpkars or harijans, in this village are mainly divided into three sub-castes, viz. koltas, doms and bajgi or lohars (blacksmiths). The bajgi used to be drum-beaters but are considered as 'sachuts' (touchable dalits).

They can even enter in the houses of the negis. The duty of doms was to lift the dead animals and the koltas were the landless labourers. The dominant caste in the village is negi equivalent to the kshatriyas of the plains. Negis though in the minority dominate every walk of life. Even their village is at a higher level so that they have fertile and plane land and also good sunshine.

The koltas and doms are not allowed to enter in the houses of the negis. They cannot touch their utensils then what to say about taking food and water in their houses. The temple is also out of bound for them. Dalits also have different water sources. And if there is no such source they have to wait till the non-dalits have filled the water. There is no social interaction between these communities except through some physical work assigned to the dalits by the negis. Negis do invite dalits to their marriages and other functions, but that is more out of compulsions, "they need but labour because of shortage of manpower among their families. Who will lift the 'pattals?' (leaf plates) once the meals are over? You can understand yourself that how much respect they have for us by the fact that they feed us separately from rest of the community and that too in the end, when everyone else has taken their meals", say the koltas. Untouchability has a religious sanction too. It is an established notion among the negis and other villagers that if someone takes food from the dalits even stealthily the local deity will punish him or her.

The domination of the negis is quite evident in the village. The basic and primary school teachers refused to divulge anything when they were asked about caste discrimination and practice of untouchability in the village. "I will not be able to tell anything about the village because I have to live in this village" said a teacher who has been living in the village for the past five years and was involved in the census process of 2001. It is because of this domination that Malaitha village has the concrete 'pakdandi', which runs through the village. While this village has electricity and water connection, just one and half kilometre down the hills these facilities are missing in Dhaiiya, Loharwa, Gamri and other 'majras' of the village, which are exclusively inhabited by the dalits. Even the grazing lands of the dalits have been taken over by the negis from different villages. The irony is that the village pradhan, Medhki Devi is a dalit and she cannot hold the panchayat in her own village because the negis have threatened her not to do so. Once she tried to do so the negis refused to come to her village and forced her to hold the meeting in their village Malaitha, revealed her husband.

It is difficult to understand this caste subordination of the dalits in the hills, as the dalits are not economically dependent on the negis or any other such caste' which is above them in the hierarchy. Almost all the dalits have land. They are not working on the lands of negis for their livelihood. Moreover there is no brutal violence against them as exists in the plains of Uttar Pradesh. This fact questions the basic premise of the Marxists that the miseries of the dalits can be eradicated with land reforms and distribution of surplus land or in a word with economic uplift of the dalits. But here in Maithala village most of the dalits have land either by 'pattas' or by succession. Moreover, except a few non-dalits, most are living in abject poverty. Even then there is this prevalence of untouchability and caste discrimination. It is pertinent for us to find out the real causes of this exploitative institution.

Similarly ask any educated non-dalit of the hills about this and he will say, "Look, untouchability exists but it is not in its crude form as in the plains. Have you ever heard about the atrocities committed on the dalits in Uttaranchal?" One fails to understand-how people can justify an inhuman institution on the basis of its intensity of crudeness and that too in this era of technological and computer revolution. Secondly, the crudeness of untouchability and absence of atrocities can also be explained on the basis of lack of assertion of the dalits in the hills. It is an established fact that till the dalits accept the dictates of the non-dalits, things are peaceful for them but once they assert their legitimate right they have to face the wrath of the non-dalits.

On the other hand the negis argue-that there has been lot of change in the caste system in the village. The doms have stopped lifting the dead animals. Today we do this work on our own they say. The dalits also boast the political empowerment, which they have felt after the policy of reservations at the panchayat level was 'implemented'. "For the first time in the political life we felt that we (dalits) are also member of the society. Earlier nobody bothered for us. We can easily approach our pradhan now and plead our case" narrated a high school-failed kolta who nourishes a desire to be a pradhan in the future. Can this speed of change break' traditional shackles of caste institution in this era of globalisation, privatisation, liberalisation and information? Will the dalits get the justice in the state?

PART II: CASTE MOBILISATION AND DEMOCRACY

7

Caste Mobilisation in Uttar Pradesh: A Survey of 2002 Assembly Elections

Political mobilisation along caste lines is nothing new to India but northern India is the epitome of caste politics. All the three forms of mobilisations, namely, vertical, horizontal, and differential, as conceptualised by Rudolph and Rudolph (1987: 24-28) in the Indian society in a different context are found in the State. Though caste mobilisation in Uttar Pradesh goes round the year, it has picked up since the last one-and-a-half year.

The storm of caste mobilisation in the State has been so overpowering that even the Communist Party of India-Marxist, which plays down the caste factor in Indian politics by fitting it into the realm of 'superstructure', was forced to organise caste conventions first at the State level and then at the district levels for Dalit rights. Not only this, parties desperate to add numbers to their kitty sought to exploit the sub-caste sentiments among the Muslims like *Ghosi-Gaddi, Chikwa-Kasai, Ansari-Momin Ansar, Jhojjha, Kunjra, Churalmr,* etc. And because of this trend in the coming Assembly elections, the saying that "the people here do not cast their votes they vote their caste" will be vindicated.

A major threat of this caste mobilisation in the coming elections is that Uttar Pradesh will again have a hung Assembly. It is certain that no political party will get a clear majority. This will have a chain reaction, which the State witnessed in the last Assembly elections. Another fall-out of this hung Assembly is that the role of the Governor of the State assumes more importance. A lot will depend on him on how he saves the democracy, that is, whether he calls the single largest party abiding by the convention or he calls the single largest coalition in order to ensure stability. But it is beyond doubt that in both the cases a lot of manipulations will take place.

Having said that we can easily substantiate our conclusions if we analyse, the nature of caste mobilisation at the grassroots. This caste mobilisation can be easily observed at two levels: one at the level of "caste conventions" organised by the different sociopolitical organisations and secondly in the form of formation of single caste based parties.

Caste/Commuunity Population of Undivided Uttar Pradesh

S.No.	*Caste/Communities*	*Percentage*
1.	Other Backward Castes	37
2.	Scheduled Castes	22
3.	Brahmins	10
4.	Rajputs	7
5.	Baniyas/Kayasthas	2
6.	Jats/Bhumihars/Intermediary Castes	2
7.	Muslims	16
8.	Others	2

Source: Rapid Census 1994.

The striking feature of this caste mobilisation through caste conventions is that these conventions cut across both party and caste lines. The Bharatiya Janata Party (BJP), Congress-I, Samajwadi Party, Bahujan Samaj Party etc. all fall in the same category on this score. Similarly, the Brahmins, Kshatriyas, Vaishyas, OBCs (Yadavs, Jats, Kurmis), Dalits (Pasis, Koris, Valmikis, Dhobis) organised the caste conventions one by one. Since the past one-and-a-half year, especially during the panchayat polls and thereafter, all the political outfits and socio-political groups have been busy organising the conventions though on different scales and levels. Hence it is difficult to hold any single caste responsible for spreading the venom of casteism in the State as had been done in the past. It is really a paradoxical milieu because the upper castes in the State call this caste mobilisation the symbol of casteism. But on the other hand the Dalits and Other Backward Castes call it the 'democratic assertion' of the castes which were relegated to the periphery in the erstwhile power matrix of the State.

Among the most important caste conventions were the Vaishya Ekta Parishad Sammelan, Akhil Bharatiya Vaishya Mahasabha Sammelan, Kshatriya Mahasabha Sammelan, Kayastha Mahasabha Sammelan, Akhil Bharatiya Brahmin Mahasabha Sammelan. Bharatiya Kori Samaj Sammelan, Akhil Bharatiya Dhobi Mahasabha Sammelan, Pasi Samaj Swabhiman Sammelan, Dalit Sena Sammelan, Ahillya Bai Holkar Sammelan, and a number of BJP-sponsored Pichari Jati Avm Anuschit Jati Sammelan to take the message of the new reservation policy for the most backwards and most Dalits at the grass-roots. One common trait of all these *sammelans* (conventions) has been that at least one or the other higher-rung political leader of a political party graced the occasion as the chief guest. The enthusiasm with which the leaders of national stature participated in the programmes underlines the importance of these caste conventions in Uttar Pradesh politics.

These caste conventions can be considered as a double-edged weapon. On the one hand the caste and communities try to impart consciousness to their caste members about their rights. On the other hand they show their numerical strength and ask the different political outfits for their increased share of representation in the political space. They also demand benefits and concessions for their communities. The most glaring example of such tactics is *Vaishya Ekta Parishad Sammelan* (Vaishya unity council convention).

Through this convention Naresh Aggarwal, the then Energy Minister in the Rajnath Singh Government, tried to mobilise the Vaishya community and to our surprise the Vaishya community leaders cutting across party lines participated in the convention. Here a slogan— *"Vote Hamara, Note Hamara, Raj Tumhara Nahi Chalega Nahi Chalega"* (our votes, our money, your rule no-longer, no-longer) was coined. In fact this slogan of the Vaishya community argues a case for their greater share in the UP power structure as they have supported the BJP both monetarily and with votes. Though this pressure tactics did not work for Naresh Aggarwal, it is true that the BJP under this pressure announced lots of concessions for the trader community in the State at the cost of the State exchequer.

Now one can ask as to why at this point in time there is an increase in the number of caste conventions. And the answer is not far to seek. One obvious reason is that elections are on the cards but there is much more substantive reason for this also. As the political democracy has taken roots each caste group is becoming conscious of their rights and possible exploitation. They all want their due share and no more like to be exploited as mere vote-banks. That is why most of the convenors of these caste conventions pointed out that their caste had been neglected for so long and hence it should be given due share in the socio-political structure. To see that their demands have maximum impact they made sure that the political leader attending the convention made some announcement for their community and predictably the leaders succumbed to their pressure. A number of statues of caste leaders were sponsored by different political parties in this manner.

That brings us to the second process of political mobilisation through the formation of single caste based parties. It is true that the dominance of the upper caste in Uttar Pradesh politics did not give any political space to various caste groupings ranked, lower in the caste hierarchy. (Hasan 1998: 132-133) Hence as they became conscious they broke the political monopoly of the Brahmins and formed their own parties. And this process multiplied with greater speed especially in 1980s and 1990s. That is why we have so many political outfits virtually based on a single caste or community. For example, the BSP has Dalits (Chamars), the BJP has upper castes (Brahmins and Vaishyas), the Samajwadi Party (SP) has Yadavs, the Apna Dal has Kurmis, the Rashtriya Lok Dal and Indian National Lok Dal have Jats, the Rashtriya Kranti Party has Lodhs, the Lok Janshakti Party and the Lok Parivartan Party have Pasis, the Shakti Dal has Sikhs as their base vote-banks.

But all these parties also know that with such exclusive vote bases they cannot sustain or develop their parties in the State and national politics. Therefore, they try to add a few more castes to their party based vote-bank. Hence, these political parties try to organise different caste rallies on the one hand and also take part in caste conventions organised by different socio-political organisations on the other. These parties have also announced many concessions to woo the masses of different castes. One such exercise was declaration of reservations for the Most Backward Castes among the Backward Castes and Ati Dalits among Dalits by the Rajnath Singh Government. It is a different matter that that has been put in cold storage after it couldn't give any mileage to the BJP's poll prospects. But the BJP tried its level best to woo the Dalits and MBCs by organising a series of Dalit and Backward rallies in the State.

Similarly, Ram Vilas Paswan has been organising rallies of Dalit Sena and Lok Janashakti Party simultaneously to woo the Pasi Community and other Dalits, the Apana Dal, Rashtriya Lok Dal (RLD), Rashtriya Kranti Party (RKP), BSP have organised Kurmi, Jat, Lodh, and Gaddi rallies in the State respectively. Further, though Sharad Yadav knows that Yadavs are firmly behind the SP, even then he is hell-bent on organising them through the JD (U). Maneka Gandhi is another leader mobilising Sikhs in her constituency.

The obvious fall-out of the aforesaid single caste/ community based party is that there will be too much of division of votes. This will reduce the percentage of votes of many political parties compared to the percentage of votes they secured in the 1996 Assembly elections. Secondly, there will be close contests in most of the constituencies where the margins of victory and defeat will be very narrow.

Seats and Votes of the Major Political Parties in Uttar Pradesh Assembly Elections 1989-1996

Parties	*1989*		*1991*		*1993*		*1996*	
	S	*V*	*S*	*V*	*S*	V	*S*	7
BJP	57	11.63	221	31.6	*177*	33.4	174	32.5
SP	—	—	34	12.5	106.	17,9	110	21.8
BSP	13	9.46	12	9.2	66	10.8	67	20.6
Cong-I	94	27.94	46	17.5	28	14.8	33	8.35

Source: CSDS, New Delhi; S = Seats, V = Votes

The aforesaid caste based parties will also affect the prospects of major political players in the State because several caste and communities have changed their loyalties since the last elections, although for different reasons. But it looks that the BJP will be biggest loser. And this can be said on the basis of the fact that two major OBC castes, namely, Lodhs and Kurmis, are no more backing the party with the same intensity as they did in 1996. Lodhs have deserted the BJP because of the raw deal given to their two leaders Kalyan Singh and Sakshi Maharaj. In the process Kalyan Singh has floated his own party and organised dozens of rallies of Lodhs throughout the western region. Kurmis have been weaned away by the Apna Dal, at least in Avadh and the adjoining region. The BJP itself knows this; that is why it is working for greener pastures and is busy striking alliances with the RLD, LJP, Samata Party, JD (U), Loktantrik Congress, KMBSP etc. and has also mooted the New Reservation Policy.

Another defection of caste which can be witnessed in this regard is that of the Pasi and Jat castes. Pasis constitute six per cent of the total 22 per cent of the Dalits in the State. In the last Assembly elections they were with the SP and BSP. It is interesting to note that the SP has three Members of Parliament from the Pasi community in the Avadh region, namely, Mohanlalganj, Barabanki, and Misrikh. But now they are being mobilised by Ram Vilas Paswan's Lok Janshakti Party. Further, Ajit Singh and Om Prakash Chautala are also busy in mobilising different factions of Jats who dominate western UP. It is also true that Ajit Singh's RLD has lost the support of the Muslims because he has joined hands with the BJP this will definitely benefit the BSP's poll prospects in western UP.

Will our democracy be the loser? Because as soon as there is a hung Assembly there will be lots of horse-trading. We have seen that in the last Vidhan Sabha elections. MLAs were bought and lured by offering Ministries. Who can forget the mockery of the Anti-Defection law when 13 BSP MLAs out of 67 defected and were recognised as a separate group. The writ against this is still pending in the Supreme Court. Above all, who can forget MLAs detained as captives and ugly scenes in the House? All these tell the horror story of a hung Assembly. Will history repeat itself? If yes, then the question is: is our democracy maturing where each caste and community is asserting for his due share in the polity or is it becoming fragile with caste factionalism?

References

1. Rudolph, Lloyd I. and Rudolph; Susanne Hober, 1987, *Modernity of Tradition: Political Developments in India,* Orient Longman, Delhi.
2. Hasan, Zoya, 1998, Quest for Power: Oppositional Movement and *Post-Congress Politics in Uttar Pradesh,* Oxford University Press, Delhi.
3. Kumar, Vivek, 2000, "Convening Castes in the Cow Belt", *The Pioneer,* New Delhi.

8

Politics of Change: A Case of Uttar Pradesh

Despite structural and normative uncertainties and the loss of 18 per cent of its area and 5 per cent of its population to Uttaranchal in 2000, Uttar Pradesh has remained the hub of the Indian politics. Whether it is political assertion of the dalits in the form of the BSP or the emergence of the Hindu nationalist Bharatiya Janata Party (BJP); or for that matter the revitalisation of Congress (I), or the peasant-dominated agricultural-capitalist political outfits, all have anchorage in this microcosm of the Indian nation. The recent development in UP saw the socialists, secularists, centrists, communists, communalists (of course clandestinely) coming together to form the government in UP after BSP lost power in a dramatic turn. But it is a forgone conclusion that the government formed with the coming together of this spectrum of ideologies will not last long. Another fallout is that the BSP, a party led and dominated by the dalits has been isolated. But this isolation also signifies that the BSP has attained a strong position in UP politics and it can thereby influence national politics decisively. The BSP's insistence on early polls in the state is testimony of its strength, as no other political party wants an early election.

The BSP has generally been projected, especially by intellectuals and the media, as a party without an ideology and principle clamouring for power. What is the mechanism by which it has succeeded in retaking its support base structural chang BSP has initiated structural changes in the most populous and castewise the most fragmented state of the country. However, it is difficult to evolve definite indicators for such changes. Nadel (1969:5) argues, "We arrive at the structure of a society through abstracting from the concrete population and its behaviour, the pattern or network (or 'system') of relationships obtaining between actors and in their capacity of playing roles to one another".

"We can then ask, what rights and obligations did dalits and the so-called upper castes have before the BSF came on the dalit liberation horizon in UP? Obviously the so-called upper castes were cumulatively dominant in the socio-economic and political realms. Their hegemonic dominance rendered dalits cumulatively without a voice of dissent. But gradually after 1984 with the formation of the BSP, the established social structure has started changing in UP."

Today no 'upper caste' can take dalits for granted in UP. They retaliate in whatever manner they can. Take the case of Mau district. Here the dalits raised their arms against the thakurs of the area. Similarly in Lucknow, village Gopal Khera of Mohanlal Ganj, the dalits raised their arms against the thakurs and in fact one thakur died [Kumar and Sinha 2001:102]. Further, Lerch (1999) narrates how dalits have forced the landlords to increase their wages with the help of the state police. Nobody could have imagined these changes in the roles of the dalits before the formation of BSP government in 1995.

The roles and statuses of dalits did not change only at the social level but also at the level of governance as well. The manner in which the dalits have become the part of the highest echelons of the decision-making institutions like legislature and bureaucracy and at the lower level in the panchayats and police stations, it has led to role reversals in the social structure of UP. It is not that the dalits were not present in these echelons but when the BSP assumed power it was qualitatively different because they acquired an independent status, agenda and leader. Before the BSP came to power the dalits used to work under the 'upper castes' but with Mayawati a dalit as head of the state, several upper castes worked under her. Similarly so many dalits became the ministers, secretaries, District magistrates and superintendents of Police etc. This forcearde reversal that has led to structural change. Today dalits do not stand outside the police station hut directly enter it and get their complaints lodged. Similarly a dalit village headman, a member of legislative assembly (MLA) or member of parliament (MP) who have won from BSP are no more accountable to the 'upper castes' of their constituency. According to many IAS officers, "Mayawati has administered a powerful and long overdue lesson to bureaucrats that their place was as servant, not master of people" [Mendelsohn and Vicziany 1998: 229].

Silent Land Reform

Another aspect of BSP-led structural change is the steps taken by the government for the distribution, regularisation and possession of land in the name of the dalits and most backward castes. Usually the BSP government is blamed for initiating land reforms in the state. But the available data show that the BSP-led government has been leading a silent land reform process. For instance, as chief minister Mayawati herself issued a letter dated September 20,1997, in which she gave details of distribution of land during her tenure as chief minister. According to her 81,000 and 500 dalits were distributed 52,379 acres of land in a special drive. Further, about 1,52,000 got possession of land in which 1,20,000 acres of land was distributed. About 20,000 more dalits benefited when 15,000 irregular land nominations were regularised in their name. The letter shows that 10,37,000 'patta' owners benefited when they got temporary rights to their land [Akhtar 1999:88; UP Information Department Lucknow, 2003]. It is difficult to narrate the changes emanating from the distribution of land by BSP-led government at this juncture but one can well imagine changes related to role and status associated with a landless labourer becoming a petty landlord.

Ambedkar Village Scheme

About 80 per cent of the dalits live in villages in UP. It is a fact that no government has given appropriate attention to their development. Though the green revolution did touch the UP village it was too limited to affect the dalits in any way. In 1995 when Mayawati came to power for the first time she energised the already existing village development programme known as 'Ambedkar' Village Scheme'. Since 1995 the BSP has come to power thrice and in total it ruled for 22 and half months in its three stints. Throughout this period it has perused its agenda of development of these villages which were chosen on the basis of concentration of dalit population. Though 36 developmental programmes were initially listed for each of such village, to start with the government took up six or seven programmes of providing drinking water, electricity, housing, school, primary health centre, toilets, link roads, etc.

Eight years after this programme was initiated it has brought changes in the lives of the dalits. Today dalits do not need schools, hospitals, source of water, roads used by the 'upper castes', which has broken the traditional shackles of caste relations. The whole process has saved the dalits from facing the perpetual humiliation inflicted by the upper castes whenever they became angry and put restrictions on the use of these facilities by the dalits. In this regard Chatteijee (2003) argues, "In Lucknow and Delhi politicians may scoff at Mayawati's *dalit ki beti* histrionics, but spend a day of these Ambedkar villages-settlements with more than 50 per cent dalit populace were declared as such and promised special development schemes... The most visible sign of change is the enthusiasm for education. In the cluster of four villages in this area - Abbasganj, Hasanpur, Kaneri, Chatauni (on Rae Bareli- Lucknow border) there are four primary schools, two junior schools and one high school. Almost every dalit parent send their sons and daughters to school".

Confrontation with Aristocracy

The BSP-led government has always been against mafia and 'goondas', which can be proved by the huge number of criminals put behind the bars during its different regimes. For instance, during her first tenure of four and a half months Mayawati put 1,45,000 rowdies, criminals, goondas, etc., behind bars [Kashi Ram: 1999]. Probably for the first time in Indian democracy an aristocrat was put behind the bars on criminal charges - the arrest of Raghuraj Pratap Singh alias Raja Bhaiya the so-called king of Kunda in Pratapgarh district who ran his parallel government under mining democratic Constitution of India even after 53 years of its commencement.

The king along with his 45 supporters was arrested under POTA and other charges in January 2003; Such was the dominance and tenor of the aristocrat that in spite of 51 cases registered against his father and 29 against himself and 17 more against their identified associates, the police and civil administration never dared to touch them *(The Sunday Express*, February 9, 2003). Now the moot question is why did no chief minister before Mayawati take any action against such subverters of democracy. And the answer is simple "as every political party benefited from him hence nobody bothered to break his dominance", narrated a brahmin who is himself is a sufferer at the hands of Raja Bhaiya. But now with his fiefdom shattered a new structural order may emerge in Kunda and other such places. As a dalit of Kunda argued "now we will vote freely according to our will, all these years we could not even see the ballot box or paper".

With the emergence of BSP dalits have deconstructed and reconstructed many identities and symbols of UP society. This whole process has created self-respect, confidence and assertion among the erstwhile deprived dalits. The qualitative changes that the BSP has brought in the roles and statures of the dalits in UP has brought new expectation from the party, leading their support of BSP and they remain with the party even when the chips are down without questioning the credentials of their leaders.

References

Akhatar, Jamil Mohammad (1990): *Iron Lady: Mayawati*, Bahujan Sungathan, New Dellhi. Chatterjee, Manini (2003): 'Maya's Gone but in These Dalit Homes the Change's for Real', *The Indian Express,* September 1, New Delhi. Kumar, Vivek and Uday Sinha (2001): *Dalit Assertion and Bahujan Samaj Party: A Perspective from Below,* Bahujan Sahilya Sasihan. Lucknow.

Lerch, Jens (1999): "Politics of the Poor: Agricultural Labourers and Political Transformation in Uttar Pradesh" in Jens Lerch (*et.al*). *Rural Labour Relations in India*, Frank Class, London. Mendelsohn, Oliver and Marika Vicziany (eds) (1998): *The Untouchables: Subordination, Poverty and the States in Modern India,* Cambridge University Press, UK.

Nadel, S.F. (1969): The Theory of Social Structure. Cohen and West, London.

Kashi, Ram (1999): In the Foreword to Mohammad Jamil, Akhatar, 1999, New Delhi.

9

Strengthening of Indian Democracy: BSP's Experiment in Uttar Pradesh

The Bahujan Samaj Party (BSP) on May 3, 2003 completed one year in power and that too in the most populous State of the country. And thereby Ms Mayawati has created some kind of history. One, she has become the first Dalit woman Chief Minister in India to remain in power for so long. Second, as the *New York Times* on May 4, 2003 wrote,

> Mayawati is the Chief Minister of India's largest State, Uttar Pradesh, in the north. It is home to 166 million people, which means she governs more people than all but one woman in the world, Indonesia's President, Megawati Sukarnoputri.

In fact Ms Mayawati broke her own record of being the only Dalit woman Chief Minister twice, first for four-and-a-half months (in June-October (1995) and then for six months (in April-September 1997). It is true that before Mayawati there have been a few Dalit Chief Ministers but there is a qualitative difference between them and Mayawati. They were/ are all products of the politics of patronage, that is, the Dalit Chief Ministers were appointed and removed at the mercy of heads of political parties led and dominated by the upper castes. But Mayawati is the outcome of an independent assertion of a Dalit political party, which is now about quarter of a century old, where Dalits decide and implement their own agenda.

With one year in power Mayawati has in many senses demystified certain established images of Dalit women and general caste women in Indian politics with her unique and aggressive life-style. First of all, she has broken the typical image of the Dalit woman— busy in her hereditary occupation and who is triply exploited on the bases of caste, class and gender. Against this image of the Dalit woman Mayawati chose first teaching as her profession and then became a full-time politician. She has proved a determined and able administrator. She has deliberately created a climate of fear to motivate officials to work to her agenda. Mayawati has demystified the image of the general caste woman as well. Most of the upper caste women in Indian politics have carried the typical image of the Indian woman wearing a *saree, pallu* draped over her head as a mark of respect for her elders (Jayalalitha may be an exception in terms of *pallu).* But Ms Mayawati has always worn a *shalvar-kurta* with a *dupatta* wrapped around her neck suggesting that there is no preferred code of dress for Indian woman even in the north where patriarchy is still very dominant. Further, it is a fact that Indian culture, especially Hindu culture, prescribes a docile and polite way of conversation for women. But Mayawati always uses rough and aggressive speeches in public. She represents a woman accepted by her followers purely on the basis of her statecraft debunking the myth that Dalits do not know the art of governance. That is why she has become an icon of Dalit women. The young Dalit girls rap their *dupatta* round their neck to imitate her. This is a significant aspect for the Dalit movement, as it did not have a popular woman icon in its history.

From an exclusive group of Dalit employees, BAMCEF, in 1978 to the first political party established by Dalits to attain a national stature— the journey for the BSP has been bumpy and marred by condemnation. The abuses hurled from every quarter at its leadership as casteist, separatist, corrupt, devoid of any vision and spoilsport etc. are still fresh in the memory of the Dalits and general masses alike. But the BSP's development has been phenomenal. And today it is ushering in a new paradigm of political mobilisation in Indian politics which is reeling under the pressure of the coalition era. Maharashtra and Bihar will soon see new coalition partners. Taking lessons from the BSP the Republican Party of India led by Ramdas Athawale is considering to align with the Shiv Sena in Maharashtra. Similarly, Ramvilas Paswan is desperate for an alliance with the Congress in Bihar. Further in Tamil Nadu, Putiatamijgam and Dalit Panthers are already in alliance with the DMK. The only drawback with these Dalit political parties is that their organisational structure is not as developed as that of the BSP. If they follow the BSP's policy of developing their own party independently without entering into coalition in governance, they can as the true heir of Babasaheb Ambedkar; that is why a slogan was mooted:

Bab a Ter a Mission Adhura

Kanshi Ram Karettega Pura.

(Babasaheb Ambedkar, your mission is incomplete, Kanshi Ram still fulfil it.)

Today Mayawati has been projected as the messiah of the Dalits in the country.

The impact of this personality cult is writ large on the forthcoming Lok Sabha elections of 2004 as the Bharatiya Janata Party has already projected Atal Behari Vajpayee as its Prime Ministerial candidate and floated a slogan:

Chauthi Bari Atal Behari.

(Fourth time Atal Behari.)

'The aforesaid slogan undermines all the institutions and norms of the representative and democratic politics where different forums and processes are involved in the selection and election of an individual to the different offices of the government and party. But it is the sheer dominance of Vajpayee's personality that he has already been declared the Prime Ministerial candidate. Can this be called representative democracy?

To conclude, we can argue that the whole phenomenon of personality cult in the system of representative democracy has made the choice of leadership very limited. You are forced to choose from the lot which the parties project. And parties project the personalities keeping primordial loyalties like caste, region, religion and hereditary status in mind which have some element of charisma in them. The candidates are seldom projected on the universalistic values. This in turn reduces the breadth of the social base from which political elites are to be recruited rendering Indian democracy reduced to a narrow base. This is why we see that only a small strata have monopolised Indian politics since its inception. As has been rightly brought out by Singh (1994: 135),

> Since still the majority of elite belonged to the upper castes, particularly the Brahmins caste, the elite structure could not be said to have been democratised in the real sense. Another fall-out of the domination of personality cult in Indian politics is that a number of institutions are compromised and the real

issues related to the masses are thwarting the development of representative democracy and making it really participatory.

It is more astonishing that even the processes of modernisation and globalisation have not been able to break this domination of primordial loyalties which give birth to this personality cult in Indian politics, though it was envisaged that these would disappear with the passage of time. On the contrary, most of the modern institutions like film, TV, politics, bureaucracy, judiciary etc. have been used to monopolise power rather than to democratise the polity and society. Will Indian democracy transform itself into a government of the people by the people or will it remain a government of a hereditary class by a hereditary ruling class.

Strengthen their Position and Increase their Bargaining Power as well

It is an established fact that the BSP is the product of two significant developments of the post-independence period in India—one, democratisation of the polity and society based on a democratic Constitution and two, the policy of protective discrimination of the state. Though there are allegations against the BSP that its politics is divisive in natures the BSP has really strengthened Indian democracy. The two most glaring aspects of this development are—it has really empowered the most deprived sections of Indian society by independently and directly speaking their language in their own idioms. By forming governments four times in UP it has made Dalits feel what state power means and what it is capable of. Today Dalits have got the space to sit in the highest echelons of power and take decisions on their own, which did not happen earlier as others decided for them or others represented them in various houses of legislatures. Above all, the BSP has successfully created a new identity, awareness, confidence and self-perception among the Dalits. And if democracy means empowerment of the lowest of the low then the BSP is seriously trying to implement it. The words of a woman sweeping the Lucknow roads early in the morning say it all. The researcher questioned the woman: "What have you got from Mayawati becoming the Chief Minister?" The answer was forthright and she replied with enormous confidence: "Yes, she has not given me any gold or silver nor has she increased my pay but now my supervisor is not asking for money and he also talks with me very politely. He used to be very rude earlier."

The BSP can take the credit for not only listening to and speaking the voice of the lowest of the low but also of punishing the most powerful individuals, if they have broken the rules of democracy. To restore democracy its coalition government has even antagonised the aristocracy and punished them. The arrest of Raja Bhaiya, his father and 45 of his supporters under POTA and other charges is a historic example in independent India when a so-called aristocrat was put behind bars for criminal offences. Such was the terror of these people that even after 51 cases were registered against Udai Pratap, 29 against Raja Bhaiya and 17 more against their identified associates, the Kunda Police never dared to touch them. *(The Sunday Express*, February 9, 2003) Pratapgarh's DM argues: Several local officers have been suspended and more are likely to face action for allowing this family to function as a private Raj. *(Ibid.)*

Imagine even after 56 years of India's independence we have an aristocracy where people have no democracy. But now restoration of democracy is on the cards. As a Dalit villager narrated,

"Now we will vote according to our free will, all these years we could not see the ballot paper."

Who knows whether this is the beginning of democracy in how many such Kundas which are still in oblivion?

Secondly, because of this independent Dalit assertion of the BSP the other stream of Dalit politics which functions as a part of the political parties led and dominated by the upper strata has got a fair share in their respective parties. In this context we are forced to argue that the independent Dalit assertion led by the BSP has really increased the bargaining power of Dalits in other parties. That is why we have seen a Dalit President, few Dalit Chief Ministers and Governors and a number of Ministers within a decade or so coinciding with the emergence of the BSP. But Dalits should be aware of the fact that this a part of the tacties of generosity of the upper strata to lure the Dalits though in effective terms they will never hand over power to the Dalits whether they are given space in the party structure or in government. Jagjivan Ram in the past and Bangaru Laxman in the present are two glaring examples. As soon as a Dalit leader in the aforesaid parties starts asserting himself he is shown the door and cut to size. Further, we should be conscious of the fact that they have also been used against their own brothers thus damaging the unity of the wider Dalit movement.

Twenty-five years down the line there have been quantitative and qualitative changes within the BSP. It has tried to project its different image. From the party of Bahujan to Sarvajan, ideologically mellowing down the tone of criticism of the Manuwadis, from a media-shy to a media-savvy leadership, from poverty-stricken, illiterate, rural Dalits to literate, petty bourgeois, upper-caste urban gentry—the whole composition of the BSP has changed dramatically. Yet the mainstream media, intelligentsia, and academia have not accepted the BSP. Instead of empathising with the BSP's leadership for negotiating in unfriendly socio-political and economic conditions, without any support from big business houses, any legacy of the freedom movement or status quoism of the Hindu.

Social order, any base of Western ideology of Marxism, they all have vehemently criticised the BSP and its leadership.

References

Weiner, Myron, Party Politics in India: The Development of a Multi-Party System, Princeton University Press, 1957.

Singh, Y. Modernisation of Indian Tradition, Rawat Publication, Jaipur, 1994.

10

Celebrating Birthday for 'Swabhiman' A Perspective from Below

But it is also true that no political party is perfect in its infancy. It shapes its agenda according to the available economic and human resources. Even then why do all these intellectuals and academicians want that the BSP should fulfill their agenda of land reforms, minimum wages act, job security etc.? Why should the BSP be guided by the whims and fancies of the so-called mainstream intellectuals and opinion-makers? If the party can survive for 25 years and has brought itself to this level that means its programmes and policies, though limited and unquantifiable, have proved functional and emancipatory for the most oppressed section of Indian society. And if it has really instilled confidence among them that it represents them it means that the BSP has strengthened Indian democracy because the main aim of any democracy is that the voice of the individual or the group of individuals placed lowest in the hierarchy should also be heard. Can Indian "democracy" be proud of the fact that Mayawati, herself a product of democracy, has strengthened Indian democracy? The vociferous criticism of Mayawati's birthday celebration by the media and other sections of the society looked very shallow and partisan. It is a fact that what looks to be the dominant perception of the society is often the perception of the dominant section of the society and the same is true in this case also. It is really heartening to read so many columns advising the Dalit movement after Mayawati's birthday, bash. But it was disturbing too that without grasping the latent functions of the programme most of the columnists condemned it. Evaluating the programme as any other event the columnists raised many questions. For instance, why should Mayawati indulge in this type of opulence when the HDI of Uttar Pradesh is one of the lowest in the country? Moreover, they argued that these types of celebrations represent status-quoism and retard the development of an alternative culture. Someone also wrote that Dalit politics should draw lessons from M.K. Gandhi's style of politics. In the same vein they blamed Dalit politics as it was, in then opinion, devoid of any emancipatory agenda; rather it was aimed at capture of power even at the cost of its principles.

The pejoratives used for Mayawati's birthday bash by the media and columnists like 'forty-seven year old birthday girl', *'falwa Maya Memsahab Ka'* etc. were not in good taste and speak volumes of the animosity with which the media approaches the Dalit leader. It was really astonishing to note the content of the stories aired by the different television channels. Every reporter had more views than the news. Not a single Dalit or BSP worker was interviewed to portray what the insiders felt. On the other hand the media totally failed to catch the imagination and consciousness of Dalits who felt elated and enthused by this unique and historical celebration. The dominant sections of the society did not capture the imagination of the teenage Dalit girls putting their veil round their necks imitating Mayawati and claiming to become like her one day. A post-graduate unemployed Dalit youth narrated the truth differently:

We have seen the landlords–Thakurs and Brahmins–organising this type of grand parties where we could not even enter and felt deprived by the glittering lights and high pitch sound, but Bahenji has made it possible for us to participate in this celebration where Dalits and other Bahujans can take part freely and that too on an equal footing.

What a pity that the critiques of Mayawati's birthday celebration could see her diamonds, dress and opulence of the occasion but failed to note and appreciate the simplicity of shawl and open sleeves of Kanshi Ram. They could not read the message, which is the priority of the Dalit movement, writ large in the nomenclature of the programme 'Swabhiman Diwas'. Why did they not capture the happiness and enthusiasm on the face of the poverty stricken Dalit who participated in the programme? But then, why would they see all these anyway? You see what, you want to see. And what you want to see is decided by your preconceived notions about a phenomenon, and that is based on values in which you are socialised because there are no spaces for alternative values, especially of Dalits, which the upper strata hardly confront.

I am sure none of the columnists visited the sight neither at Lucknow nor in Delhi; otherwise they would have written some insightful things about the programme as well. For instance, about the play *'Parivartan ka Maseeha'* (Messiah of Transformation) in Delhi's Talkatora Indoor Stadium which highlighted the 'alternative hegemony' with which Dalits are being equipped. The identities and symbols projected in the play included King Pururava, Buddha, Kabir, Raidas, Narayan Guruswamy, Phule, Periyar, Sahuji and Ambedkar, and ably constructed a parallel value system for the Dalits. Not only that. Dalit cultural artistes presented their own songs and dances, like the Bundlkhandi Raee dance, Gazipuri Dhobia dance, Rawat folk dance, Rajasthani Kalbeliya dance, Biraha, Lachari, Ambedkarite songs, etc. One can easily argue on the basis of the whole programme that Dalits at least for a day deconstructed the dominant identities and symbols of the Hindu social order which have hegemonised the Dalits since ages and constructed their own independent ones.

The barbaric killing of five Dalits, when they asserted that they will not bribe the police, in Dulena, Jhajjar in Haryana on October 16, 2002 is the first case in point. The mob had no sympathy with the Dalits because of a psyche that Dalits are to be treated shabbily and are worse than animals. This was evident when after the lynching of Dalits instead of ordering for an inquiry, the authorities ordered the post mortem of the cow as if the life of a cow is more precious than five human beings. Not only that, though the sacred texts of the Hindus have assigned this stigmatised job to the Dalits, yet the same Hindus look down upon them and take refuge in the cow which has been declared as sacred by the *shastras.* Once again the objective is: establishing the hegemony of caste Hindus with their sacred symbol of cow. The second incident of Dalit atrocity for maintaining the hegemony of the caste Hindu is of Chakwara in Jaipur. Here the caste Hindus denied Dalits access to the water tank and temple on September 22, 2002, lest they defile both. And when they asserted their right to do so they were beaten. Again the caste Hindus took refuge in the sacred symbol of the Hindus, that is, sanctity of the Hindu temple. Similarly on September 5, at Kaundampatti in Dindigul district, a Dalit agricultural worker was forced to drink urine for having lodged with the police a complaint of trespass against a caste Hindu. This was done precisely because the caste Hindu felt offended that a Dalit can question his hegemony even though he is a thief or a rogue! These are a few but significant cases of atrocities in contemporary times, which prove the fact that the atrocities of the second category are becoming dominant with each passing day. But the disturbing part of the whole issue is that the total number of cases of atrocities on Dalits has been multiplying with every passing day.

The exciting paradoxical socio-political context in which these atrocities on Dalits are inflicted is further complicated by the onset of the process of globalisation in contemporary India. The process of globalisation, alongwith its appendage processes of information revolution and privatisation has not had any impact on the stigmatised status of the Dalits. Regarding globalisation, it was argued that with the onset of these processes the interaction pattern on the basis of primordial loyalties would be replaced by global identities. Needless to state that the national leadership also had more or less the same hope with the processes of modernisation and industrialisation in Indian society after the adoption of the Consti-tution. But the irony is that this neither happened then nor is it happening now. We can ourselves observe that still the caste Hindus are interacting with the Dalits on the basis of the same primordial identities as is evident from the aforesaid incidents. To prove the point further we can take the atrocity data of the Sixth Report of the Commissioner of Scheduled Castes and Scheduled Tribes, 1990-2000 and 2000-01. The report depicts 23,742 atrocity cases against the Dalits in the year 2000 alone. Out of these 23,742 cases, there were 1034 cases of rape of Dalit women and 3241 cases of murder of Dalits. This means approximately three cases of rape and nine murders per day respectively. And mind you, these are all reported cases though it is a fact that a substantial number of cases of Dalit atrocity go unreported.

It becomes evident from the above analysis that despite constitutional safeguards, legislations, modernisation, industrialisation and now the era of globalisation, information revolution and 'saffronisation of Dalits', atrocities on them are going on unabated. Therefore, one is forced to argue that these processes are not enough to check the rate of atrocities on the Dalits committed by the caste Hindus. Further, in the same vein one is also forced to ask a question: don't we need a cultural, rather than an economic, approach to find out the different sources of atrocities on Dalits committed by the upper castes?

While examining the sources of atrocities on Dalits from the cultural perspective, we can take the help of the Gramscian notion of hegemony. Though he analyses this phenomenon in a class society, we can very well apply it in a caste society also. According to him, hegemony means "the ideological/cultural domination of one class by another, achieved by 'engineering consensus' through controlling the content of cultural forms and major institutions". (David Jary and Julia Jary, *Collins Dictionary of Sociology,* 2000, p. 261) It is in this way that the caste Hindus have controlled the Dalits and kept them in the fold of Hinduism. But now as the Dalits are becoming conscious of their exploitation, they are moving outside the fold of the Hindu society. This they are doing by establishing their own identities and symbols like identity of the Dalit, conversion to Buddhism, establishing the idols of Ambedkar and so on so forth. The caste Hindus do not like this counter-hegemony of the Dalits because this challenges their hegemony and hence on the one hand they want to coopt them into their fold and on the other they perpetuate atrocities on them to keep their total control on them. Therefore, in the near future the atrocities on Dalits will increase because they are not ready to take things lying down and this will in no way be liked by the caste Hindus.

Despite these processes of deconstruction and reconstruction by the Dalits, the sarcasm with which newsreaders read the news and columnists wrote the columns revealed the partisan nature and ignorance of the media about the symbols and activities of the Dalits. In both these acts their hegemonic perceptions looking at the Dalit phenomenon from their own vantage-point was writ large. I think before evaluating such events not only mediapersons, columnists but also the so-called mainstream intellectuals should take a lesson in concepts like 'alternative hegemony' propounded by Gramsci or 'pedagogy of the oppressed' of Paulo Freir. One needs conscientisation rather than socialisation to understand the latent functions of the processes in which Dalits are involved today. Otherwise they will give only such simple explanations as they have given sitting in their cozy rooms and writing about deaths because of the cold wave.

Granted, no one should empty the state's exchequer for personal use. But why blame only one. It is a fact that since the inception of the modern state its exchequer has been used for self-aggrandisement by the upper strata that controlled it and this continues even today. The budget allocated for each Kumbh Mela, for instance, is more than a million rupees. The last Kumbh in Allahabad had the same budget. The moot question is: for what? People can argue that it relates to the religious sentiments of the masses. But everyone knows that the whole Kumbh is only" for a particular section of the society. If you can spend millions of rupees just to facilitate people to take a dip in the dirty water (as was just highlighted by the devout *Sadhus* in Allahabad, UP), they by the same logic it can be argued that few lakhs can be spent for celebrating to respect the feelings of the Dalits. And mind you, in comparison to the expenditure incurred by the state in organising religious functions round the year for a particular *varria* of the Hindu social order, which helps no one and are used as a ploy to keep the masses under false consciousness, devoid of any scientific temper, the expenditure incurred on Mayawati's birthday was insignificant. It was a state-sponsored programme not only for Mayawati but also for the whole Dalit community. Now, one can ask about the importance of this programme in this era and the answer is simple. A collectivity subjected to multiple depravation will protest first against those disabilities which it perceives to be most inhuman and unbearable; and hence this social gathering and projection.

Further, opulence versus simplicity—the same moral issue erupted when Ambedkar wore his suit and was criticised while the *dhoti*-clad Gandhi was hailed. But the Dalits argued that Gandhi, a son of a *Dewan* of an empire and a *Vaishya* by caste, had to wear *dhoti* to get accepted by the masses. On the other hand Ambedkar had no problem of acceptance but had to project an image which Dalits could follow. He had to act as a reference-point for the Dalits. Gandhi took Dalits to temples while Ambedkar took them to politics and Buddhism. Today, Dalits have understood that their salvation lies in politics in the realm of power and in Buddhism for spirituality; therefore they are carving out their own path. They have learnt the tricks of the trade where opulence and self-projection play a dominant role.

Analysing the positive function of the aforesaid programme further we can argue that for Dalits, the birthday celebration was totally a new experience when they saw, possibly for the first time in the history, their own icon celebrating her birthday. Till now they have heard of Nehru's, Gandhi's and now Shyama Prasad Mukherjee's and Deen Dayal's birthdays being celebrated. Jawaharlal Nerhu's birthday is celebrated as 'Children Day'. By doing so it is projected that they are the only 'significant individuals' who have contributed to the development of the Indian society. In turn the contribution of the Dalits were ignored. Hence the Dalits were devoid of any 'cultural capital' which could boast that they also have individuals who have contributed to the construction of this society and hence have status of some worth. The BSP since its inception has been trying to establish new icons who can be revered by the Dalits. Buddha, Raidas, Kabir, Guru Ghasi Das, Birsa Munda,

Jotiba Phuley, Narayan Guruswamy, E. V. Ramaswamy Naicker (Periyar), Sahuji Maharaj, Babasaheb Ambedkar, Jhalkaribai Kori, Uda Devi Pasi, Maharaja Bijli Pasi etc. have been highlighted as parallel national figures at par with Gandhi and Nehru. Her birthday celebration is another step in that direction which was legitimately called *'Swabhiman Diwas'* (Self-respect Day).

Easy collection of funds for the party's development was another functional aspect of the birthday party. Since 1999 the Bahujan Samaj Party has made a ritual of collecting funds from its well-wishers and supporters on the occasion of Mayawati's birthday. In fact in 1999 the party collected Rs 12 million and in 2002 this collection went up to Rs. 43 million. This is part of the party's long-drawn strategy so that masses could pay for the development of their movement. Kanshi Ram, the BSP supremo, has always highlighted the need of funds for the party. He perpetually asks this question in workers' meetings: who will fund the Dalit movement? And answers: definitely not the upper strata; hence we should develop a habit in our supporters to contribute financially for the movement. It is in this context that he popularised the slogan *'Ek Note Ek Vote'* (one rupee and one vote), and started charging fee for addressing rallies whenever his supporters called him. Kanshi Ram was for the first time paid a fee of Rs 12 thousand equivalent to his weight as he was weighed in one-rupee coins. He addressed 100 meetings with the same fee. Later Kanshi Ram started charging Rs 52 thousand after his fiftysecond birthday and thereafter he went on increasing his fee for addressing rallies. But today because Kanshi Ram has stopped political mobilisation in Uttar Pradesh Mayawati has started reaping the benefit of this habit developed among the Dalits and other Bahujans. Of course, now the party has a bigger network because it is now a *Sarvajan Party* (party of everyone) and also because it has come to power four times, once with the Samajwadi Party and three times with the Bharatiya Janata Party.

This collection of funds through the masses assumes importance when we compare the BSP with the other established political parties in the country. It is true that most of these parties are funded directly and indirectly by some or other business houses. Moreover they also represent mostly affluent sections of the society. Compared to this the BSP is still funded by individuals of the proletariat secton of society. Hence it is a fight between unequals, as was ably put by Kanshi Ram in his speech at the Janurary 15 celebration. He argued:

> After making the poor section conscious, pitting the poor section against the rich, making the poor section victorious we have achieved the target I want to see in my lifetime that the BSP, which is the party of the poor, should become the number one party leaving behind the parties of the rich.

In this context, if the birthday celebration has so adversely affected the upper strata psyche, may I add that Mayawati's larger purpose has been served? She has conveyed the message, to one and all, of Dalit assertion. Further, she has been successful in demoralising the oppressors for a day and has conveyed that state power can change the mantle. Contrary to this, she has been successful in arousing the sentiments of the demoralised Dalits further with the help of the few lakhs of rupees from the state exchequer which is not an expensive deal specially when we look at the amount usurped by the upper strata in scams. Can anyone buy the happiness of approximately 20 million people with so meagre an amount?

Last but not the least, to evaluate the BSP's performance one must locate it in the context in which it has emerged and is functioning, especially in the era of coalition politics and state led societal development. In all the BSP has ruled for 18 months and that too as a minority party with 49, 65, and 99 MLAs. Against a political and bureaucratic set-up which is 53 years old with the commencement of modern Constitution, and a social order that has a history of two thousand five hundred years, this is just a fragment. Yet, Mayawati has not compromised with the values of her party. Had she done so, the BJP would have not withdrawn support from her (in 1995) or she would have not withdrawn support from the BJP (1997)! Her decision to revamp the status-quoist bureaucracy to implement the agenda of her party, would not have been criticised. She would not have been condemned when she punished the Mafia don Raja Bhaiyya. The critics without taking note of the perception of the people of that area to which the name Raja Bhaiyya is terror, debated on political vendetta only. She would have been hailed for taking firm action in deterring a mass VHP mobilisation around the Keshav Das temple/Idgah/mosque in Mathura in mid-1999. She would have been also hailed for not only distributing *pattas* of land but also possessions on the land. Has anyone visited the sight where the Sub-Divisional Magistrate is himself present and completes formalities of the possession of land given to Dalits? Similarly, she would have been appreciated for the Ambedkar Village-Scheme, Taj Express Highway, and the proposed International Airport at Dhankaur eighty kilometres from Delhi. I think these facts will suffice to prove the point that the emancipatory agenda of Dalit assertion is moving from the realm of ideas to the economic and political realm.

References

Kumar, Vivek, 2002, *Dalit Leadership in India,* Kalpaz Publications, Delhi.

Kumar, Vivek, 2003, "The birthday and party poopers", *The Indian Express,* January, 24, New Delhi.

11

Understanding Patterns of Mobilisation: A Case of BSP

If Indian political democracy can be proud of one thing it should be that a dalit woman has become chief minister of India's most populated state, Uttar Pradesh, not once but four times. Mayawati's ascendance to the post of the chief minister in 2007 is the greater historical event because she has occupied office on her party's own strength, without outside support or in coalition. The Bahujan Samaj Party's (BSP) recent victory in UP is also historical because for the first time in modern Indian politics a political party led and dominated by dalits has come to power on its own* intelligentsia and academia have been interpreting BSP's victory in an over-simplified manner. Earlier they labelled the BSP as a movement spreading the venom of casteism, a party without ideology, a "power hungry" outfit without any agenda of emancipation and only committed to erecting Ambedkar's statues and gardens, celebrating birthdays, etc. In each election they predicted its doom and in poll surveys of 2007 gave the BSP only 120-160 seats. Now these analysts are evaluating BSP's victory in terms of a dalit-brahmin social engineering programme led by brahmins, an anti-incumbency effect and the effectiveness of the Election Commission in overseeing the elections, etc., without substantiating why only the BSP has benefited from these factors.

Media's Myopia

The media's projection that the BSP's victory in UP was the result of a dalit- brahmin alliance raises a few questions. For instance, why

Out ironically the intelligentsia and academia

Table 1: Party-wise Seats in Uttar Pradesh Assembly Elections (1989-2007)

Year/Party	*1989* •	*1991*	*1993*	*1996*	*2002*	*2007*
BSP	13(9.4)	12(9.4)	69(11.3)	97(11.2)	98(23.19)	206(30.46)
SP	-	109(17.9)	109(21.80)	143(25.43)	97(25.45)	
BJP	57(11.6)	221(31.5)	178(33.3)	174(32.5)	88(20.12)	50(16.93)
INC	94(27.9)	46(17.4)	28(15.0)	33(8.4)	25(9.00)	22(8.56)

Note: The figures in brackets represent the percentage of votes polled.
Source: Chief electoral officer Uttar Pradesh, Lucknow.

has only the BSP been successful in successfully building a dalit-brahmin equation? Why did the Congress not succeed in reviving its brahmin-Muslim-dalit arithmetic? Why was the Bharatiya Janata Party unable to make its 'samrasta' slogan functional? Moreover, the BSP has been contesting elections since the days of the Dalit Soshit Samaj Sangharsh Samiti (DS4) in 1981, yet why is it that only now it has been so successful?

One can argue that the BSP did not earlier welcome brahmins as it does now. But the question is, why did the brahmins earlier not support the BSP in the same proportion as they were given a share in seat allocation? We can argue that the brahmins came to the BSP once the party crossed a threshold with its traditional votes and they were convinced that the BSP could give them a sure victory. Moreover, the new elite and its younger generation have been stagnating in the Congress and BJP, as the established leadership has not given them any space for their development. Brahmins will stay with the BSP as long as the party has power and they themselves do not have space for development in other parties. Secondly, this alliance will not take a pan-Indian shape unless the BSP crosses threshold in different parts of the country?. In sum, the dalit-brahmin alliance in UP is not part of any social engineering process but abjure political adjustment.

That means the reasons for BSP's success in 2007 assembly elections are to be found in the historical feature and struggle of the "Bahujan Movement because the BSP is an offshoot of a movement and is also a movement in itself rather than only a political party [Kumar 2006]. This article is an attempt to analyse BSP's victory historically.

End of 'Chamcha Age'

The BSP's first step in politics was establishment of an "independent dalit political leadership" instead of a "dependent dalit political leadership" [Kumar 2003a]. The latter was present in the political parties that were led and dominated by the so-called upper castes and was a product of the politics of patronage - the 'ma-baap' culture. Against this Kanshi Ram produced an "independent dalit political leadership" in a party that was led and dominated by the dalits with an independent agenda. As a result, the BSP made the dalit leaders in other political parties redundant. The 2007 UP election was a witness to this phenomenon, with all political parties giving Mayawati a virtual walkover as far as the dalit votes were concerned. Except for giving tickets to dalits from reserved seats no political party tried to mobilise the dalits. Even during the election campaign no political party could present a dalit leader for mobilising the dalits, though they did have a number of such candidates for leadership.

This has happened because of the emergence of Mayawati. She has not only effectively mobilised the dalits in the BSP's favour but her style of governance and performance of her successive governments has consolidated dalit support. The dalits have virtually lost faith in dalit leaders from other parties. That is why this time in UP, BSP won a record 62 out of 89 reserved seats, i.e., almost 70 per cent of the seats and garnered 77 per cent of them were organised across the state with a specific membership drive, which culminated in the "Brahmin Maha Rally' on June 9, 2005 in Lucknow, it was a tactical move because it changed the preconceived notions of brahmins about the BSP. To convince them further Mayawati groomed an upper caste leadership in her party and changed the party's slogan from 'Jiski Jitni Sankhya Bhari; Uski Utni Bhagedari' (representation of each (caste) according to its population) to 'Jiski Jitni Taiyari; Uski Utni Bhagedari' (representation of each (castes) on the basis of their ideological preparedness to accept BSP's ideology).

To bring in a larger number of savarnas, the BSP constituted 'Bhaichara Baraho Committees' (develop brotherhood committees) in every assembly constituency. The economically poor among the upper castes were made a target. Mayawati vehemently criticised former prime minister Atal Behari Vajpayee, a brahmin, for not paying attention to their problems. Finally, in a pragmatic move she distributed 86, 38 and 14 tickets to brahmins, rajputs and vaishyas respectively, in the recent UP elections. In spite of making all these efforts and political manoeuvring Mayawati was not suffering from any illusion about the political commitment of so-called upper castes to BSP. Her speech on June 3, 2005 is a pointer in this regard;

Bahujan Samaj should not trust the upper castes who are joining the party... because...it will take some time to change their hearts. At once they should not rely or trust the upper caste in the constituencies where the candidates are from the Bahujan caste. The upper castes will not cast their votes in the favour of the Bahujan caste candidate. But Bahujan caste voters should transfer their votes totally in favour of the upper caste candidates in every constituencies where they are contesting on the BSP ticket though in such constituencies also the upper castes will not voteen masse for the upper caste candidate contesting on the BSP ticket. But in this process, even if the upper caste candidate gels 2 to 3 per cent of the upper Caste voles, the BSP as a party can enhance its tally from the dalit votes. Earlier it used to win only 22 to 25 per cent of the reserved seats. This can be called the end of what Manyavar Kanshi Ram used to call the "Chamcha Age" and the BSP has become the sole custodian of dalit votes.

Other Backward Classes

The other backward classes (OBCs) have always been the core component of Bahujan Samaj. A strong notion prevails among the general public that OBCs perpetrate atrocities on dalits. However, in UP as well in the rest of India, the OBCs do not form a monolithic whole. There are 79 castes, which come under the rubric of the OBCs in UP. Of the lot, the yadavs, kurmis, jats, lodhs and gujjars can be termed as economically and politically mobile. Internally differentiated on the class lines, these are still socially stigmatised and excluded from the higher bureaucracy. These castes cannot match the brahmins in UP as far as bureaucratic power is concerned.

Granted these five castes are aggressive; what about the other 74 castes, which can be termed as most backward castes like the rajbhars, nais, mauryas, kushwahas, bindhs, sainis, nishads, kevats or mallahas, pals, noniyas, kumhars, etc., to name a few. Most of these castes have lost their traditional occupations and have had no access to political power. Their economic political status is akin to dalits, especially in the countryside. How then can they be seen as exploiting dalits or brahmins? Moreover, in UP even the yadavs are not a monolithic whole as western and eastern UP yadavs have different lineages.

Over the years the BSP has developed an amicable relationship between the dalits and OBCs by propounding a common history of exploitation by the Manuwadis. The pantheon of bahujan leaders which includes Jotiba Phule, Narayan Guru, Sahuji Maharaj, Babasaheb Ambedkar and E V Ramasamy Naicker Periyar helped further to unite bahujans in the Hindi heartland. Moreover, the BSP has developed a committed leadership among each sub-group of these OBCs. If the leaders failed to win direct elections they were nominated to the vidhan parishad and Rajya Sabha so that they could be visible in their communities. The BSP also directed OBC leaders to mobilise members of their castes in the reserved constituencies. Now these leaders and their castes have become the second pillar of BSP politics. That is why in the recent UP assembly elections, out of 110 tickets given to OBCs about 50 per cent have won, 27 per cent of OBCs (non-yadavs) voted for the BSP and 8 yadavs have also won. It is surprising that mention of minorities is missing in most analyses of the BSP's historical victory though a record 29 Muslim candidates out of 60 tickets given to them have won on the BSP ticket. Never before in the history of BSP have so many minority candidates won. Why is there no discussion of the significance of the increased presence of Muslim MLAs in the BSP despite the fact that the party joined hands with the BJP not once but thrice?

The BSP has always included religious minorities in its definition of bahujans and since its inception has tried to bring them in its fold. Kanshi Ram's strategy was to mobilise the lower castes of Muslims - the ansaris, chikwas, kasais, ghosis, gaddis, churahars, lalbegs, etc., to name a few. To instil confidence among Muslims, the BSP appointed four cabinet ministers from the community in 1995 when the party formed its first government. Mayawati wrote a booklet entitled, 'Muslim Samaj Soche Samjhe Aur Tab Apne Vote Ka Istemal Kare' (Muslims Should Think, Understand and Then Vote) to woo the Muslim voters in 1999.

The BSP's efforts have slowly but surely convinced Muslims to support the party; this has ensured a regular flow of Muslims to its hold. Even in 2002, 12 MLAs had won on the BSP ticket. In the 2007 elections Mayawati deliberately gave a free hand to Naseemuddin Siddiqi, a Muslim face of BSP, who was projected as a leader with independent stature. He prevailed on the leadership to distribute tickets to candidates of his choice and he was given a separate aircraft for campaigning in the Muslim-dominated constituencies. This has paid rich dividends to BSP in the recent elections in which 17 per cent of the Muslims voted for the BSP.

From Bahujan to Sarvajan Party

BSP had started mobilising the upper castes in 1998-99 and in the 1999 parliamentary elections Kanshi Ram distributed approximately 12 per cent of tickets to the 'savarnas'. In the 2002 assembly elections BSP gave 38 tickets to brahmins, of whom only seven won and the party got only 4.7 votes of 'sarvajans'. But since the beginning of 2005 Mayawati started mobilising brahmins, kshatriyas, vaishyas and kayasthas vigorously. 'Brahmin Jodo Sammelan' (mobilise brahmin conferences) present by 50 to 60 seats. This will give the BSP a chance to form a majority government for a full five years term in the state cited in Kumar 2007: 265J.

In all, the BSP's leadership followed a different strategy, in this era of coalition politics, by directly forging an alliance with castes and communities instead of having an alliance with political parties. Along with its core constituency of dalits, OBCs and Muslims, the BSP mobilised the so-called upper castes and they also voted for BSP (Table *2).*

Table 2: BSP and Caste-wise Support in Assembly Elections, 1996-2007

Castes/Communities	*Percentage of Voters*	*1996*	*2002-2007*
Dalits	62	69	77
OBC (non-yadav)	13	20	27
Muslims	12	10	17
Upper castes	4	5	16

Source: Centre for the Developing Societies (CSDS), New Delhi.

Superior Organisational Machinery

Apart from consolidating its core constituency of dalits, OBCs and Muslims and adding savarnas, the BSP's success in the assembly elections of 2007 should be seen in terms of its superior organisational preparedness. For instance, the party had announced its prospective candidates almost one and a half years in advance. Further, while the national parties formed coalitions, the BSP contested elections alone. Moreover, in a shrewd political move BSP did not contest the civic polls held in November 2006 to avoid the embarrassment of defeat, as it knew its weakness in urban areas. That also helped the party avoid inner party bickering and prevented factions political manoeuvring. Mayawati has developed a charisma of an able administrator and hard taskmaster, cutting across caste and religious boundaries. She is considered to be the only political boss able to teach bureaucrat a lesson that they are the servants and not the masters. People remember her treatment of the sell-styled aristocrat of Kunda to prove the point that no one is above the law. As far as commitment to her ideology is concerned, by pursuing the Ambedkar Village Scheme, effective implementation of the Atrocities Act overseeing a communal riot-free regime in 1995, 1997 and 2003, she has justified her commitment to dalits, minorities and other marginalised sections of the state [Kumar 2003b], By wooing the savarnas she projected herself as the leader of an umbrella party, which can carry all the castes/communities together.

Conclusions

The BSP's victory in the UP elections 2007 is the result of a "social engineering" process started some three decades ago by Kanshi Ram, which divided India's population into two imaginary group, 85 per cent bahujans and 15 per cent Manuwadis. Different castes in the social hierarchy were brought together via construction of a common history of exclusion. Lower caste Muslims were also made conscious of exclusion within their own religion and handed an agenda of development with independent leadership. While other parties offered food, shelter and employment BSP offered them "self-respect". After the demise of Kanshi Ram - the founder of 'Bahujan' ideology - Mayawati window dressed the so-called upper castes with the slogan 'Sarvajan', which is not a part of the social engineering as discussed earlier. But it is sure that dalits and OBCs and minorities have become more confident that their party can come to power on its own and are joining the BSP in different states.

References

Kumar, Vivek (2003a): *Dalit Leadership in India,* Kalpaz Publications, Delhi.

____, (2003b): 'Uttar Pradesh: Politics of Change'. *Economic and Political Weekly,* Vol. XXXVIII, No 37, September 13-19, Mumbai.

____, (2006): India's Roaring Revolution: Dalit *Assertion and New Horizons,* Gagandeep Publications, New Delhi.

____, (2007): 'Bahujan Samaj Party: Some Issues of Democracy and Governance' in Sudha Pai (ed). *Political Process in Uttar Pradesh,* Pearson Longman, New Delhi.

PART-III: DEMOCRACY AND INDEPENDENT AGENDA FOR YOUTH

12

Problems of Youth in Era of Globalisation

The Process of Globalisation

Explaining the process of globalisation Oommen (2004) has emphasised that during this epoch because of increase in the impact of communication a common communication system has converted the universe in a 'world society'. This can be said so because whatever happens in one part of the world can instantly be communicated to the rest. Therefore we can broadly conceptualise the universe as a world society. However, he argues that one world culture is different from one world society. It is different because there are four interrelated processes involved in the creation of what is called the global culture. These processes are (1) homogenisation, (2) pluralisation (3) traditionalisation and (4) hybridisation. Hence to understand the impact of globalisation on the Indian society it is very important to look at how these four processes are at work. In this context Oommen (2004) emphasises that the vast network of communication system which produces a world society results in the process of homogenisation. That means the traits of culture or institutions say jeans or institution of democracy all has become global.

However, underlining this process is the process of pluralism. This means that it is one thing to adopt an item from the package of global culture but it is another thing to use it on a regular basis. For instance considers Indian democracy, with its numerous parties anchored in the values of caste, religion or region etc. Now it is quite a different phenomenon compared to democracy in USA with two party systems. They both are said to democracies. Oommen has called this process as pluralisation, which is necessary to adapt to the needs of local/national situation. The third interrelated process which Oommen mentions in the process of globalisation is that of traditionalisation which emerges out of the process of assimilations of minority and weaker groups into the mainstream dominant culture. According to him the process of homogenisation leads to the process of hegemonisation and hence the weaker and the smaller cultures have a tendency of search for their roots which forces them to go back to the roots of the little tradition.

Last but not the least, the process of hybridisation also accompanies the process of globalisation. Oommen explains lucidly that in the process of adaptation, we often try to mutate some aspect of the alien culture when it interacts the indigenous culture and add to the alien culture some indigenous traits. In this process of mutation of the modern culture and merging it with the traditional culture elements a hybrid product is produced resulting in the process of hybridisation. For instance take the case of local adaptation of McDonald's Burgers in which beef and pork has been replaced by potato cutlet. Similarly Hindi version of MTV programs. Therefore we can see that the local adaptations of cultural traits differ from the original process ruling out any possibility of a world culture.

Further Oommen suggests that by cultural globalisation, we mean spread of cultural elements which has been happening all along from the days of Colonialism. The only difference is that because of superior technological advancement there has been greater and greater compression of time and space. But we have to take into account advantage and disadvantages of these technological advancements as well. One disadvantage of this process of globalisation can be withering away of primary groups because of high technology and that might effect whole civilisation. Secondly, there is also the element of availability and accessibility of the modern technology, the great instrument of globalisation which increases disparities in the society and diminishes the possibility of a common humanity.

Defining Youth

Youth is a category. We define youth as social category between 15 to 35 years. That is a category based on age. If you take content of age; then what is the content of this age category? The content is more important. This age group has immense psychic and physical energy and enthusiasm, which need proper outlet. Hence, we can say that youth is a combination of psychic and physical energy. The category youth possesses immense enthusiasm, which needs a proper channel of release. If this energy is not channelised for creative and constructive purposes, then it is likely that is can be destructive in nature. Therefore, it becomes pertinent on the part of elders to guide the younger generation carefully so that this energy can be constructively used in the process of development of self and nation.

Lack of Independent Agenda for Youth

According to Oommen (1990) the role of the youth is to be viewed not in isolation or independent of the needs and goals of a given society. That means that the role of youth, transitory as it is in character, varies from society to society and at different points of time in the same society. In the absence of an independent agenda, the youth takes up the agenda lying before the nation. For example, during the Indian youth became the freedom of the nation. A long list can be prepared of the youth who sacrificed their lives Bhagat Singh, Madan Lal Dingra, Sukhdev, Rajguru, Khudiram Bose etc. Rani Laxmi Bai scarified her life at the tender age of twenty-three. Subhas Chandra Bose asked the Indians 'give me blood'. I well give you freedom'. He was in fact asking for the energy, that content of energy was blood, and only youth was capable of given that energy. Later on, Subhas Chandra Bose formed the Azad Hind Army by collecting the youth only. Gandhi indirectly called students to leave their schools and join the freedom struggle and all of a sudden, everybody came in. This proves the point that actually, the youth do not have their own agenda.

In the same vein after the freedom struggle, occurred Jai Prakash Narayan's 'total revolution'. He assigned the youths against an agenda and all of a sudden, youth came in big numbers on the road. They participated in the movement against emergency and in fact, overthrew Indira Gandhi's rule. Till date, youth have been participated in various movements, whether it is Naxalbari Movement of Bengal, Telengana Movement of Andhra, Extremist movement of Punjab, Assam Students' movement, to name a few. All of these movements have been ridden with violence but are not related directly to youth problems only. Hence, we can say that the youth do not have their own independent and exclusive agenda and their elders assign them the agenda. Therefore, it is the duty of elders to guide youth to lead a constructive path. If elders of the society do not give right direction to youth, then the youth will lead an undisciplined and in-subordinated life and will be harmful for the solidarity of the society.

Another problem that emerges out of the non-availability of an independent agenda for the youth is that the elders for their own can misuse them. For instance, the politicians misuse youth for political violence, communal violence or caste violence. Therefore, we see that youth as a category is always involved in performance of an act with the content of its energy; whether it is psychic or physical and makes things happen (Kumar 2005).

Sociologically, the concept of youth is a new concept in society. In western society itself, youth as a category emerged very late. For the first time, the French Philosopher Rousseau talked about the young persons in 1762 (Oommen 1990). Otherwise, there were only two statuses in society, based on age that of a child and that of an adult. Now the question is why there emerged a concept of youth. According to Oommen (1990), it was so because an individual learned everything at his home as an assistant to his father and family members. There was no exclusive institution of training and hence no disassociation of status. However, with industrialisation and expansion, there is intense specialisation of roles and division of labour. Hence, society assigned specific role to the category between 15-35 years that is to be engaged in learning and wait for their specialisation. Hence, they have marginal role in society (Oommen 1990).

In the traditional Indian society as well, there was no such notion or youth. Due to early marriage people entered from childhood to adulthood. Even in the *Varna Ashram* system *Brahmacharya, Grahasta, Varanaprasta* and *Sanyasa* only *Brahmacharya* was related to youth, when you were allowed to unfold your creativity with the learning process. But here also the Shudras, Women and ex-untouchables were not allowed to learn Vedas or take part in educational activity; hence they were devoid of any such category as youth (Kumar 2003).

Overall, Indian society did create a sense that even through there is a population between 15-35 years, it cannot be left independent. For instance, even during *Vanaprastha Ashrama,* when the father temporarily goes for renunciation, there is no complete transference of power from father to son. The total power and independence come to the son only when the father went for *Sanyasa* and it is certain that by that time, sons have lost their youth and became old. Hence, we see that the process of formation of youth was delayed in Indian society by traditional Hindu social order (Kumar 2005). With the advent of the British, who brought along with them industrialisation, modern education, new army etc., the category of Indian youth started emerging, though not in its totality. The different institutions, which were brought by the British, facilitated the Indian youth to learn different professions independent of family. The migration of youth from rural to urban centers also gave them an independent status and disassociated them from families.

Hence, we can argue that in traditional Indian society, there was no concept of youth. The formation of youth identity ushered in only in Modern India with the advent of the British when the differentiation of occupation started emerging (2005). Even then, we tell this population between 15-35 to wait for its turn. We do to assign it any specific duty. We advise them he/she should be involved in his studies and things will change when his services will be needed. Thanks to the freedom movement, some youth took an independent stand towards the freedom of the nation. Then and only then did we argue 'Yuva Shakti, Rashtra Shakti' (Youth power is nation's power). Today, we argue that youth are the future of tomorrow.

Types of Youth in Indian Society

Youth is not a monolithic category in a hierarchical and diversified society like India. The diversity of caste, class and region will emerge if we make a typology of Indian youth. On the basis of certain criteria Oommen (1990) tried to divide Indian youth into Rural, Urban and Western category. I have tried to develop the concept of Dalit Youth (2003). We will evaluate Indian youth in the light of the above while adding one more category of globalised youth.

Rural Youth

In this context, we observe that after independence, three streams of youth have emerged in India. What are these three types of youth? The first types of youth can be called as rural youth. You can see rural youth in the whole country, because 70 per cent of Indian still lives in villages and therefore, 70 per cent of Indian youth is rural in nature. Therefore, only 30 per cent of youth lives urban areas. This rural youth is undereducated unenlightened and is not aware of his rights. This youth has narrow vision as he forced to lead an insulated life in the villages. This rural youth is caught in the labyrinth or primordial loyalties of the traditional society such as caste, family, region, religion etc., and has no freedom whatsoever. As he bound to many institutions like caste, family etc. and the lack of knowledge, he feels alienated. This section of rural youth has to be taught about his rights and should be imparted modern knowledge so that it can relate itself to the mainstream society. Due to lack of employment opportunities, the extremist groups such as PWG, MCC etc. attract them and they associate themselves with violence. Hence they think that violence is the right path and change can be brought through this means.

Urban Youth

Another type of youth is urban youth. This category is the offspring of the first generation rural migrant to the city. The first generation, which came out from the villages and settled in the urban centre, keep a constant touch with the villages. That is why they are caught in the compulsions of tradition and modernity. As the urban youth has energy and traditional values, he respects and obeys his elders. This trait of this youth also becomes the cause of exploitation. Mostly politicians exploit these types of youths and you can find them in different universities and cities in large numbers, being exploited by the politicians. Not only politicians, but also *goonda* elements exploit this youth of the city. This type of youths are easily misguided and the goons and politicians can easily hire them by paying small amount of money. As they have enthusiasm, they are unable to differentiate between good and bad. The goons give them firearms and initiate them into the world of crime. Thus, it is certain that in both cases, the youth is exposed to crime and youth energy is wasted. Most of the middle class youth fall in this category and their main aim is to get a government job. Government job gives them tenure security and they fall in the rut of 10 to 5 job through out their life without any innovation.

Westernised Youth

There is third type of youth also in Indian society that can be called as westernised youth. The reference point of this type of youth is western society and he is fascinated and overpowered by the culture of western society. The process of westernisation as defined by Srinivas (1972) emerged in India because of 150 years of rule of British. And because of this rule there were far reaching changes in the Indian society. Hence the westernised youth tries to initiate and imbibe the values and ethos of western society without understanding it. Therefore, they are uprooted from the Indian social system and, are in search of an identity. This youth tends to reject the prevalent Indian values and norms and bears contempt for Indian commodities. This youth is educated and capable of understanding and appreciating an independent agenda but though he is rebellious in thought, he is passive in action. Hence, he feels alienated from the society. Therefore, generally he is waiting for the first opportunity to go abroad. Hence, we see that all these three types of youth are alienated in Indian society. They are alienated in Indian society. They are alienated because of over-integratedness in the society as in the case of the rural and urban youth and on the other hand, alienated because of total detachment from the society as in the case of western youth.

The situation has been further complicated in the contemporary society for all youth. As youth grows and achieves knowledge, spending lots of his time of life, say 20 to 25 years, money and energy, he is faced with rampant corruption, nepotism, regionalism etc. His ambitions are shattered when he doesn't get a job because of these values rampant in the society. Therefore, he takes his own route, which he deems, fit under these circumstances.

The Crises of the Globalised Youth

Here we have tried to evaluate the Indian youth in the light of the recent development specifically in the context of process of globalisation. One can argue that what is so different about westernised youth and globalised youth. Both the processes, westernisation and globalisation have thrown many opportunities for the youths in India and have also taken away many of them. Both types of youths have to face the crises of onslaught of alien culture. Both of them pass through the dilemma of imbibing foreign culture etc.

But it is a fact that the globalised youth is different from westernised youth. He is different in many senses. One he is not imitating west only. His reference group is the whole universe. He has exposure to so many cultures of the world. He is ready to imbibe and imitate all of them as the silent and inert recipient. Today very few youths are ready to rationalise it and let go many cultural elements, which are not useful to him/her. The real problem in cultural realm is that he is overpowered by the onslaught of the media. Media in the era of globalisation through advertisements has become more and more powerful. It is media, which has been responsible, for creating and dismantling choices of the globalised youth. For instance, look at the icons created by the media in last half a decade. It is not astonishing that they are all from sports, film, fashion, and television world. Not only that these icons have not been stationary rather they keep on changing rapidly on the basis of their success and failure in the profession during that period. In this way media has deprived the globalised youth from the real world icons say from politics, social movements, education etc. Moreover media has acclimatised the youth minds to forget the cognitive societal values and beliefs of honesty, hard work, endurance, etc. Instead it has taught them lesson of instant success and individualism away from the societal good. This is alienating to many youths because everyone cannot become instant success like sports persons, film and fashion personalities do.

Another crisis the global youth faces is the rapid change because of technology. He has to perpetually update himself. For instance, within half a decade so many computer languages have become obsolete and whatever he learnt then has also become redundant. If he has to survive then he has to update himself otherwise he will not be competent enough to carry his job. Further the globalised youth feels alienated because there are limited opportunities. No doubt the process of globalisation has brought new opportunities. Today many Multinational Corporations have come in the country. Number of NGOs, CBOs has come to recruit youths. But these opportunities are not enough for the vast army of different types of youths in the country. The opportunities, which have emerged during this time period, are only for technically trained youths. The youths from management background and computer knowledge are being preferred. Even within these streams there is intense competition. Youths from IIMs and IITs themselves are finding it difficult to find a job.

Ray of Hope in the Era of Globalisation

In this era of intense competition Indian youth can survive if it captures the following areas:

1. Culture
2. Service
3. Education
4. Civil Society
5. Indigenous Knowledge System

Culture

Let us take one by one. If we really understand our culture then we can market it also. We will always have an edge over the foreigners in understanding our culture. Therefore if we package it well then we can sell it to the global market. From Indian folk songs, dance forms, festivals, culinary to art etc. every element of Indian culture is at our disposal. If we can collect information about them and search for the demands in the global market then there is lots of potential in this sphere. Look at China how minutely it has studied our culture and today we are using goods made in China even for our religious purposes. For example, the lights on Divali festival came from China.

Service

We have numerical strength. If we can train this man power then we give service in every sphere. From security guards to mechanics are required on contracts by the MNCs and Indian companies. The MNCs cannot bring this manpower with from abroad and therefore they will need the assistance of Indians.

Education

With the development of time education and literacy is bound to increase. Not only that in the era of globalisation foreign education is bound to spread. Already approximately sixty foreign universities and 150 foreign Institutions are functioning in the country. As the time will pass their numbers will grow. These institutions cannot bring the trained teachers from their countries. They will need teachers and we can supply them if we have enough teachers. But after the privatisation of technical education we have not been able to meet the demands of the number of medical and engineering colleges, and management institutes. There is dearth of trained faculties in most of these institutes. Because of dearth of efficient and competent faculties thousands of seats in number of such institutes go vacant. Hence we can tap this gap.

Civil Society

As the government is withdrawing because of the processes of privatisation in the era of globalisation it is transferring many of its functions to Non Governmental Organisations (NGOs) or Community Based Organisations (CBOs). Government will need more and more such organisations, which are run by trained, honest and efficient persons. Moreover in the era of globalisation the foreign NGOs are increasing their activities in India. India is their preferred destination. Already hundreds of foreign NGOs are working in India or thousands of Indian

NGOs are being funded by foreign funding agencies. This whole functioning of NGOs and CBOs need trained manpower. And there is no trained manpower to fit the bill. The worse scenario is the rural area. There is only one Institute in the country, i.e. Institute of Rural Management (IRMA), which trains the individuals to work in the rural sector. One can imagine how many students it can prepare when we know that 70 per cent of India still resides in the rural sector. Can we really think in this direction.

Indigenous Knowledge System

Knowledge is the basis of global society. He who controls the knowledge will rule the world. That is why the Patent Law has become so important. Every country and business industry is rushing to get its process and product patented. But India is lagging behind.

That is why we had to fight to get the *Neem* and *Haldee* patented. In the same way India has a vast resource of fauna and flora, if we search their uniqueness and qualities only through oral knowledge system and get it codified it will help us in getting our product patented. Otherwise we will be loosing precious articles and commodities because some other country gets them patented. We have to shed our arrogance of book knowledge and literacy to appreciate un-codified oral indigenous knowledge system to score a point on others because it is we and only we are blessed with this treasure.

References

Kumar, Vivek, 2003, Emergence of Dalit Youth: Some Sociological Reflections in, Vinod Chandra (ed.) Construction and Reconstruction of Indian Youth, Circle for Youth and Child Research in India, Lucknow.

_____, 2005, Violence and Youth: Carving Out an Independent Agenda for Youth, Indian Journal of Youth Affairs, Vol. 9 (2); July-December, Vishva Yuvak Kendra, New Delhi.

Oommen, T.K.1990, State and Society in India: Studies in nation-building, Sage Publications, New Delhi.

_____, 2004, Approaching cultural change in the globalisation; interview with Anand Kumar and Frank Welz. Social Identity, Vol. 9. Taylors and Francis ltd. London.

Srinivas, M.N., 1972, Social Change in Modern India, Orient Longman. New Delhi.

13

Violence and Youth: An Independent Agenda for Youth

According to sociological definition, "an infliction of physical harm to human body or to human property by physical force using the body or external force is called violence". However, in Indian society, we have defined violence even deeper.

According to Jain philosophy, violence can be divided into three kinds. First type of violence is physical violence. If you injure or kill anyone or harm anyone bodily, it will be called physical violence. The second type of violence is verbal; that means if you abuse someone or if you are using harsh language against someone that means violence in words. There is a third type of violence, which is mental violence. If you think ill of others, you are committing violence.

In contemporary societies, even state becomes a source of violence. The state tries to monopolise the power of the people and hence monopolises the means of violence. But the state is restricted to use the power frivolously because the subject class has lots of power as well. The masses make the state defensive and therefore, rulers are always afraid of or cautious in using violence against the subject class. The state through its institutions like police, military etc. inflicts violence on the subject class. For example; lathi charge on a democratic sit-up; the military firing on a communal mob or on extremist groups, etc.

Violence is Eternal

Violence is not a new thing in the world in general and in India in particular. Violence is an eternal fact. Violence has been present since the inception of human society. If you analyse the presence of violence in Indian society, then you will see that our vedas, puranas as well as other sacred scriptures, our epics such as 'Ram Charit Manas' or the 'Gita' depict the presence of violence in Indian civilisation. Even in European civilisation, there are traces of violence. For instance, the famous quotation of Karl Marx is apt proof of the fact "the history of all hitherto existing societies is the history of class struggle".

In Indian civilisation also, we find a tussle between number of warring groups. For instance, in Ancient India, there occurred a long battle between 'Arya' and Anarya' or 'Arya' and 'Dasa'. After that, the Shakas, Hunas, Kushans, Seythians, Parthians all came to India and settled here after a long drawn physical battle. In Medieval India, Karl Marx wrote that Arabs, Turks, Tartans and Mughal captured India and ruled over it. Moreover, of course, this rule was established through the might of the sword resulting in violence.

In Modern India, we see Dutch, Danes, Portuguese, French and British tried to establish supremacy over India and in the end, the British captured India. This struggle created lots of violence proving the point that violence was present in India from times immemorial.

Violence is Negative and Positive

Violence is not negative only. Violence is both positive and negative. For instance, when a soldier is on the border and kills the enemy, as we did in 1971, or we fight and save our borders, then that violence is not considered negative. A soldier may be awarded for killing some one at the borders with medals like 'Param Veer Chakra', 'Veer Chakra', 'Police Medal' etc. Hence, we can argue that violence in itself is not negative, but if the rate of violence is abnormal and its rate keeps on increasing day-by-day, that becomes a cause of concern.

In contemporary societies, there is a steep increase in the rate of violence. Each country is faced with this problem of rising rate of violence. Within the country, every institution family, religion, bureaucracy etc. is marred by violence. That is, we can say that violence is playing a negative role in societies.

Individual and Groups as Sources of Violence

In this context, let us now look at the sources of violence. At times, individual can be a source of violence and at the other on some pretext violence can emerge in a group. The group violence may also have many forms especially in Indian Society. This violence can be in the form of communal violence, caste violence, racial violence and also based on human rights. Violence may start for genuine demands like legitimate rights but when denied it may take an ugly turn and become negative. For instance, extremist movement in Punjab for rights started peacefully but soon took a negative form. When there is discrimination of democratic rights of individuals, first they ask for their rights democratically and if rights are denied, then undemocratic means are employed, resulting in violence. Similarly, there is violence based on caste, especially the castes located higher up in the caste hierarchy commit lots of crime against the castes located at the lower level of caste hierarchy. There have been more than three and a half lakhs of atrocity cases on the Dalits from 1981 to 1995; that means 61 cases of atrocities per day. Therefore, we can say that this type of violence is negative because it has acquired an abnormal rate.

Sociological Explanation of Changing Social Structure and Violence

Two sociologists, Emile Durkheim and Robert King Merton have helped us in understanding violence indirectly. They have both defined deviance in the society, which can be used here in understanding violence. Durkheim has talked about normlessness in the society. This means that when there are fast changes in the society, there is dilemma among the individuals, because old rules have not vanished away and new ones have not yet taken roots. Therefore, an individual does not know which rule to follow. Hence, individuals are confused, start inventing shortcuts, and make their own rules, which hurt the collective conscience of the society. Indian society is a typical example. There are so many traditional rules but at the same time, there is modernity, which has produced new laws and hence people are confused. For instance, today, youth is trapped in the labyrinth of modernity and tradition. On the one hand, the traditional society stipulates that you have to obey the elders, live in a family and abide by the societal norms or group in which you live. On the other hand, modernisation forces you to inculcate individualism. If you want to develop yourself, you will have to leave the family.

Hence, to develop himself economically, professionally etc., an individual, mostly the youth, came out of villages and small towns to earn his livelihood. Such individuals migrate to big cities or cosmopolitan cities in search of better opportunities, in this manner, many traditional ties are broken. In a traditional society like India, he faces a dilemma as to whether to follow modern values or remain with the tradition.

Society thus loses control over the individuals. In addition, where there is no societal control, the youth in search of fast mobility create their own rules, which may not be commensurate with the societal norms. This can result in deviance, which can give rise to violence. The youth taking to crime for attaining economic mobility is a case in point.

Further, once you are in the complex urban society, it is difficult to follow the traditional values and hence you again create short cuts. For example; in Indian society, performing 'puja' in the morning is considered a cherished value. Till individuals are in villages or in small towns, they can practice this value, but once they move into a cosmopolitan city or in an industrial area, then there is constraint of time and they cannot carry on this value. If you try to maintain it, then you will have to leave your job. Therefore, most of the individuals find different ways and means of worship but in doing so, the real function of religion, i.e.; social control is lost. People only think of externalities and rituals of the religion. The fear that religion evokes the consciousness about the virtues and vices that religion evokes are all gone.

Hence, an agency of social control is lost because of formlessness, which is created in the society because of its transition. On the other hand, there is no effective institution, which has replaced religion that can make you realise what is virtue and what is vice. You can say that there is law, but the problem is law takes its own course and people may not be aware of the law because of their location in the social structure. Due to their location in the social structure, individuals are differentially exposed to the rules and regulations. According to Merton, those groups which are located at the lowest rung of the social structure are least exposed to the laws of the society. Therefore, this group produces maximum deviance. Hence, we can argue that no institution can replace religion in the society. Therefore, as there are no effective means of social control in a society, which is in transition, people behave in such a manner that they deem easy. Hence, we see in modern complex society lots of corruption, nepotism, arson etc., which are all sources, and/or manifestations of crime. Indian society is full of this and youth is the victim as well as the carrier of all these processes.

Therefore, it becomes pertinent on the part of elders to guide the younger generation carefully so that this energy can be constructively used.

Contemporary Malfunctioning of Indian Society and Youth Violence

The situation has been further complicated in the contemporary society for all youth. As youth grows and achieves knowledge, spending lots of his time of life, say 20 to 25 years, money and energy, he is faced with rampant corruption, nepotism, regionalism etc. His ambitions are shattered when he doesn't get a job because of these values rampant in the society. Therefore, he takes his own route, which he deems, fit under these circumstanced.

Nation Building as the Agenda for Youth

Now the job on hand is to mobilise these alienated youth for an independent agenda of its own: Otherwise, different groups will misuse the energy of this youth for their vested interest. Now, what could be the independent agenda for the Indian youth? I think nation-building is the most important agenda for the Indian youth. He has to contribute his energy in the nation building. To begin with, Prof. Oommen has argued that Indian youth can start their action taking into account the elements of fundamental duties enshrined in Article 51A of the Indian Constitution. If Indian youth internalise and practice the values contained in the fundamental duties, they could be making a singular contribution towards the creation of a first and humane society.

Religion and Violence

But I don't think that any religion teaches you to fight. All religions state that actually there can be co-existence. If you take Islam, it talks about Muslim brotherhood and if you take Hinduism, it talks about 'Vasudeiva Kutumbakam', that whole world is our family. Christianity, Zorasterism etc. every religion talks about co-existence. But the problem is that these teachings take you in the different directions and you only follow externalities of the religion. That is why in Indian society, the saint poets like Kabir criticised the externalities of religion long ago. He said that:

1. कांकर पाथर जोर के मस्जिद लई चिनाय
   ता चढ़ मुल्ला बांघ दे क्या बहिरा भया खुदाय।।
2. माला फेरे टोपी पहने छाप तिलक अनुमाना
   कांकर पाथर पूजै लागे मरम न कोई जाना।।

That means that he was criticising that people have forgotten the basic ethos and value of the religion and they are only concerned with the rituals, which in turn create violence and animosity. Even Buddhism a religion that taught peace all over the world has been dragged in violence in Sri Lanka. Hence, we have to watch the roles of the leader the religious and political who are actually responsible for leading the masses against the very ethos of the religion. Therefore, if religion is followed in its true spirit and ethos it can act a dominant agency of social control, because it is the only agency, which teaches you self-control. If you have self-restrained and control then, there will be order in the society. Even law alone cannot create social control in society. Look at the plight of the ex-untouchables of the Indian society, there are so many laws for their upliftment and also to stop atrocities on them yet we see 61 cases of atrocities per day, 2 dalit women are raped per day and 3 dalits are murdered, which proves the point law alone cannot act as an agents of social control, religion is also needed.

The other thing is that diversity is the reality of Indian society. Hindu, Muslim, Sikh, Christian, Parsis all have contributed in making Indian civilisation a rich civilisation. They all have contributed culturally, materially and economically starting from their advent to freedom movement and till date they are contributing in the maintenance and development of this nation. Look at the Tata, one of the most developed businessman contributing in the economic development of the country. Mohammad Azharuddin, Mohammad Kaif, Irfan Pathan or Zahir Khan when score runs and take wicket for Indian cricket team and India wins then we are all happy, that means they are also contributing in bringing glory to our nation. You can add many examples but I think this will suffice to prove that diversity is the reality of Indian society and we can live with our differences. We can co-exist with these differences of region, race, caste, religion etc. peacefully.

Youth: Carving Out its Independent Agenda and Leadership

It is important for the youth to carve out their own independent agenda otherwise they will be misused by different politicians for different purposes. Look at the political parties how they use youth in communal violence, no elder leader of any political party goes to commit violence it is the youth, which is roped in. Hence, the youth have to carve out their own agenda. Moreover, this agenda is "Agenda of Nation Building". The Article 51A of the Indian Constitution provides fundamental duties for the citizens of Indian society. These are:

(a) To abide by the Constitution and respect its ideals and institutions, the National Flag and the National Anthem;

(b) To cherish and follow the noble ideals which inspired our national struggle for freedom;

(c) To defend the country and render national service when called upon to do so;

(d) To promote harmony and the spirit of common brotherhood among all the people of India transcending religious, linguistic and regional or sectional diversities; to renounce practices derogatory to the dignity of women;

(e) To value and preserve the rich heritage of our composite culture;

(f) To protect and improve the natural environment including forest, lakes, rivers and wild life, and to have compassion for living creatures;

(g) To develop the scientific temper, humanism and the spirit of inquiry and reform;

(h) To safeguard public property and to abjure violence;

(i) To strive towards excellence in all spheres of individual and collective activity so that the nation constantly rise to higher levels of endeavour and achievement.

Therefore, it is the duty of Indian youth to contribute their bit in nation building. It is their duty to preserve and promote the political unity and integrity of India.

This in turn would bring uniformity. At the same time, it is also their duty to nurture the desirable elements of Indian culture. Given the multiple cultural stream in India, this implies plurality. Moreover, as Prof. T.K. Oommen says, "political uniformity and cultural plurality can co-exist without contradiction".

Therefore, it is pertinent for Indian youth to carve out their own agenda. Unless and until they have it, there is no hope. As the villagers once told me:

> Literally translated it comes to be, "The battle is whose issue it is and therefore leadership is whose battle it is". Hence, it becomes amply clear that if the youth have to emancipate

themselves they have to take the leadership in their hand. Till now their issues are being highlighted by others that means others are fighting their battle and hence it is not effective and youth remains victim of negligence and exploitation.

The civil society has yet to realise its duty. It is true that in Indian society unless the sufferers have themselves not taken up their issue nobody has cared for them. For instance, take the issue of women, dalits, or tribals all have started their own movement in their own leadership. Baba Saheb Ambedkar gave the leadership to the Dalits and then only they were recognised as a category to be fit for rights. Otherwise, until that time, they were neglected and were not considered even as human being. But after an intense battle Dalit movement has become quite prominent and today they are asserting in every field whether politics, education, literature, NGO or even at the international level. The tribal movement was against their exploitation by the moneylenders, the British officers and outsiders. Birsa Munda, Tana Bhagat, Mopilla all were tribal groups, which raised their issues and got implemented many laws for their human rights. Similarly, Chipko Movement gave birth to the women's movement in the hills and women fought for not cutting the trees, as they were the real sufferers. It was women who use to go to fetch the fuel and fodder from a great distance. Hence, it can be proved from the above example that one can emancipate and empower him/her by fighting his or her own battle under his own leadership. Yes, other forces can facilitate and help from behind or from side but should not take up the leadership in their own hand.

Selection of Cultural Traits in the Agenda

Another important agenda for the Indian youth could be how to select the right moral, beliefs and norms for their life. Today in this Indian society where westernisation has set in its deep roots and today when under the name of globalisation western culture is being imposed it is the duty of the Indian youth to select what is good and bad, what is asset and which part of the culture is liability. It is in this context, we have to search the Indian values as well. I am not saying that all Indian values are or were assets, there are values which are liabilities as well, for instance, the practice of untouchables and subjugation of women are really degrading values. On the other hand, the values of corporatism which plays down individualism, the values of 'Santosham Param Sukham' (contentment in the life), respect for the elders and neighbors etc. are assets and should be inculcated by the youth. This will give us strong confluence of tradition and modernity and we can strengthen our society on our as well as their principles, it is certain that we cannot stop the onslaught of the western culture through mass media and foreign state intervention but we have definitely made its impact a bit slow. !n addition, it is the youth, which is the dominant carrier of day-to-day fashion and life style, can take the mantle in his own hand for the selection of assets of the culture.

14

Dalit Youths: Construction of Different Personality

The present paper tries to highlight the construction of differential personalities among the Dalit youths in the Indian society. We have also analysed most crucial role played by the Hindu social order in the formation of these personalities. This has been done purposely because, though Dalits are treated as part and parcel of the Hindu society yet their position in it is not ascertained. On the other hand, Dalits themselves have been clamouring for an independent status from the Hindu Social order. This chapter of the book also probes into the demands by the Dalits for a counter identity with reference to Hindu Society. This they do so as they feel that the aforesaid society has always given them a stigmatised identity and a degraded status, which has been justified by sacred texts of the Hindu Society. It is worth mentioning here that the Dalits in general and Dalit youths in particular face status inconsistency in the Indian society. On the one hand, they have a stigmatised and unequal social status in Caste hierarchy. And on the other hand they have an equal status of a Citizen based on Constitutional rights. Hence they have a paradoxical socio-political milieu of persisting social inequality and contest for equality. Further aforesaid milieu contributes in the formation of the differential personalities and self among the Dalit Youths. It is more so as the Dalit youths throw up differential responses depending upon their consciousness, material resources and 'Cultural Capital', which they posses. The Chapter is a modest attempt to:

> Before we come to analyse this we will have few conceptual clarifications. The first concept here is Dalit knowing this we will come to know the target group for whom we are concerned in this paper.

Locating Dalits in the Hindu Social Order

The location of a group or an individual in a social structure has far reaching effects on the total being of the group or individual. It also affects the process of construction of consciousness among them and their production of knowledge. Therefore it is necessary to locate Dalits in the Indian Society because then we will be able to understand that Dalits are different from the rest of the Indian population. And hence the Dalit youths are also a different category, which cannot be treated at par with the general youths in India.

It is a well-known fact that the Hindu society is divided into four Varna namely, *Brahman, Kshatriya, Vaishya* and *Shudra.* "In Rig Veda, ...three classes of society are frequently mentioned, and named Brahma, Kshatra, and Visha... It is only in one of the later hymns the celebrated *Purusukta,* that a reference has been made to four orders of society as emanating from the sacrifice of the Primeval Being. The names of those four orders are given there as Brahmana, Rajanya, Vaishya, and Shudra,... The *Taittiriya Samhita,* for example, ascribes the origins of those four classes" (Ghurey 1979: 44). It is clear from the above statement that there is no mention of the Dalits (Untouchables) in the Rigveda hymn. Srinivas (1985: 150-151) writes, "...in the Rigvedic hymn *Purusukta,* the four *varna* or orders formed the limbs of primeval man (*Purusha*), who was victim in the divine sacrifice which produced the cosmos. The Brahmins emerged from his mouth, the Kshtriyas from his arms, Vaishyas from his thighs and Shudras from the feet. The untouchables castes find no mention in the hymn." Similarly Dumont (1999:67) argues, "There is in actual a fifth category, the untouchables, who are left outside the classification." Hence we can observe ourselves that though the presence of the Dalits (Untouchables) cannot be denied in the Indian society but they have no legitimate place in the order. This itself speaks the volume of the discrimination and degradation they are subjected to in terms of their location in the Hindu Social Order.

It is not only that these four varnas are mentioned in the sacred texts but also they have been assigned their duties or jobs (*Dharma*). For example, " in the hymns of the *Rig-veda,* the job of the Brahmin *varna* was to read and write, teach and preach, offer and officiate sacrifices. The Brahmins were obliged by this tradition to undergo a life of study, meditation, and penetration into the mysteries of God and *dharma"* (Mathur 1991:68). Ghurey defines the occupation the Kshatriyas, "must have consisted in administrative and military duties...In the prayer for the prosperity of Kshatriya, he is said to be an archer and good chariot-fighter" (1979: 48). The Vaishya formed the third order and was supposed to be a trader. Further Ghurey argues, "The name of the fourth class, the Shudra... It seems the class represented domestic servants, approximating very nearly to the position of slaves. The Shudra is described as "the servant of another", "to be expelled at will", and "to be slain at will". The Panchvimsha Brahmana defines this position still more precisely when it declares that the Shudra, even if he be prosperous, cannot be but a servant of another, washing his superior's feet being his main business... The Shatapatha Brahmana goes to the length of declaring that the shudra is untruth itself'(*Ibid:* 50-51). Again we do not find any mention of such duties for the Dalits (untouchables) in the sacred texts which mention the same for the other varnas.

Apart from these aforesaid duties assigned to various Varnas except for the Dalits (untouchables), Hindu Social Order also prescribed an elaborate arrangement of the various socio-economic, political and religious activities by an individual to be performed in various stages of his life. In fact these stages are named as *ashrams,* which are four in number namely-*brahmacharya, grihastha, vanaprastha,* and *sanyasa.* The male members of *Brahmin, Kshatriya,* and *Vaishya* varna pass through these four stages in their life. The first *ashram* is called *brahmacharya ashram* from which the forth varna, viz., Shudra and the women of the first three *varnas* were barred. It is to be noted that this *ashram* is very important of all the *ashrams* in the individual's life. Kakkar has eloquently portrayed its importance. In his own words, "*brahmacharya,* in which the school child, growing into youth, learned the basic skills relevant to his future adult working role while he lived together with other students and the guru. The myriad duties prescribed for this stage can be subsumed under two headings: (a) the social importance placed on the learning of skills, and (b) the student's unquestioning devotion to the guru's person". Kakkar further points out, "The task of the *brahmcharya* stage, I would say, lies in the knowing of one's *dharma,* which would consist in acquiring the skills in one's caste and in winning an identity based on a caste identity and the identification with and the emulation of the guru. The strength issuing from this stage would then correspond, to 'competence' and 'fidelity'" (Kakar 1982: 8-9). It is evident from above that Dalits (Untouchables) were kept out of this scheme of development of their 'self'. Hence we can objectively argue that the Dalits (Untouchables) were located at such a place in the Hindu Social Order that they had no rights for their development in any realm of the society. They were left in lurch to find their own salvation. While others had all the rights and privileges-social, economic, political, religious for their own emancipation and empowerment Dalits had none.

Injured Psyche and Atrocities on the Dalits

Against this discriminatory socio-economic and political background a Dalit youth grows with an injured psyche. The cumulative dominance of the Upper Castes injures the psyche of the Dalit youth. The modus-operandi if simple. The upper strata inflict atrocities on the Dalits and to maintain its hegemony through physical and cultural dominance in every realm of the society. From physical intimidation to verbal abuses by the Upper Stration to the Dalits perpetually demoralises and eliminates them from the mainstream of the society. We can see ourselves the incidence of the atrocities committed on the Dalits by the Upper Castes and mind you these are all government data and the registered cases. If we add to them the number of unregistered cases then the plight of the Dalits become more unbearable.

Atrocities Committed on Dalits during 1997-2000

Year	*Crime against Scheduled Castes*
1997	27944
1998	25638
1999	25093
2000	23742
Total	102417

Source: National Commission for Scheduled Castes and Scheduled Tribes, Sixth Report, 1999-2000 and 2000-2001, pp. 208-9.

It is shocking that Uttar Pradesh (6122), Rajasthan (5623), and Madhya Pradesh (4667) have highest incidence of crime against the Dalits. These three states accounted for 65.4 per cent of the total cases of atrocities on the Dalits in the country during 1999. These three states had highest number of cases against Dalits in the previous years also.

The process of discrimination in different forms of atrocities from murder of a Dalit to ridicule and Taunts has resulted in the development of a differential personality among Dalit Youths. Those Dalits who accept these atrocities of the Hindu Social order develop a submissive personality and also try to imitate the life style of the Upper Strata of the dominant castes of their region – a process, which was called as Sanskritisation by M.N. Srinivas. Those who protest choose political process of assertion by establishing political parties and number of social and political organisations. And those Dalits who revolt against the existing social exploitation choose the process of conversion to different religions. But in most cases it is certain that Dalits face lots of difficulty in getting integrated in the mainstream of the society, as has been rightly brought out by Kulke. He argues,

> "The consciousness of having repeatedly to suffer discrimination and of belonging to a group that is branded 'untouchable' manifest in the form of latent psychological barriers which hinders the efforts of socially mobile 'Scheduled Caste' members towards social integration. Frequently, this consciousness is not even based on direct personal experience but rather on unconscious group solidarity or the conscious effort to detach and free oneself from the group of origin is very difficult for socially mobile (Scheduled Caste) members" (Kulke 1983: 141).

It is a well-known fact that the Dalit youths have protested against the exploitative Hindu social order at different point of interval. They have protested and launched vigorous movements to change the nature of hierarchies of the Indian society. Number of social movements launched by young Ambedkar is a case in point. Similarly, Namdeo Dhasal was 23 years old when he founded the Dalit Panthers. He has studied up to SSC and was a bachelor. Raja Dhale was about 30 years old when he joined the Dalit Panther's movement. Besides, them there were number of angry youths who joined the movement to take revenge from the unjust Hindu Social Order. That is why Murugkar, points out very clearly, "The rise of the Dalit Panthers had brought forth a new type of leadership... Their youth and immaturity and their premature fame prevented them from understanding the social situation in its true perspective" (Murugkar 1991:97). In contemporary period number of Dalit youth forums like- Dalit Sahitya Akadmi, Dalit Bahujan Intellectual forum, number of Dalit Student organisations, publications of number of weekly, fortnightly magazines and Newspapers are testimony to the fact that the Dalit youth has become quite conscious about its subjugated position. It is in this context that the Dalit youth wants change.

Dalit Youth and Reservation Policy

To understand the concept of 'Dalit Youth' it is inevitable to go through the history of its emergence. At a glance, the sum total of all the developments in this regard was a revelation of the growing potential of the Dalits and the perspective of their coming together with the other backwards, which was viewed by the upper caste layer of the Society with anxiety and indignation. The very emergence of the Dalit educated nucleus was perceived as a fulfillment of the main task of the reservation system, a breach of the Hindu tradition of banning education and intellectual activity to the untouchables. These perceptions were reflected in the process of a changing realignment of forces illustrated best of all in the division of society into pro- and anti-reservationists.

While the upper caste youths were very much certain about their anti-reservation stand from the very beginning, the mass of the Other Backward Classes, who were used to practice discrimination against the untouchables, sided with the anti-reservationists. It took some time before the Backward Classes movement began to take shape in the Northern States of India substantiated by the recommendations of the Backward Classes Commission headed by B.P. Mandal (1978-1980). The main focus of the Commission was on the Other Backward Classes (OBCs) which, according to the Commission's calculations, were made of two groups - backward Hindu castes and communities (43.8 per cent of the Indian population) and backward non-Hindu communities (8.4 per cent). Along with the SCs and STs (together they make up 22.5 per cent), the OBCs form the backward classes of citizens for whom, in accordance with the constitution of India, the state may make special provision for their advancement, including the reservation of appointments or posts in the services under the state (Articles 15 and 16 points 4).

The Commission recommended 27 per cent reservation of jobs in the public sector undertakings, both under the Central and State Governments, in nationalised Banks as well as 27 per cent of seats in all scientific, technical and professional institutions run by the Central and State Governments for the representatives of the OBCs.

When the very principle of reservation began to be severely attacked by the upper-caste anti-reservationists, accompanied by a rising militant Hindu chauvinism, a very important change in the perception of the problems of the whole category of the Backward Classes took place. As a result, the middle class from the Backward Classes citizens came forward to answer the challenge. They formed a number of Backward Classes organisations, entered a lot of unions. Naturally, these organisations and unions were comprised mainly of the youth belonging to these communities, because this was youth which found himself directly concerned with the benefits of this reservation policy (or polity). Indeed, in the post-independence period, particularly in the last two or three decades, shrinking job market and stagnant economy have begun to effect important changes in the process of politicisation of castes which gave Dalit youth an identity. Lowering of the voting age, as was attempted by the young prime-minister Rajiv Gandhi's government, enhanced this regimentation by inviting a remarkable mass of young people between the age of 18 to 21 years to manifest their caste-consciousness in the field of political decision making. According to Rajani Kothari (*The Times of India*, 29th September, 1990), "contrary to the belief that democratic politics and adult franchise were providing a new lease of life to caste, what was in fact happening was a transformation in the nature of caste under the impact of competitive politics". He asserts that the key process was politicisation of caste structure in a competitive but stagnant economy – and limited resources – which gives birth to power due to struggle for it.

Dalit Youth and Education

Dalits have realised the need of education for their upliftment along with other processes of change. Even Ambedkar had greatly emphasised as early as in 1920s and 1930s on education of the Dalits with the view that only education could liberate them from their traditional bondage and subordination to the upper castes and classes. Not only that but education, in his opinion, would enlighten them and expose them to the outside world. It would sensitise them to realise their long cherished goal of embracing equality, liberty, fraternity and justice. Besides, it would also prepare them to collectively strive for achieving a respectful identity, which in no case would dither to identity of the nation.

It is a well known fact that educational opportunity was categorically denied to Dalits in traditional Indian society as stated earlier. It is only after the advent of the British that education was opened for them. Especially the Christian Missionaries opened the gates of education for the Dalits. Phuley also took special interest in imparting education to the Dalits during this period. After the Independence things changed further for the Dalits. The State itself has started giving the Dalits so many privileges.

But even then things have not moved in the desired directions. One of the major hindrances in this has been, "the expected contributions of the SC/ST (Dalits) students to resolving the socio-economic problems of their family, community, and society as a whole. It has been pointed out .. .that most of these students are supposed to economically contribute to their family subsistence while pursuing their study" (Ram 1995: 122). This means they suffer from socio-economic problem, which should be addressed by the state to improve their educational standards.

The second problem of Dalit Youth in the education realm is lack of dominant culture to which Bourdieu calls 'cultural capital'. Though he and his associates have analysed this issue in class terms we can very well apply it in Indian context of upper and so called lower castes (Dalits). Bourdieu (1973) argues that students with upper class background have a built-in advantage because they have been socialised into the dominant culture. He further claims that the success of all education depends fundamentally on the education previously accomplished in the earliest years of life. Children from the dominant classes have internalised these skills and knowledge during their pre-school years. The educational attainment of social groups is therefore directly related to the amount of cultural capital they posses. Seen in the above light, as the Dalits never had the culture of education among them they suffer in good performance and then ridiculed for lacking in merit. Though the very section Upper Castes are not bothered about the merit of the general caste students in the professional colleges run on the basis of capitation fee.

Yet Dalits have started performing well in the educational realm. Today after 54 years of independence the literacy among Dalits has reached only up to 37 per cent at all India levels. There is an increase in the number of graduates and post-graduate students among Dalits along with other professional courses (See Table).

Scheduled Castes Studying at Graduate, Post Graduate and in Professional Courses

S.No.	*Course*	*Scheduled Castes*		*Total*
		Boys	*Girls*	
1.	B. A./B.A. (Hons.)	249850	99040	348890
2.	B.Sc./ B.Sc.(Hons.)	67539	28205	89744
3.	B.Com./ B.Com.(Hons.)	52996	22688	75684
4.	B.E./B.Sc. (Eng.)/B.Arch.	24021	6172	30193
5.	M.B.B.S./Ayurved	7791	4824	12615
6.	B.Ed./B.T.	9366	3638	13004
7.	M.A.	33489	10604	44093
8 .	M.Sc.	6877	3257	10134
9.	M.Com. 4967	1467	6434	*Xkllf*
10 .	Ph.D./D.Sc./D.Phil.	1429	469	1898

Source: National Commission for Scheduled Castes and Scheduled Tribes, Sixth Report, 1999-2000 and 2000-2001, p. 180.

But even then Dalit youths suffer from a deep sense of anxiety because of the societal pressure exerted on them at the pretext of reservation policy. On the one hand government has blown out of proportion the magnitude of the policy which has made Dalit youths target of criticism. Dalit youths in general and students in particular are ridiculed by their friends, fellow classmates and even by their own teachers, who are supposed to play a decisive role in harnessing the potential creativity among them. A term *'Sarkari Damad* (Government Son-in-Law) has been coined for them meaning there by a privileged status as is enjoyed by the Brahmins in the traditional Hindu society. But in reality the government has not filled the quota of seats enshrined in the Constitution for the Dalits even after 54 years of Independence. Now the government is rolling back with the onslaught of the processes like globalisation and privatisation. The percentage of the filled quota of reservation at the central government is given in the following table. This tells the reality of the story that the number of jobs provided to the Dalits in the form of reservation is very small compared to the number of educated Dalit youths. Hence the society in general and the general caste youths in particular should understand that the Dalits are not taking away their share of jobs and therefore they should not look at them with contempt.

Representation of Scheduled Castes in the Services of Central Ministries, Departments and their Subordinate Offices as on 1.1.1999.

Group	Total	Scheduled Castes	Percentage
A	93520	10558	11.29
B	104963	13306	12.68
C	2396426	378115	15.78
D	949353	189761	19.99
Sweepers	96435	63233	65.57
Total including Sweepers	3640697	654973	17.99

Source: National Commission for Scheduled Castes and Scheduled Tribes, Sixth Report, 1999-2000 and 2000-2001, p. 182.

Conclusions

Based on these socio-political and religious realities prevailing in the Indian society, we can conclude that, the Dalit youths lacking 'cultural capital' have responded differentially to these conditions. Some have tried to live within the Hindu social order by *sanskritising* themselves and accepting their subjugated position. It is this section which tries to hide its stigmatised case identity because even after *sanskritisation* the caste stigma haunts their psyche. Therefore they suffer from an inferiority complex which emanates from their degraded status in the caste hierarchy.

The second response of the Dalit youth has been their protest against the Hindu social order. For this they have launched number of social and political movements. Ambedkar can be regarded as the pioneer in this realm. He was just 28 years of age when he started the struggle in 1919 against the suppression, exploitation, and isolation of his Dalit brethren. Similar is the case of the Dalit Panthers movement, which was stared by Dalit youths in Bombay slums. Even in the contemporary India Bahujan Samaj Party's movement is led and dominated by the Dalit youths. Except for Kanshi Ram all the leaders in the BAMCEF (the employees wing of the BSP) and DSS (the mass organisation, which preceded BSP) were very young. For example, Mayawati, who has now occupied the post of UP's Chief Minister three times, was only 25 when she joined the BSP movement. The movement for the Dalit Human

Rights led by National Campaign on Dalit Human Right (NCDHR) is also a case of Dalit Youths' protest. It is worth mentioning here that NCDHR has today formed a network of 26 NGOs at the International level. This section has been more revolutionary than their elders and has retaliated against the existing subjugation and exploitation. Besides, this section of Dalit youths has posed its faith in capturing the political power through Ambedkarism rather than depending on the social reform. It has also tried to highlight its stigmatised identity to mobilise the community horizontally, which has paid rich dividends to them as Dalits today have attained a separate political identity.

The third response of the Dalit youths has been that of shedding their stigmatised identity either by the process of de-sanskritisation or by conversion. In the former attempt they have launched number of movements claiming their indigenous status and declaring the Aryans as outsiders. For their assertion they launched movements like- Adi-Hindu, Adi-Dravida, Adi-Dharma, Adi-Andhra etc. Conversion to different religions like- Islam, Sikhism, and more recently to Buddhism has been another response of the Dalit Youth. Though it is debatable whether all these aforesaid processes have helped the Dalit youths in enhancing their self esteem and image in their own eyes and in the eyes of the general masses but it is amply clear from the above discussion that location of the individual in the social structure has far reaching affects on the formation of individuals personality. This in turn also influences the formation of worldview of others about the community as a whole.

References

1. Bourdieu, P., 1973, Cultural Reproduction and Social Reproduction in R. Brown (ed.) Knowledge, Education, and Cultural Change, Tavistock, London.
2. Dumont, Louis, 1999, *Homo Hierarcihicus: The Caste System and its Implications,* Oxford University Press, New Delhi.
3. Ghurey, G.S., 1979, *Caste and Race in India,* Popular Prakashan, Bombay.
4. Kakar, Sudhir, 1982, Setting the Stage: The Traditional Hindu View and the Psychology of Erik H. Erikson, in Sudhir Kakar (ed.), *Identity and Adulthood,* Oxford University Press, Delhi.
5. Kulke, E., 1983, The Problem of Educated Middle Class Harijans, in John P. Neelsen, (ed.), *Social Inequality and Political Structures,* Manohar Publications, New Delhi.

6. Mathur, K.S., 2000, Hindu Values of Life: Karma and Dharma, in T.N. Madan (ed.), *Religion in India,* Oxford University Press, New Delhi.
7. Murugkar, Lata, 1991, Dalit Panther Movement in Maharashtra: A Sociological Appraisal, Popular Prakashan, Bombay.
8. Srinivas, M.N., 1985, Caste *in Modern India and Other Essays,* Media Promoters & Publishers Pvt. Ltd. Bombay.
9. Ram, Nandu, 1995, *Beyond Ambedkar: Essays on Dalits in India,* Har-Anand Publications, New Delhi.

PART IV: DEMOCRACY AND ISSUES OF REPRESENTATION

15

Democracy and Self-Representation

After intense political debate it has been decided that for the first time in the 218-year old US democracy a Black will be contesting for the prestigious presidential elections. Is it out of blue that the world's "most developed democracy", the US, is going to choose its first Black President or is this a new stage in the evolution of US democracy? If the latter is true, then US democracy is moving up and reaching a higher level. This means it has created an atmosphere in which the excluded and the marginalised are asserting for self-representation rather than being represented by White males. Democrats have been clever enough to capture the mood of their society. That is why they fielded both a woman, Hillary Clinton, and a Black, Barack Obama, as their candidate in the primaries for the presidential elections. Democrat Obama justified his inclusion by asking for a comprehensive debate on racism and raising problems of poverty and emerging unemployment in the US. Isn't it astonishing that somebody is frank enough to ask for a debate on poverty and unemployment in the world's most developed economy? Obama also boasted of his acquaintance with the socio-economic conditions of the underdeveloped and developing countries as he has lived and visited these countries unlike his rival who have never visited these places.

The debates by Obama reminded one of the American Civil Rights Movement (1955-1968), an integral part of the reform movements in the United States aimed at abolishing racial discrimination against African Americans and restoring suffrage in the Southern states. It refreshed the memories of the Black Power Movement, which lasted roughly from 1966 to 1975 and enlarged the aims of the Civil Rights Movement to include racial dignity, economic and political self-sufficiency, and freedom from White domination.

If we take US politics of the last decade into account, it is not that Republicans were not aware of this social fact of their society. However, instead of giving the marginalised self-representation they opted for another strategy. The strategy was of co-option and giving them a dependent status. Republicans co-opted these excluded categories in their Administration. Colin Luther Powell was the first Jamaican American to be appointed as the United States Secretary of State by the Republicans from 2001 to 2005. Later on he was succeeded by Condoleezza Rice—the first Black woman and second African American to become the Secretary of State. Maybe Republicans wanted to kill two birds (woman and Black) with one stone. In the process the White governing elite among Republicans have not been able to leave their lust for power and therefore they relied on symbolic representation of the African Americans and women. Another thing which should be kept in mind here is that the treatment meted out to Colin Powell and his silent disappearance after the Iraq war is still fresh in the memories of the marginalised American community.

Here I am not arguing that if a Black is in the process of becoming or becomes the US President there will be structural change in American society or in the lives of the millions of excluded people in the US. However, I want to emphasise here that with this change at the helm of affairs in US politics, the excluded and the marginalised can emphatically declare three things. One, they can assert that it is a historic moment for the Blacks that they are having a choice of their own—a Black as presidential candidate in 218 years of democratic history. Otherwise they were supposed to elect a White even against their will. Secondly, the Black can stress that they have also arrived. And thirdly, they will make the point that they are no more passive onlookers; rather, they can also directly influence the policies and make laws for others.

It is a fact that Indian democracy is still at a nascent stage. However, the Indian political elite should learn some lessons from this political process in contemporary US 'democracy'. Indians should not only be content that Obama carries a small statue on Hanuman; rather, we should look at the democratic values this election has emphasised. One thing the political elite in India should learn is the culture of inner-party democracy. The way Obama and Hillary Clinton, both belonging to the same political party, contested for their candidature in the primaries is unimaginable in India. We have seen political bosses—the 'High Command' of different political parties—nominating candidates for different executive posts in India. Or the political parties have got bifurcated just because there are ambitious leaders for one post. Parties have become captives of families and individuals and leaders are not able to differentiate between the Party and the Parivar (family). And now the political constituencies are handed over to the sons and daughters by their parents as if it is their empire. Against this in the US even Bill Clinton couldn't influence his wife's candidature. In the end the people's choice prevailed. In this context we have a long way to go.

Another thing which the Indian political elite should realise, faster the better, is that like in the US the days of representing the marginalised by according them a symbolic or nominal representation in India are coming to an end. The marginalised groups—Dalits, tribals, women, etc—in India, are also asserting for self-representation. The demand of the 'Women's Reservation Bill' and the disappearance of Dalit leaders with substantial following from the parties led and dominated by the so-called upper castes are testimony to the above fact. Gone are the days when the Scheduled Castes and Scheduled Tribes were restricted to the 'Cells' specially established for them or made Vice-Presidents in the different political parties and they felt obliged to cast their votes in favour of that party. In the coming days it will be difficult for the Dalit candidates, contesting from the Congress, BJP or any other political party with so-called upper-caste domination, to win a seat from a reserved constituency. The Dalits and other marginalised sections are slowly but surely realising that their emancipation lies in their self-representation rather than being represented by those who do not belong to them. That is why we are witnessing a number of region and community-based parties emerging day by day. However, one should realise that this has not happened in a day. This evolution of Indian politics has a history.

Ambedkar had long back emphasised the point of self-representation in Indian politics by asking for separate electorates for the Dalits. He did so because he was convinced that representation of opinions by itself is not sufficient to constitute a popular government. To ensure its true meaning it requires personal representation as well. A government with representation of opinions is sure to educate some into masters and others into subjects. Therefore, Ambedkar argued that it is not enough to be electors only. It is necessary to be law-makers; otherwise those who can be law-makers will be masters of those who are electors. But Ambedkar could not win the demand for separate electorates because of Mohandas Karamchand Gandhi's opposition. However, after two decades of Indian's political democracy Kanshi Ram started the quest for self-representation of the marginalised communities with the slogan "Vote Hamara, Raj Tumhara—Nahi Chalega, Nahi Chalega (Our Vote, Your Rule Shall No Longer Prevail)". By establishment of the Bahujan Samaj Party and installing Mayawati as the first Dalit woman Chief Minister of UP he laid the foundation of self-representation of the Dalits and other marginalised sections of the Indian society. Mayawati, on her part, has further strengthened this quest for self-representation by winning the UP elections and forming the government on her own in 2007 and is now igniting aspiration among her followers to capture the Prime Ministership of the country.

Therefore, the sooner the political elite realise that it is futile to visit the thatched huts and distribute cheap rice or liquor to Dalits the better. They should start a comprehensive debate on casteism, poverty, unemployment, gender discrimination, communalism etc. For instance, if they are honest enough they should ask why even after 60 years of India's 'political democracy' a social group (Gujjars) is demanding Scheduled Tribe status although they have been already accorded OBC status. Why in this epoch of globalisation when economic development is said to be the highest in the history of India, with a high Sensex, a nine per cent growth rate, huge foreign direct Investment and increasing number of multinational corporations coming to this country, is a community ready to sacrifice hundreds of lives for the sake of reservation? Why after the launch of series of satellites successfully, ten in a row, the announcement of the National Rural Employment Guarantee (NERGA) and following the waiver of loans for small and marginal farmers, are they forced to embark on such a violent agitation?

But we know that they will not raise a debate on the aforesaid issues as these issues never affect them directly or indirectly. Rather, these leaders are conscious of the fact that they can represent the people till the people remain marginalised and exploited. However, as the people are becoming more and more conscious about their fundamental rights, they are asserting more and more for self-representation. Here the leaders should realise that self-representation by the marginalised is the future of Indian politics which will wipe all the 'isms' from Indian politics. The dictum at the grassroots says it all—"Jiska Mudda Uski Ladai, Jiski Ladai Uski Agwai (Leadership should be in the Hands of the Sufferer)". Can the 'people' in India change the attitude and thinking of the ruling elite?

16

Representation of Marginalised Sections and Indian Political Parties

Introduction

This chapter analyses the issue of representation of one of the most marginalised section of Indian society called Dalits. We can observe the increasing aspiration of Dalits for self-representation in the contemporary Indian politics by analysing the formation of their own political parties or by asserting within mainstream political parties for their effective representation. This process has created an uneasy situation for the main stream political parties who want to give only notional representation to Dalits in their parties. Further, in the absence of effective means of countering this aspiration of self-representation of Dalits they have suffered great losses at least in north India, specifically Uttar Pradesh. It is in this context this paper analyses the history, nature, development and scope of Dalit politics. The paper has also reflected upon how different mainstream political parties, both national and regional have treated Dalits in terms of the representation of their issues and Dalit as political actors.

However, before we do that we would explain in brief certain terms and concepts used in the paper for better understanding of the reader. Therefore we have explained the meaning of term Dalits, Dalit leadership and the concept of mobilisation.

Defining the Collectivity Dalits

The term Dalit has been used here strictly used for ex-untouchables of Indian society who are constitutionally known as Scheduled Castes and number approximately 170 million. They were excluded from every sphere of life (see Appendix I) and hence occupied a unique structural location in it. Here the term structure has been used in terms of pattern of inter-related roles and statuses, which the actors of a specific society occupy in the spheres of rights and obligations. Nadel (1969:5) argues, 'we arrive at the structure of a society through abstracting from the concrete population and its behaviour the pattern or network (or "system") of relationships existing between actors and in their capacity of playing roles to one another'. Going by the definition of structure Dalits by allotted the role to perform stigmatised occupation and serve other classes of Indian society. They had no rights whatsoever and hence were excluded in every walk of life. In this context the term 'social exclusion' can be defined as, 'a multi-dimensional process, in which various forms of exclusion are combined: participation in decision making and political processes, access to employment and material resources, and integration into common cultural process. When combined, they create acute form of exclusion that find a spatial manifestation in particular neighbourhoods' (Madanipour *et. al* 1998:22). However in the Indian context as far as social exclusion of Dalits is concerned we have to add to the elements of religious justification of such exclusion based on Dharma and Karma. Moreover social exclusion for Dalits is ascriptive in nature. Accordingly, exclusion of Dalits can be depicted in the following manner (see Appendix I):

The aforesaid prescriptive and normative role and status of Dalits for centuries have produced the objective condition of exclusion of Dalits like low literacy rates, extreme poverty, and high dropouts which is self evident from Table 1.

Table 1: Socio-Economic Status of Dalits in Different States of India States

Sr. No.	*State*	*Percentage of SC Population (2001)*	*Percentage of SC Literate Population (2001)*	*Percentage of SC under Poverty line (1993-1994)*	*Drop-out rate of SC at Secondary stage (1990-1991)*
1.	Andhra Pradesh	16.20	53.5	34.92	86.00
2.	Arunachal Pradesh	0.60	67.6	--	--
3.	Assam	6.90	53.94	29.86	62.42
4.	Bihar	15.70	28.5	62.91	89.39
5.	Goa	1.80	71.9	--	81.07
6.	Gujarat	7.10	70.5	38.62	71.29
7.	Haryana	19.30	55.4	35.07	78.12
8.	Himachal Pradesh	24.70	70.3	27.70	67.78
9.	Jammu & Kashmir	7.60	59.0	--	79.09

Sr. No.	*State*	*Percentage of SC Population (2001)*	*Percentage of SC Literate population (2001)*	*Percentage of SC under Poverty line (1993-1994)*	*Drop-out rate of SC at Secondary stage (1990-1991)*
10.	Karnataka	16.20	52.9	54.00	75.03
11.	Kerala	9.80	82.7	34.01	51.05
12.	Madhya Pradesh	15.20	58.6	55.41	61.58
13.	Maharashtra	10.20	71.9	52.10	71.96
14.	Manipur	2.02	72.3	--	81.70
15.	Meghalaya	0.50	56.3	--	30.57
16.	Mizoram	0.10	89.2	--	--
17.	Nagaland	No SC	No SC	No SC	No SC
18.	Orissa	16.50	55.5	48.2	81.54
19.	Punjab	28.90	56.2	25.02	79.34
20.	Rajasthan	17.20	52.2	43.50	82.07
21.	Sikkim	5.00	63.0	--	91.51
22.	Tamil Nadu	19.00	63.2	52.77	77.32
23.	Tripura	16.36	74.7	--	87.29
24.	Uttar Pradesh	21.10	46.3	58.50	72.20
25.	West Bengal	23.00	59..0	41.51	88.81
26.	Delhi	16.90	70.8	--	65.36

Source: Census of India 2001, Primary Census Abstract Scheduled Castes: Tables A-8, *Sixth Report of National Commission for Scheduled Castes and Scheduled Tribes, 1999-2000 and 2000-2001,* New Delhi, pp. 40, 41, 172-4, 177.

The structural location of the Dalits and the process of their social exclusion, as discussed above, results in construction of unique consciousness of Dalits, which is depicted through their worldview, their orientation towards life and nature etc. This consciousness cuts across the boundaries of different castes found among the Dalits and unites Dalits cutting across the caste, regional and linguistic identity.

Therefore sociologically speaking, the Dalits can be defined as social group who have following characteristics:

1. Unique Structural location in Indian Society
2. Face social exclusion on the basis of collective identity
3. Suffer from Cumulative Social exclusion
4. Long history of social exclusion
5. The construction of consciousness, which is anchored in their structural location, cumulative social exclusion and long history of social exclusion.

This definition of Dalits also highlights the fact that Dalits are different from Scheduled Tribes (STs), women and poor persons belonging to caste Hindus.

Understanding the Difference; Dalits vis-à-vis Other Marginalised Groups

The logical question then would be how are Dalits different from other groups? At the outset economically poor person is different from the Dalits because he (or the group of economically poor persons) may be deprived in economic spheres especially in terms of income necessary to participate in the economy. But he may not be necessarily deprived in social and cultural spheres i.e. he may not face the same type of exclusion in the social and cultural life either in his neighbourhood or in the society at large as Dalits face. We can argue that a poor may be economically or politically deprived or may be in both but he is generally not excluded from the social and cultural spheres. But an ex-untouchable is deprived in all the three–social, economic and political realms. And therefore Oommen has rightly pointed out, 'If proletarian consciousness is essentially rooted in material deprivations... Dalit consciousness is a complex and compound consciousness which encapsulates deprivations stemming from inhuman conditions of material existence, powerlessness and ideological hegemony' (Oommen 1990:256).

The social exclusion of an ex-untouchable is so overpowering that even though he attains economic and political mobility or even goes beyond the national boundaries through his hard labour, he is not accepted by the castes located higher up in the caste hierarchy as an equal. His social identity remains stigmatised and his achievements are basically associated with that social identity. Some examples in this regard can make the fact clearer. One, it is a fact that as soon K.R. Narayanan became the President of India in spite his high educational achievements and political experience, every one tried to evaluate his ascendance to Presidential post only on the basis of his caste identity. Most of them argued that Narayanan was elevated to the post of President because he belonged to Dalit community (Kumar 2007 b). Secondly, if we take the Dalit Diaspora as another example the issue of social exclusion of Dalits becomes further clear. It is true that amongst Indian Diaspora, 'that caste was increasingly an aspect of culture rather than social stratification per say...[however] the stigma of caste did not die out completely' (Jain 2003, Kumar 2004). Jain (2003:74) makes amply clear how the caste stigma exists with the Dalits even though they have transcended the national boundaries. In his own words, 'Women of high caste married to low caste men...looked down upon their husbands ...and even told their children how their fathers were of a lower caste than them'. The caste stigma and consciousness haunts the Dalits in Diaspora in spite of their economic mobility, whenever they visit to their ancestral village. The villagers still looked down upon them. Another impact of social exclusion on Dalits is that the loss of 'social capital' that could give them the potential to develop consciousness and motivation for their amelioration. Moreover, because of lack of this consciousness, they could not revolt against the existing unequal Hindu Social Order for long. Their cultural co-option in the Hindu Social Order, even though they were formally not the part of *Varna* hierarchy, was affected by the artificial consensus. The artificial consensus was of course part of Hindu hegemony legitimised by the Karma theory, which makes people believe in the deeds of previous births determining one's status in the present.

Apart from these Tribals exclusion comes more from their geographical location and independence of their social system. As far as women are concerned their primary exclusion comes from patriarchy and the role which they have assigned. Hence we will not include economically poor, tribals and women in the definition of Dalits. Having defined the term Dalit on the basis of their structural location, exclusion, history of exclusion and construction of unique consciousness and understanding the difference between Dalits and other marginalised sections of Indian society let us not analyse nature of Dalit politics.

Nature of Dalit Politics and Leadership

Emergence of Dalit politics can be traced back to the British rule in India in general and introduction of separate electorate for different communities by them in particular (Kumar 2002:49-50). Although it is part of and partial of Indian politics and functions under the same constitutional provisions as other political parties function Dalit Politics can be defined as the political processes led by the leaders who are by birth Dalits and have taken politics as their vocation. They may be full timers or may be part-timers following multiple occupations or jobs. Some of them might adopt politics as their vocation from the very beginning of their lives and are second generation politicians for instance – Mukul Vasnik, KM. Shelja, Meira Kumar to name just a few. On the other hand some of them might enter by accidents or making a deliberate choice usually after the retirement from government jobs as officers or teachers. It is interesting to note here that the number of Dalit officers joining the political parties after their retirement from government job is increasing day by day. Usually, the mainstream political parties prefer such types of leaders instead of rearing the leaders from the grassroots and launching them at the state or at the national level. This may be so because they are educated and their credentials are well known to the parent political party. Secondly, these leaders, because they come from services directly, do not have mass following and remain harmless to party's interest even if they leave or defect change the party. On the basis of the nature of the organisation, agenda, idioms of mobilisation and identity of leadership etc. this political process led by Dalits themselves differ in nature and scope. That is why Dalit politics can be divided into two streams. Further, the political process is actuated by the Dalit leaders we can also divided Dalit Leadership into two types. Then the two types of Dalit politics producing two types of Dalit Leadership will be:

(a) Dependent Dalit Politics (Dependent Dalit Leadership)

(b) Independent Dalit Politics (Independent Dalit Leadership)

Dependent Dalit Politics

Dependent Dalit politics and its leadership can be defined with the help of Dalit political leaders who are found in thc political parties led and dominated by the so-called upper castes/and class. They are found at the national and regional level both. In the aforesaid political parties Dalits are found usually in the 'Cells' specifically created for Dalits and Tribes known as Scheduled Castes and Scheduled Tribes Cells or *Anusuchit Jati avm Janjati Prakosht*. That means they are never considered as the mainstream of the political party although they may constitute numerically a majority. In such political parties Dalits contest only from the reserved constituencies. They are never given prominent organisational positions which play decisive role in policies formulations and programme implementation even for the Dalits. Apart from the organisation in the event if the same political party comes to power Dalits get insignificant ministry portfolios in the government. Usually we have seen that 'Empowerment and Justice Ministry' in the government is reserved for the Dalit leaders only. Moreover, Dalit leaders in these parties do not enjoy any freedom whatsoever to raise their issues in the party forum or in the state or national legislature independently. The Dalit leaders in such party do not have an independent voice and have to speak the language of their political bosses in the name of party discipline. If any Dalit leader raises his voice or starts gaining popularity with the masses he is either denied ticket for contesting the elections or he is chucked out the party (Kumar 2002). Jagjivan Ram is one such Dalit leader from Congress who was thrown out of the party as he challenged the leadership of Indira Gandhi.

Independent Dalit Politics

On the contrary Independent Dalit politics is that politics which is practiced by the Dalit leaders who establish and lead their independent political parties. Such parties are led and dominated by the Dalit themselves. In such an organisation Dalits play a vanguard role in the formulation and implementation of programmes and policies of the party on the one hand. On the other hand they also play a significant role in mobilisation of people not only of their own caste but other caste as well. In this type of political party Dalits form the mainstream and have their own and independent parlance and icons. They have their own style and slogans for the mobilisation of the people. The leaders do not have to take any lessons and permission from the so-called Upper caste leaders to raise their issue. No doubt such parties lack the legitimate structures of a democratic polity and are usually one person or personality dominated parties. They remain functional till the person who has established the party is alive. However, the strength of such party is their organic linkage with the poverty stricken, illiterate, and rural masses that form the party's backbone (Kumar 2002). Till recent times no business house has supported such type of parties. The unique feature of such politics is that they mostly try to alien with some dominant political parties for contesting elections. It may be pre-poll alliance or post-poll power adjustment.

Caste and Mobilisation in Indian Political Parties

Mobilisation of people belonging to different castes has been conceptualised by Rudolph & Rudolph (1987) as vertical, horizontal or differential. However since then the Indian politics has changed a lot. Specifically if we analyse the mechanism adopted by the Bahujan Samaj Party (BSP) (Kumar: 2007 c) on the principle of "*Jiski Jitni Sankhya Bhari, Uski Utni Bhagidari*" (representation of each (caste) according to its percentage of population). This has not been analysed earlier rather it did not exist when the Rudolphs were doing their research. Therefore the caste mobilisation in India needs a fresh understanding.

It is a fact that BSP initially mobilised Dalits, Minorities and OBCs under the epithet of Bahujanas. However, now it is also mobilising the so-called twice born castes the Brahmins, Kshatriyas and Vaishyas. This pattern of mobilisation of so-called twice-born castes by BSP does not fall in any of the categories viz. vertical, horizontal or differential as given by Rudolph & Rudolph (1987). This is a new phenomenon in Indian Polity. For the first time the Dalits are able to mobilise the so-called Upper Castes through their own independent political party and are ready to provide them patronage. I have called this phenomenon as '*Arohi*' mobilisation' (Kumar 2007c). *Arohi,* is a Hindi word which means ascending. Accordingly, *Arohi* mobilisation can be described as the process of mobilisation in which the lower strata try to mobilise the so-called upper castes through their own political parties. It is interesting to analyse the nature of the mobilisation of political parties led and dominated by the so-called upper castes and class and the mobilisation of the political party led and dominated by the so-called lower castes and class. We have observed that when the so-called upper castes mobilise the lower strata (in this case lower castes) they do it for monopolising power and party both. On the contrary when the parties led and dominated by the lower-castes try to mobilise the so-called upper castes is has a democratising effect (Kumar 2007c).

Having defined the terms like Dalits, nature of Dalit Leadership, and process of Caste mobilisation let us discuss the contemporary scenario of the mobilisation of Dalits in modern politics.

The Contemporary Scenario

One can safely argue that the political rights of the Dalits were established between 1916 to 1935. Since then they have tried to mobilise themselves independently by forming their own regional and national parties like ILP (1936), AISCF (1940), RPI (1957), Dalit Panthers (1972) and now BSP (1984). However a large chunk of Dalit population is still mobilised by the so-called mainstream political parties like Congress (I), Bhartiya Janata Party etc. Conceptually, the mainstream political parties have the dependent Dalit political leaders who in turn mobilise Dalits for their respective political parties. This mobilisation is not devoid of allurements. However, effectively Dalits get only notional power both at the Party's organisation level and in the Government if their party comes to power. Let us see representation and mobilisation of Dalits by the other so-called mainstream political parties. And towards the end we will analyse the mobilisation of Dalits by Bahujan Samaj Party which represents the independent Dalit politics in contemporary Indian politics.

The mainstream political parties have obliquely raised the issues of the marginalised sections of the Indian society (Ambedkar 1991). There has been only a lip service to their problems although they have enjoyed their support throughout the history of Indian politics (Kumar 2002). This continues even today if we analyse the functioning of the mainstream political parties. For instance, the Congress did not raise any specific issues of the Dalits in the 2009 general elections. However, it was astonishing that it increased its tally of seats and formed the national government consecutively second time. Similarly the 'Shining India' and 'Feel Good' campaign led by NDA government led by Bhartiya Janata Party (BJP) in 2004 general elections had effectively marginalised the burning issues of Dalits and thereby a debate on social justice. On the other hand, in 2009 the Bahujan Samaj Party (BSP) and Third Front concentrated more on making Ms. Mayawati (a Dalit leader) Prime Minister of the country on the basis of tactical alliances and numbers in this era of coalition politics. Hence we can argue that there is no mainstream political party that can highlight the pathetic condition of the Dalits in contemporary India (see Appendix -I). In fact no political party, baring a few, have a Dalit leader of any repute with mass following who can raise these issues, although though according to the *Reference Handbook, General Elections 2004* released by the Press Information Bureau, ministry of information and broadcasting, there are in all seven national parties, 40 state parties, and about 110 registered (unrecognised) political parties in India. The irony is that most of the national and state parties contest from seats reserved for Dalits and add them to their kitty to grab political power.

Let us now analyse the status and representation of Dalits in different political parties at the national and state levels. We have analysed the case of Dalits first in three 'national' political parties led and dominated by the so-called upper castes separately and then we have lumped the state political parties together for the analysis. We have also analysed the representation of Dalits in the Bahujan Samaj Party separately.

Indian National Congress and the Question of Self-Representation of Dalits

Indian National Congress[1], which has always opposed the independent political status for Dalits (Ambedkar 1991) after independence

1. Henceforth referred as Congress. In contemporary period, by Congress we mean Congress (I), the ruling Congress.

boasted for having Dalit leaders of mass following. Congress also highlighted the fact that it captures maximum numbers of reserved seats. Rudolph and Rudolph have underlined the fact why Congress enjoyed the power. According to them, 'The electoral successes of the Congress party under Jawaharlal Nehru and Indira Gandhi were largely enabled by support from India's largest minorities, Muslims and the scheduled castes' (1998:48). However Congress did not win these votes directly. Late Jagjivan Ram was the Congress's Dalit icon and through him Congress captured Dalit votes without much effort and bagged most of the reserved seats and could rule for so long. During 1980s and 1990s Buta Singh, Meira Kumar, Shusheel Kumar Shinde, Mukul Wasnik, Mata Prasad, Mahavir Prasad etc. to name just a few came to rescue Congress (I). However the scenario changed after the emergence of BJP and BSP (1984). Today Congress has not got even one Dalit leader with a national or even regional following specifically in the north India. At the state level for instance in Uttar Pradesh the present Dalit leaders were no match for BSP's Mayawati. Yet Congress relied on them for mobilisation of Dalits. Very recently in 2009 election for Lok Sabha Congress has got a retired bureaucrat P.L Punia, elected Member of Parliament from Barabanki and Meira Kumar, daughter of Jagjivan Ram, who shifted her base from Delhi to Bihar where she faces the towering personality of Ram Vilas Paswan, could hardly revive Congress and attract Dalit voters and supporters in UP and Bihar respectively.

However, it is interesting to note that, Meira Kumar has been now elected to the post of Speaker of the Lok Sabha, the first Dalit woman to do so in the history of modern Indian politics. It is interesting to note that, she was earlier Minister for Empowerment and Justice in UPA-I government 2004-2009. It is general perception of the Dalits she did not do any significant work for the empowerment of the Dalits during her tenure. Rather she was more interested in furthering the glory of her father Jagjivan Ram. She established 'Jagjivan Ram Foundation' on the lines of 'Ambedkar Foundation'. To propagate the legacy of her father 'Jagjivan Ram Chair' was also established in Benaras Hindu University for the research on his life and works. It is interesting to note that she did not do any thing to strengthen the 'Ambedkar Chairs' which exist in nine universities for researching on the life and works of Babasaheb Ambedkar. Rather she was involved directly in countering Ambedkar's legacy. The seriousness of the Ministry is visible by the fact the "Empowerment and Social Justice Ministry" does not have any preamble or blueprint for empowering the Dalits. Further, even though successive ministers belonging to Dalit Community have headed this ministry but there is no attitudinal change in the officers and employees of the ministry.

It is not that today Congress does not have a single Dalit leader from UP, Bihar who has substantial following only this situation exists in other parts of the country. Rajasthan, Madhya Pradesh, Punjab, also go unrepresented by any Congress Dalit leader who has substantial grass-root following. This means the cow belt, which accounts for 187 parliamentary constituencies in general and 35 of the reserved constituencies has no effective representative of Dalits who can raise their voice in the party forum or in the government. In Maharashtra Congress is trying to ride on the back of Republican Party of India, Sushil Kumar Shinde and Mukul Wasnik, (they have been inducted in the cabinet) but here also it is facing a stiff challenge by different political parties. Specifically, the Republican Party of India although it is now fragmented in number of factions and led by Dalit leaders like Prakash Ambedkar, the grandson of B R Ambedkar, R S Gavai, Ramdas Athawle, Jogendra Kawade, etc. are organising Dalits independently. Further the Shiv Sena's slogan, Bhim Shakti and Shiv Shakti (followers of *Bhim Rao* Ambedkar and Shivaji the King) is making a dent in the traditional Dalit vote bank of RPI and Congress. The BSP is also making its presence felt especially in the Vidharba region where it has von number of seats in the local body elections. In the rest of Indian also there is a dearth of Dalit leaders in Congress. However, Congress is cleverly trying to arrest its fast diminishing Dalit vote bank by co-opting Dalit intellectuals via locating them in the high profile government offices or by nominating them in the Upper House of the Parliament. At least a dozen of Dalit intellectuals have been given these offices.

Congress and Scheduled Castes in Contemporary Times (2004-2008)

Apart from organisational conflicts with the Independent Dalit organisation and co-option of ineffective Dalit leaders Congress (I) led UPA government during its last tenure, it seems, pursued an anti Scheduled Castes agenda. In doing so it did virtually nothing positive for the Dalit community. For instance, it did not launch any programme specifically for uplifting the Scheduled Castes in the last five years. Prithviraj Chuhan, Minister of State Prime Minister's Office and Ministry of Personnel, Public Grievances and Pensions government of India's letter, dated 11th Feb is proof of the same. The letter sent to various ministers of the government reflects that the UPA has taken certain policy measures for improving the quality of life of the marginalised sections of Indian society. There were eight brochures highlighting the programmes for empowering Scheduled Tribes, Religious Minorities, Farmers, Students, and National Employment Guarantee (Act), Rural Health Mission. However there was no specific programme for 16 per cent of Scheduled Castes. Secondly, the Congress Manifesto of 2004 before going into election promised for the Scheduled Castes that,

> The Congress will create a national consensus on the issue of Dalits and *Adivasis* getting a reasonable share of jobs in the private sector. A dialogue with private industries will be initiated to identify how best Indian industry could fulfill in tangible measures the aspirations of youth, especially those belonging the weaker sections of society. Determined efforts will be made to promote a culture of entrepreneurship among the Dalits and Adivasis by providing business run by them with preferential treatment in government procurement and by extending bank credit at affordable terms." (Congress Manifesto-2004, pp. 21-22; Subsection: Dalit and Adivasis).

However, when the Congress led UPA government in 2004, came to power and released the Common Minimum Programme-2004 it deleted the most important portion of its commitment i.e. "Determined efforts will be made to promote a culture of entrepreneurship among the Dalits and Adivasis by providing business run by them with preferential treatment in government procurement and by extending bank credit at affordable terms." This shows the attitude of the Congress towards the Dalits. Before going to election when it needed Dalit votes Congress assured them some expectations. And once the elections were over it forgot all its promises.

Promises of Congress to the Scheduled Castes and Scheduled Tribes

The UPA is very sensitive to the issue of affirmative action, including reservation in private sector. It will immediately initiate a national dialogue with all political parties; industry and other organisations to see best private sector can fulfill the aspirations of Scheduled Castes and Scheduled Tribe youth." (Common Minimum Programme of the Congress led United Progressive Alliance May 2004, Subsection: "Scheduled Castes, Scheduled Tribe" Page 5). Further the Congress Manifesto of 2004 also promised, "All reservation quotas, including those relating to promotions will be fulfilled in a time bound manner. Especially recruitment drives particularly for Class I and Class II vacancies will be launched" (Congress Manifesto-2004, Page 22; Subsection: Dalit and Adivasis). Moreover, "A Comprehensive national programme for minor irrigation of all land owned by Dalits and *Adivasis* will be introduced. Landless families will be endowed with some land through the proper implementation of land ceiling and land redistribution legislation" (Congress Manifesto-2004, Page 22; Subsection: Dalit and Adivasis).

But five years have passed in the UPA-I and almost one and half year has passed of UPA-II still nothing has happened on any of these promises.

Congress and Scheduled Castes and Scheduled Tribes (Anti-Reservation in Posts and Services) Bill 2008

If this was not enough the Congress led UPA-I government towards the fag end of its tenure wanted to hurt Dalits by bringing 'Scheduled Castes and Scheduled Tribes (Reservation in Posts and Services) Bill, 2008.' This bill could have been disastrous for the future development of Scheduled Castes and Tribes. The bill smacks vendetta against Dalits because of the style in which it was passed in the Rajya Sabha. The bill was passed in Rajya Sabha within two minutes without any debate and clause by clause reading of the bill. A number of Dalit members of the Rajya Sabha told the author the story in which the bill was passed. Before passing the clause by clause reading of any bill is convention in the house. This was not followed. Further, the said bill had a clause which had a provision to debar the SCs and STs from the reservation to posts 'above the group 'A' and technical posts in the 47 specified institutions considered to be Institutions of National importance. It is matter of grave concern for one and all because the bill did not specify the legal or constitutional definition of "Institutions of National importance". The bill did not also specify which competent authority had declared these institutions as institutions of national importance. Moreover, the Congress led UPA government before formulating the bill did not take or consult Scheduled Caste Commission or Scheduled Tribe Commission which is mandatory under article 338 (clause 9) of the constitution for formulating a bill related to Dalits. Above all Congress brought a Bill in Rajya Sabha, a Bill which was going to affect the SCs and STs, knowing fully well that Dalits do not have any representation in Rajya Sabha. Therefore one is forced to say that this bill smack vendetta against Dalits.

In this manner we can see that Congress has been against the independent Dalit movement and politics of the Dalits and thereby against the uplift of the whole Dalit community. Although the Congress has never given the Dalits what ever was due to them but it has tried to garner their votes by giving them some falls promises or co-opting their leaders. For example, even after 60 years of independence the prescribed percentage of reservation quota has not been fulfilled and Dalits live on the margins. It has deliberately sabotaged their movements and if not succeeded in doing the same it has implicated Dalits in falls cases.

Bharatiya Janta Party and Dalits

On the other hand, the BJP which won the bulk of SC reserved constituencies in the 1999 general elections, i.e., 25 out of 79 has the same status, that is the absence of an effective Dalit leader with some mass following who can put their point of view effectively. The Bangaru Laxman experiment to attract Dalits towards the party miserably failed with his unceremonious ouster after the Tehelka episode. Then elevation of Suraj Bhan, a Dalit leader from Haryana, first to the post of governor of Uttar Pradesh and then his shifting to the same post to smaller state of Himachal Pradesh also angered the Dalits. Later he was totally neglected in the party without any function and then was made Chairman of the Scheduled Caste and Scheduled Tribe Commission, a ceremonial post. The same fate was bestowed on the veteran Ambedkarite turned saffornite leader Satya Priya Gautam who was the vice-president of BJP and also a cabinet Minister. However, he could never raise his voice for the plight of the Dalits, neither in the party forum nor in the Parliament. BJP was hoping to reap electoral benefits in Uttar Pradesh with the help of BSP but in the 2004 general election that has also failed. So BJP had to debunk the Dalit agenda which it had adopted by elevating its Dalit leaders to the prominent position in the party and by aligning with Bahujan Samaj Party. Later BJP tried its level best to align with the Other Backward Castes instead of Dalits by elevating Uma Bharti as the chief minister of Madhya Pradesh, recalling an abusive Kalyan Singh back to the party in 1999, and helping Mulayam Singh Yadav form the government in UP. BJP has once again trying to bring in some change in its policy when they have inducted Ram Nath Kovid, the former Rajya Sabha member when he was made spokesman of BJP in the new arrangement with the new Chief of BJP. However BJP does not have any programme to attract Dalits towards its party. Most of the Dalits are still are kept in the 'Anusuchit Jati avm Anusuchit Janjati Prakkosth' without any say. Satyanarayan Jatiya who was the cabinet minister from 1999 to 2004 and held portfolios of Labour and Social Justice and empowerment is also not having a significant position in the party.

Left Parties and Dalits

The Left parties are even worse. The Leftists dominate West Bengal where Dalits constitute approximately 24 per cent of total population of the state. Here the Left coalition grabs all the eight seats for the Dalits but we cannot name a single leader who represents dalits here. In fact their representation in the state cabinet is a testimony to the fact that they have been denied their representation; today Dalits are devoid of any dalit leader of repute and mass following in the state. Atul Kohli (1990:374) remarks that how meager the representation of dalits was in the Communist-led government in West Bengal. In his own words, 'In the case of governments led by the Communist Party of India (Marxist) between 1977 and 1982 there were even more Brahmins than in the Congress governments, over 35 per cent; the number of kayasthas (31 per cent) and vaishyas (23 per cent) was almost the same as in the Congress governments, while Scheduled Caste representation was marginally lower at 1.5 per cent'. Hence one can argue that the Leftists never groomed any leadership among the Dalits though they reaped a good harvest of their votes.

Dalits and other State Leved and Regional Political Parties

DMK, AIDMK, TDP, SP, BJD, RJD, SAD, AGP, INLD, etc., are some of the state political parties which have ruled different states at different points in time, but here also there is dearth of effective Dalit leadership. We cannot name a single leader, who has any voice in their respective political parties or any following at the state or national level. It is difficult to understand that why south India which has witnessed the anti-Brahmin movement, seen an assertion of both Scheduled Castes and their political parties is devoid of independent Dalit assertion like Maharashtra and Uttar Pradesh? Though there is a faint assertion of Dalits through Puthiya Tamizgam and Thirumaavalavan's the Revolutionary Dalit Panthers in Tamil Nadu, they have yet to make any substantial mark at the state level. It has been reported by many Dalit activists that here in Tamil Nadu Dravid parties DMK, PMK, AIDMK etc., have deliberately suppressed the independent Dalit movement.

That is why Pandian has argued that in contemporary politics Dalits in Tamil Nadu treat the DMK as a sign of betrayal. Their hostility is so complete that a number of Adi Dravida political groups active in the state willingly let gleeful Brahmin off the hook while projecting the DMK as the exclusive villain (Pandian 1994: 221). It is a fact that under both the regimes DMK and AIDMK the atrocities on Dalits have gone unabated and without guilty been punished (Gorringe 2005:82). Off late although Thirumaalavan asserts that, "...the upper castes bias of the Dravidian parties – the DMK and AIDMK can only be resisted if Dalits organise themselves independently" (Basu 2006:33). However, he himself is not able to snap the ties from these political outfits. On the other hand NGOs led by Dalit themselves have also blunted the edge of Independent Dalit political movement in Tamil Nadu. These NGOs have taken up the human rights issues of Dalits with the help of International NGOs and Supra Institutions like UNHRC, UNDP etc.

In Orissa, where Dalits account for approximately 17 per cent of total population of the state, the situation is similar. Biju Janta Dal (BJD) which has been in power in Orissa for past ten years has not taken any special interest in developing a separate Dalit agenda and thereby a Dalit leadership in the state. As far as status of Dalits is concern it is worse than any other state because Dalits cannot muster courage to raise their legitimate voice and demands. Rashtriya Janata Dal (RJD) led by Laloo Prasad Yadav is another such state party, which though swears to being the savior of Dalits have neglected Dalit issues and that is why today, Laloo has to forge an alliance with Ram Vilas Paswan's Lok Janshakti Party in the ongoing 2010 state legislature elections. Punjab is the state where the highest percentage of Dalit population resides i.e., 28 per cent, yet Akali Dal has no adequate representation of Dalits in its leadership either at the national or the state level. Nobody knows a single Dalit leader from Punjab representing the Dalits effectively. The Samajwadi Party (SP) in UP and Indian National Lok Dal in Haryana also shows the same type of neglect of Dalits and their agenda. SP which has Uttar Pradesh has its core political centre had aligned with BSP to form a coalition government in 1993 till June 1995 but latter both the parties have become political adversary. The main reason for this competition is that they both have a common vote bank and with that only one party can survive. But one thing is sure that this competition has made Samajwadi Party totally indifferent to Dalits and their demands. Had there been no political reservation the party would have not given any share to Dalits, which any way true for all the political parties.

Mainstream Parties, Dalits and Self-Representation

The above survey of the mainstream national and regional political parties amply explains that there is utter lack of self-representation of Dalits and concerns of their issues in the mainstream political parties, which are led and dominated by the so-called Upper castes. There are no leaders belonging to these sections with substantial following or we can argue that the mainstream political parties have never allowed a Dalit leader to have mass-following otherwise he will become strong enough to bargain. Hence the result is that they neither have any political power or clout within the party structure at the functionary level. Nor they have any effective portfolio in the government when their respective parties come to power. If at all a Dalit leader becomes powerful and starts enjoying a little bit of clout in the organisation he is shown the door or he is denied a ticket for contesting an election or he is denied a position in the cabinet or ministry. Jagjivan Ram, Buta Singh, Mukul Wasnik, Shushil Kumar etc. are glaring example from Congress (I), Bangaru Laxman, Sanjay Paswan from BJP, to name just a few.

If on the one hand the mainstream political parties have denied the opportunities to the self-representation to the Dalits within their own parties the very same parties have thwarted or tried to thwart the development of an independent Dalit political organisation and leader both. They have used all the sources– social, political, economic and judicial to create impediments in the path of development of an independent Dalit Politics and thereby Independent Dalit political leadership. To be specific, social movements, big-business houses, courts, bureaucracy and other institutions have been used to stop the march of an independent Dalit party or movement (Kumar 2007: 247-47). That is why one is forced to conclude that Indian political democracy has dual nature. On the one hand it has created some avenues for the assertion of the erstwhile deprived and excluded section of the Indian society by enshrining their political rights in the Indian Constitution (Zelliot 1970, Beteille 1992, Kumar 2007d). On the other hand it has erected hurdles for the independent politics of the Dalits. The modus operandi is simple. The dominant mainstream political parties have used the existing political democracy for co-opting the Dalit leaders from the emerging Dalit political parties. This is done either by allurement by offering party post or a ministry. Secondly, the Indian political democracy has failed to check use of money power by the mainstream Indian political parties. Specially, the political parties which have enjoyed political power at the Centre or in the state use this money power indiscriminately by indulging in horse trading and engineering defections. In doing this they have off course taken help of big business houses. Not only indulging in co-option of leaders, engineering defections, and horse-trading the mainstream political parties have influenced the court proceedings for delaying the justice in the event of a case of anti-defection or lack of strength in the legislature. Therefore, these tactics have proved detrimental for the development of Independent Dalit politics which is directly related to excluded and marginalised, rural, illiterate, poverty stricken Dalits.

Bahujan Samaj Party; Casteism vs. Caste Assertion

Under these circumstances few independent Dalit political parties emerged using the Caste exploitation as the basis of mobilisation. However, from their inception till date they have been stigmatised as divisive in nature and spreading venom of casteism. Social Scientists and lay man have argued that these parties have not only divided the politics but they have divided the society as well. In this context it is necessary to understand the difference between Casteism and Caste-assertion. Casteism means the process by which the dominant caste groups exclude the members of other castes by denying them the access to the institutions of power and governance. The dominant twice–born castes deny them the other castes their legitimate rights on the basis of their stigmatised identity. On the other hand Caste-assertion is a process to mobilise the stigmatised and exploited castes for asserting their legitimate rights. Here exploited and stigmatised castes do not want to usurp the rights of the others. Further, we have to understand, "…caste can be oppressive but it can also provide a basis for struggle against oppression. It can at once be a traditionaliser and a moderniser. It has the potential of being a two pronged catalyst: as purveyor of collective identity and the annihilator of the same hierarchical order from which the collective identity is drawn. Furthermore, certain type of case mobilisation are also pitched against communalism of the religious sectarian type, hence…as a secular upsurge" (Kothari 1997: 444). Last but not the least when we evaluate functioning and performance of Bahujan Samaj Party we should keep temporal history also in mind. We all know that the Bahujan Samaj Party is only 25 years old and has in all it has ruled for six years and that too in four stints. Out of these four stints three times it has ruled with minority government. However, BSP is up against a history of 2500 years of exploitation of Dalits. Hence we will now evaluate Bahujan Samaj Party's performance in the context of self-representation of Dalits and highlighting their grievances.

Dalits and Bahujan Samaj Party

Under such circumstances of criminal neglect of issues and self-representation of one-fourth of Indian population, the political space was available for a political party to assume leadership exclusively of the Dalits in the country. The seed for such a political organisation was sown with the establishment of political parties at the national level. The Scheduled Caste Federation (1942), Republican Party of India (1957), Dalit Panthers Party (1970s) were political parties established at different point in times that were exclusively led and dominated by the Dalits as discussed earlier. These aforesaid parties made some attempt to uplift the Dalits and made them conscious that caste exploitation could be one of the bases for mobilising Dalits for achieving for independent Dalit assertion in the realm of Indian politics. But they could not go beyond a point. However, on April 14, 1984 there emerged the BSP which had exclusive agenda for the Dalits and also had its core base among them. The studies have shown in contemporary politics that after the emergence of the BSP, Dalits have felt more comfortable within this party, identifying with it "yeh apni party hai" (this is our party).

They form the mainstream and play a vanguard role from grassroots mobilisation, in the party organisation and in the government. It is they (Dalits) who represent themselves outside the political party, in the society, in the legislature and in the institutions of governance as well. It is they who decide their agenda and mode of campaign during the elections. Within a short span of time BSP has become the first political party led and dominated by the Dalits to be a national political party. In the last general elections it polled 6.17 per cent of total votes in the country and thereby has acquired third position after Congress and BJP in terms of votes (See Table III). In terms of numbers of votes, it garnered 2,57,28,920 votes that means today it represents approximately 25 million people which is not a mean achievement when we know that its base is illiterate, poor and rural masses. It still is a predominantly rural party. It is really the hard work of Dalit leaders to bring their party to this level without the support of any business house, landed and literate gentry. It is in this context it becomes significant that the BSP is also developing in the different states of the country. Today it is present in every state and union territory where the national and state parties have neglected the Dalits deliberately. Although its development and spread is slow but it is spreading its wings in every part of the country where it was not present. Secondly, what is significant of BSP is that it has given Dalit leaders and issues a prominent place in its functioning.

Bahujan Samaj Party: From State Leved to National Political Party

No doubt that BSP has created aspirations among Dalits at the grass roots level for capturing political power with forming its government five times in a state i.e., UP. But what was important for the 14th Lok Sabha election in 2004 was that the BSP gave a call as to why a daughter of a Dalit cannot become the prime minister of the country? This is a very significant demand by a Dalit political party because never before have Dalit political parties stated such aspirations in the annals of Indian politics. This phenomenon could be seen as the channelisation of Dalit aspirations from local to national level. Before the formation of BSP two decades back Dalits were satisfied with their suppressed position. After that they were offered political offices at the mercy of political bosses of the parties led and dominated by the upper strata. But with the formation of their own political party they started aspiring to become *panchayat* presidents, member of legislative assemblies, members of parliament, member of legislative councils and *Rajya Sabha* and even the Chief Minister of a state on their own without any patronage. No doubt all this has happened within last two decades and during which BSP has shared political power in the largest state of the country five times (1993, 1995, 1997, 2002, 2007) and Mayawati has become the chief minister four times. In 2007, BSP came to power on its own a historical moment in the UP politics because it was after 16 years that a political party was coming to power independently. Today BSP has become the largest party in the state leaving behind the two national political parties Congress (I) and BJP (see table 2).

Table 2: Performance of Political Parties in UP Legislative Assembly Elections (1989-2007) - seats (per cent votes polled)

Party	*Year*					
	1989	*1991*	*1993*	*1996*	*2002*	*2007*
BSP	13 (9.4)	12 (9.4)	69 (11.3)	97 (11.2)	98 (23.19)	206 (30.46)
SP	--	--	109 (17.9)	109 (21.80)	143 (25.43)	97 (25.45)
BJP	57 (11.6)	221 (31.5)	178 (33.3)	174 (32.5)	88 (20.12)	5 0(16.93)
INC	94 (27.9)	46 (17.4)	28 (15.0)	8.4 (33)	25 (9.00)	22 (8.56)

Source: Chief Electoral Officer Uttar Pradesh, Janpath, Lucknow-226001.

BSP Channeling the Dalit Aspiration: From Local to National

Now a moot question is that why these local aspirations have reached the national level? The answer is simple. Till now most of the political parties took the Dalits for granted as their vote banks without taking their independent aspiration into account. These parties, kept them in special cells opened for them like – Scheduled Castes and Scheduled Tribe Cell or '*Anusuchit Jati avum Jan Jati Prakoshta*'. Though these parties thrived on the votes and labour of the Dalits but they never allowed the Dalits to become 'mainstream' group in their parties as it was led and dominated by the so-called upper castes/ classes. Also the aforesaid parties never gave Dalits a platform within the party or in the legislature to divulge their grievances. Dalit issues never occupied centre stage. They all paid lip service to the issues of the Dalits both at the local and national level which is evident from the wretched condition of the Dalits (see Table). However, this trend of the Indian politics changed very rapidly with the establishment of BSP. With its formation Dalits started moving towards BSP specifically in Uttar Pradesh the most populated and politically sensitive state of India because it sends maximum number of Members of Parliament in national legislature. In BSP Dalits have moved from the margins to mainstream and to the frontiers of the party. The party has its own parlance in which Dalits can air their pain and agony in straightforward manner. Moreover, the Dalit leadership has its own priorities. Where the other political parties talk about *Roti, Kapda, aur Makan* (food, clothes and shelter) as the priority, BSP gave the slogan for *Swabhiman* (self-respect) and 'capturing of political power' as the priority area. All these elements have changed the whole mobilisation pattern of the Dalits and that is why BSP is spreading slowly but surely in every nook and corner of the country.

Further, after tasting power in UP, the BSP leadership has deputed leaders from the state to organise the party in different states of the country on UP pattern. Local leaders from UP share their experiences with local leaders of different states and invoke in them the aspiration of capturing state power. Today the local level leaders of BSP in different states have started thinking differently because of Mayawati's clarion call to capture political power at the centre. They yearn to be part of a national cabinet as and when BSP comes to power. The local level leaders who were stagnating in UP after the formation of five governments have a channel now for moving up the ladder if BSP forms or plays a role in the government at the national level. This in reality is the channeling of Dalit aspirations from local to national level. That is why BSP as a political party has become significant for both Dalits and national political parties. BSP's existence has created a pressure on the political parties led and dominated by the upper strata that they cannot form a government without the representation of Dalit leaders. Secondly, they have to take up Dalit issues in right earnest.

BSP and 2009 General Elections

Let us see now what has been the strategy of BSP for giving this aspiration a practical shape. It is true that after her thumping victory in 2007 UP elections and formation of BSP led government on her own Mayawati started nursing the dream of becoming first Dalit Prime Minister of the country. Of course in this era of coalition politics any thing is possible. One can remember Chandrashekhar who became India's Prime Minister with only 60 Members of Parliament. Deve Gauda, Inder Kumar Gujral, Vishwanath Pratap Singh all of them became Prime Minister without any majority in Lok Sabha. However to realise her dream Mayawati on her part popularised her aspiration from local to national level through her party structure. For doing so she has organised 'Bahichara Bano Rallies' (Brotherhood Rallies) in every state of the country. This has further strengthened her party structure and she injected aspiration among the local leaders who have never ever thought of being part of the national government with a party led and dominated by the Dalit and other marginalised communities. BSP cadres and followers popularly call this preparation "Mission 2009". It is in this context we have to understand and analyse the legitimacy granted to BSP led by Mayawati by the different political parties. One can easily argue that before the 2009 general elections BSP was never considered to be part of a national coalition. Every political party debunked it as communal party because it had formed governments with the support of BJP. However it was because of 2007 victory at the state level and because of BSP's maneuvering 'Mission 2009' got support not only from within the BSP but it has found supporters from outside.

The whole political process made Mayawati the fulcrum of a formidable alternative political coalition taking shape in the name of 'Third Front'. Almost ten parties from left to center are ready to join hands. The prominent among them were CPI (M). CPI, TDP, TRS, JD (S), Forward Block, RSP, INLD. There were some other political parties which were single member parties but they all made significant contribution in this age of coalition. What is more significant in this emerging coalition it was not BSP which initiated the exercise of political alignment. Rather it was initiated by the other political parties. To begin with TRS, TDP and the Left parties went to Mayawati one by one. The expectation of other parties from BSP has given BSP a different recognition. This also proved the point that BSP has become a force to recon with not only in Uttar Pradesh but also in other states as well and it can play a crucial role at the national level politics.

Table 3: Bahujan Samaj Party's Performance in Lok Sabha Elections (1996-2009)

Year	*1996*	*1998*	*1999*	*2004*	*2009**
Seats Contested	117	251	225	435	
Seats won	11	5	14	19	21
Per cent of votes polled	3.64	4.67	4.17	5.3	5.78

Source: Reference Handbook, General Elections 2004, Press Information Bureau, Ministry of Information and Broadcasting of India, New Delhi, p.80. And Election Commission of India. *for 2009 election source is Election Commission of India-General Elections 2009, http://eci.nic.in/results/frmPercentVotesPartyWiseChart.aspx (21.05.09)

Table 4: Bahujan Samaj Part's Performance in States (Lok Sabha Elections 2009)

State	*Percentage of SC Population*	*Vote share in*
Andhra Pradesh	16.2	0.91
Assam	7.40	-
Bihar	14.56	4.42
Chhattisgarh	11.6	4.25
Delhi	19.05	5.34
Goa	2.08	-
Gujarat	7.41	1.62
Haryana	19.75	15.75
Himachal Pradesh	25.34	1.59
Jammu & Kashmir	7.6	3.10
Jharkhand	11.8	3.52

State	*Percentage of SC Population*	*Vote share in*
Karnataka	16.38	1.66
Kerala	9.92	1.28
Madhya Pradesh	14.54	5.85
Maharashtra	11.10	4.83
Orissa	16.20	1.90
Punjab	28.31	5.75
Rajasthan	17.29	3.37
Tamil Nadu	19.00	0.77
Uttar Pradesh	21.04	27.42
Uttaranchal	17.9	15.24
West Bengal	23.62	1.00
Chandigarh	17.5	17.88
Pondicherry	16.2	0.61

Source: Census of India 2001, Primary Census Abstract, Scheduled Castes: Tables A-8, Registrar General and Census Commissioner., India Pg.xivii. For election Data source: Election Commission of India-General Elections 2009, http://eci.nic.in/results/frmPercentVotesPartyWiseChart.aspx (21.05.09)

BSP and Politics of Statues: Democratisation of Public Space

It is not that BSP has consolidated its position at the national level but it has done so at the state level also. It has succeeded in doing this by its own style of mobilisation which needs a mention here. Mobilisation through building statues, monuments, parks and gardens in the name of Dalits and Bahujan leaders. There has been an ongoing debate on this because BSP's government is democratically elected government. The dominant section argues that government is wasting tax payer's money. BSP's workers and leaders on the other hand defend this. They argue, 'How can anyone call it a waste of tax payer's money?' One can do so if one doesn't know leaders like Jotiba Phule, Sahuji Maharaj, Babasaheb Ambedkar or Kanshi Ram in whose name these statues and monuments are constructed. It can happen because knowledge systems in schools and universities have never taught them about these icons. By training the mainstream society has known only about Mohandas Karamchand Gandhi, Pandit Jawaharlal Nehru, Rabindra Nath Tagore, Vallabh Bhai Patel, Indira Gandhi etc. to name just a few. Had UP government made these monuments in their names they would have never called it a waste of tax payer's money. Therefore, if the society had been conscious about the contributions made by Dalit and Bahujan leaders in uplift downtrodden and thereby to the whole humanity, it would have not declared these constructions as waste of money. Moreover, society should understand that when BSP contested elections it made very clear its party's ideology. BSP leadership since its inception has made it clear that they abide by the path shown by the social reformers like Jotiba Phule, Narayna Guru, Chtrapatti Sahujii, Babasaheb Ambedkar and will honor them as and when it comes to power. Secondly if the UP government is spending rupees two thousand *crores* for the section of the society who were excluded for two thousand five years to accord them a dignified status, it is an economical deal. What would have happened if Dalits ask compensation for their centuries' exploitation by the so-called upper castes? This should be considered as a service to nation because the government is rectifying mistakes committed by earlier national and state governments for not according due respect to Dalit and Bahujan leaders.

This debate is selective because so-called conscience keepers have specifically chosen construction works of Lucknow by willfully avoiding the developmental programmes and policies launched UP government. For instance since 1995 (when BSP had formed its first government) it has village development scheme 'Ambedkar Gram Vikas Yojana'. Government has given possession of thousands of acres of land to the members of the marginalised communities. Under Kanshi Ram Shari Vikas Yojna plots it distributed plots to the urban youths to start their business. Recently government has announced reservation in the construction works amounting up to five lakhs. This is sufficient to make the point clear. Further it looks that intellectuals are targeting UP government because they have never filed any PIL against the hundreds of monuments made in the name of Gandhi, Nehru, and Tagore or even in the name of Indira Gandhi or Rajiv Gandhi. They have not called the money spent in the preparations of Commonwealth Games in Delhi even though Delhi government is not able to provide basic amenities like drinking water and electricity to the people, as a waste. In Delhi Dalits have died in manholes and still carry excreta on their heads. But no PILs have been filed against this inhuman practice in the capital of the nation. No one files a PIL against the 'day and night cricket matches' played in India even though Lakhs of Indian villages don't have electricity. Moreover government provides Law and security, land on concessional rates to build stadium where now IPL matches are played. It is because of government's support that IPL teams are able to buy players for millions of rupees in auction, even though Indian farmers are committing suicide although 70 per cent of Indians live on Rs. 20 a day. However no one has filed a PIL to stop all this.

Therefore one should understand meaning of development or economic progress. Economic development does not necessarily result in breaking of existing social, economic, political, religious, educational structures of society. The ruling class values do not change with economic development and ruling elite keeps the exploitative social and political structures alive. The modern institutions – judiciary, bureaucracy, universities, industry, media remain biased in favour of upper strata. For instance Dalits remained marginalised in the mixed economy even after four decades of Independence. Globalisation, after 1990s has further marginalised 260 Million Dalits (Dalits and Tribals together). Another fact is that Upper Strata has not always preferred development. In fact, they chose Independence over development that is why they demanded Independence from British rule though they were developing India in different spheres. Hence we should understand that through the construction of these symbols Dalits are also demanding independence from the clutches of dominant and hegemonic symbols of the Indian society in general and Hindu society in particular. That is why BSP leaders have argued that Dalits have to understand the difference between of 'Economic Development' and 'Social Transformation'. Dalits do not need only economic development in which they have no share. Dalits need 'Social Transformation' that changes existing power structure of the society and gives them their legitimate rights. For this it is necessary to create an alternative hegemony, a parallel thought process and symbols which are different from existing ones with which Dalits can relate.

Hence the symbols in the forms of monuments, statues and parks become essential for social transformation in a caste-ridden society, where masses are illiterate. These statues of icons and parks have long-lasting impact on the memories of excluded communities, because they have nothing to call as their own. Hence if Dalits want a permanent change, they will have to go for 'Social Transformation' rather than mere 'Economic Development'. Lastly, this condemnation of monuments reflects deep sense of frustration of the non Bahujans because of two reasons. One, their exploitative, feudal and hierarchical social structure is crashing under the pressure of emerging democracy. They are not able to bear that Dalits, who till yesterday were forcibly restricted to

Dalit 'Busties', 'Maharwadas' or 'Chamrauties' have today occupied the spaces at the crossings of the city and they are not able to stop them with their all might. Secondly, they are afraid of these democratically elected Governments which erect such statues and monuments which have demoralising effect on them. Hence, these monuments, parks and statues of the Dalits and Bahujans symbolise the emerging consciousness among the Dalits to claim their spaces. They should be seen as the processes of democratisation of public spaces of the society, correction of the exclusion imposed by the society and the governments and assertion of the Dalits.

Crises of Dalit Political Movement

In spite of their many achievements the Independent Dalit political movement faces number of crises as well. First and foremost, the movement has failed to unite the different shades of independent Dalit political leadership functioning in different parts of the country. The independent Dalit political movement has been victim of factionalism and has seen divisions a number of times. It happened in RPI, Dalit Panthers and now it is happening in BSP. Every time, it has been observed, an independent Dalit movement emerges, flourishes for some time but gets fragmented either because of ideological differences or because of personality clash between leaders. The second crises of the Independent Dalit political leadership is its inability to provide a unified pan-Indian identity to Dalits. Some movements want to have an alliance between Scheduled Castes, Scheduled Tribes, Other Backward Castes, and converted religious minorities under the nomenclature of Dalits however some others want to unite them under the name of '*Bahujans*'. Beyond this, yet another group wants to unite them under the name of '*Moolniwasi*' (original inhabitant of the land or indigenous people). Thirdly, Dalit politics has failed to search a genuine political ally in the Indian polity. Hence they keep on changing the alliance with political parties. Fourthly, the Dalit political movement has not taken any initiative to establish a dialogue between different shades of the Dalit movements. Fifthly, the political movement at times looks sectarian to general public because it never reveals its economic, educational and nationalistic agenda. The leaders have failed to claim the nation. Last but not the least Dalit Political parties have failed rise the issue of corruption although Dalits are the worst sufferers of it because majority of them are poorest.

Conclusion

We can conclude that in spite of the aforesaid crises faced by Dalit politics, it has made significant contributions to Dalit movement and different institutions of Indian politics. The Dalit politics as a whole has not only contributed in the development of the Dalit movement but it has also strengthened the Indian democracy (Kumar 2006, Gorringe 2006) by making the Dalit politics and Dalit movement more effective to bring the erstwhile excluded collectivity into the fold of democratic processes.

The logical corollary is that, the independent Dalit political leadership has given separate identity to Dalits and has carved out a distinct community with a vast vote bank. On the other hand it has given Dalits self-confidence that they can also make things happen and are no more silent spectator in the democracy or they are not the passive recipients of democracy. It has also infused in them a new type of aspiration that they can also hold the highest offices of the country on their own without the blessings of the upper-castes. In doing so independent Dalit political movement has brought Indian democracy nearer to masses. In fact it has changed the nature of Indian democracy from representative to the participatory. Earlier Dalits were represented by the so-called upper castes in the upper caste led and dominated parties in which dependent Dalit political leadership use to function at their mercy and patronage. Today independent Dalit political leadership plays a vanguard role and organises not only Dalits but also the members of other castes as well (Kumar 2007c). They themselves organise meetings, mobilise people to cast their votes in their favour on their own agenda, take up their problems with the local and regional administration without taking help of the upper-castes etc. Further, leadership of the Independent Dalit political movement has been successful in keeping the Dalit in the fold of democratic politics by stoping them not to be lured by the violent politics of Naxalite groups. In doing so they have taken Indian democracy much closer to the erstwhile-marginalised sections, which is a process of inclusion.

Another fall out of this process is that the Independent Dalit political leadership has not only challenged the political hegemony of the so-called upper castes but has started mobilising them to bring them within its fold - a process, which is quite evident in Uttar Pradesh (Kumar 2006). This has weekend both the liberal Congress (I) and right wing BJP in Uttar Pradesh (UP). Though in UP the independent Dalit leadership led by BSP entered in post-poll alliance with the right wing BJP but it never succumbed to their pressure to allow them to implement their communal agenda. Rather by forming three governments with them BSP weaned out Dalits from their fold by making them conscious that there is fundamental difference between 'Jai Bheem' (Symbol of Dalits) and 'Jai Shri Ram' (religious symbol of so-called upper-castes). Not only that, it also created a secular environment by mobilising the lower strata of the Muslims which was never given a representation in the politics. This has saved Uttar Pradesh from communal conflicts which were a regular features of UP during Congress, BJP and Samajwadi Party's regimes.

In the same vein Independent Dalit politics has helped the Dependent Dalit political Leadership by forcing indirectly their parent parties to give them dignified recognition not only in the government but also in the party organisations as well. It is a fact that because of the pressure of the former the latter has been given due recognition in different echelons of power structure by their parent organisation, a phenomenon which did not existed earlier at all and mainstream intelligentsia has forgotten to record this phenomena. Following examples amply prove the point. Dr. K.R. Narayan was elevated to the post of Vice President of the country by the Congress in 1992. Five years later the Congress elevated him to the post of President of India. Needless to say that it happened for the first time in the country when a Dalit occupied the highest constitutional position of the land. Similarly Congress during the same period nominated Mahavir Prasad and Mata Prasad as the Governors of Haryana and Arunachal Pradesh respectively. It is interesting to note here that both the Congressmen hailed from Uttar Pradesh. A question here is that why at all Congress picked up these Dalit leaders and that too from UP, an act which it never did in 45 years of its history in the state after the commencement of the Constitution? Couple of years later for the first time in the history of Indian parliament G.M.C. Balyogi – a Dalit from Andhra Pradesh was elected as the speaker of Lok Sabha. It is interesting to note here that though his candidature was mooted by Telugu Desam Party but it was readily supported by the National Democratic Alliance (NDA) of approximately 24 political parties.

The BJP-led NDA appointed Haryana politician Suraj Bhan as the Governor of Uttar Pradesh (UP) (April 1998-November 2000) and Himachal Pradesh (November 2000 - May 2003). Can we rule out the ulterior motive of (Bhartiya Janata Party) BJP in his nomination specifically as the Governor of UP? Further BJP crossed all the limits when amidst lots of opposition from its national executive it elected Bangaru Laxman, a Dalit from Andhra Pradesh, as its national president. In the same vein it is difficult to give a list of ministers in the Central and State Governments without a significant department and responsibility, who were appointed by Congress and BJP respectively in their governments. In the same vein we have to take note of the nominations of number of Dalits by these parties to the post of Vice-Chancellors of Central and State universities, as well as at the other statutory positions in the government. And, in 2010 Meira Kumar was been elected as the Speaker of the Lok Sabha, the first Dalit women to become the Speaker.

The success of the leadership of the Independent Dalit political movement apart, Dalit politics as a whole has some negative aspects as well. First and foremost it has failed to unite the different shades of independent Dalit political leadership functioning in different parts of the country. The independent Dalit political movement has been victim of factionalism and has seen divisions a number of times. It happened in RPI, Dalit Panthers and now it is happening in BSP. But worst part is that the main stream political forces have been creating hurdles for the development of the independent (of) Dalit political movement by either co-opting their leaders or by co-opting their agenda. Therefore we can argue that democracy not only provides space to Dalits but creates hurdles for them as well. Second, the Independent Dalit leadership has failed to provide a unified identity to Dalits. Some movements want to have an alliance between Scheduled Castes, Scheduled Tribes, Other Backward Castes, and converted religious minorities under the nomenclature of Dalits though others want to unite under the name of 'Bahujans' and yet another group under the name 'Moolniwasi'. Further, they have failed to search a genuine political ally in the Indian polity. This has retarded the development of independent Dalit movement and confused the Dalit masses to choose their path of assertion and emancipation (Kumar 2002). Therefore we can argue that the Dalit political movement should not be treated as a monolithic whole. The evaluation of internal differentiation of this movement is sine qua non to understand the real nature and contribution of the Dalit political movement in the Indian society and politics.

Abbreviations:

AIADMK: All India Anna Dravida Munnettra Kazhagam

AGP: Assam Gana Parishad

BAMCEF: Backward and Minorities' Employees' Federation

BJP: Bhartiya Janata Party

BJD: Biju Janata Dal

BSP: Bahujan Samaj Party

CPI : Communist Party of India

CPI (M): Communist Party of India (Marxist)

DMK: Dravida Munnettra Kazhagam

INLD: Indian National Lok Dal

JD: Janata Dal

JD(S): Jajata Dal (Socialist)

NDA: National Democratic Alliance

RPI : Republican Party of India

RSP: Revolutionary Socialist Party

PT: Putiya Tamizhgam

TDP: Telugu Desham Party

TRS: Telangana Rashtra Samithi

UPA: United Progressive Alliance

References

Ambedkar, B.R., 1979. 'On Constitutional Reforms: Evidence before the Southborough Committee', in *Dr. Babasaheb Ambedkar Writings and Speeches,* Vol. 1. Education Department, Government of Maharashtra, Mumbai.

_____1991, 'What Congress and Gandhi have done to the Untouchables', in *Dr. Babasaheb Ambedkar Writings and Speeches,* Vol. 9, Education Department, Government of Maharashtra, Mumbai.

Basu, Sekhar, Raj, 2006, 'Dalit Politics in Tamil Nadu', *Seminar*, 558, February.

Beteille, Andre, 1992, *Society and Politics in India: Essays in Comparative Perspective*, New Delhi: Oxford University Press.

Chandra, Bipan, 1989, *India's Struggle for Independence*, New Delhi: Penguin Books.

Gokhale, Jayshree, 1993, *From Concession to Confrontation: The Politics of an Untouchable Community*, Mumbai: Popular Prakashan.

Ghurye, G.S., 1963, *The Scheduled Tribes*, Bombay: Popular Prakashan.

Gorringe, Hugo, 2005. *Untouchables Citizens: Dalit Movements and Democratisation in Tamil Nadu,* New Delhi: Sage Publications.

Kohli, Atul 1987, 'From Elite Activism to Democratic Consolidation: The Rise of Reform Communism in West Bengal' in Francine R Frankel and M S A Rao (eds.), *Dominance and State Power in Modern India: Decline of a Social Order*, Vol. 2, pp. 367-415, London: Oxford University Press.

Kothari, Rajni, 1997, 'Caste and Modern Politics', in Sudipta Kaviraj (ed.), *Politics in India*, pp. 57-70, New Delhi: Oxford University Press.

Kumar, Vivek, 2002, *Dalit Leadership in India*, New Delhi: Kalpaz Publication.

_____, 2006, *India's Roaring Revolution: Dalit Assertion and New Horizons*, New Delhi: Gagan Deep Publications.

_____, 2007a, 'Bahujan Samaj Party: Some Issues of Democracy and Governance', in Sudha Pai (ed.), *Political Process in Uttar Pradesh*, pp. 241-270, New Delhi: Pearson Longman.

_____, 2007b, 'Governance and Development in the Era of Globalisation: Understanding exclusion and assertion of Dalits in India', in Kameshwar Choudhary (ed.) *Globalisation Governance Reforms and Development in India*, pp. 302-331, New Delhi: Sage Publications.

_____, 2007c, 'When the Marginalised Mobilise: A Case of the Bahujan Samaj Party', *The Indian Journal of Social Work: Special Issue on Dalits and Development: A Reappraisal*, 68 (1), pp. 88-100, Tata Institute of Social Sciences, Mumbai.

_____, 2007d, *Social Exclusion and Different Shades of Dalit Movement*, Punc: Pune University.

Lohia, Rammanohar, 1979. *The Caste System*, Hyderabad: Rammanohar Lohia Samata Vidhyalaya Nyas.

Lynch, Owen M., 1974. *The Politics of Untochability: Social Mobility and Social Change in a City of India*, New Delhi: National.

Madanipour, A., 1998, 'Social Exclusion and Space' in A Madanipour, G Cars and J. Allens (eds.), *Social Exclusion in Europe Cities*, London: Jessica Kingsley.

Murugkar, Lata, 1991. *Dalit Panthers Movement in Maharashtra: A Sociological Appraisal*, Bombay: Popular Prakashan.

Nadel, S.F., 1969. *The Theory of Social Structure*, London: Cohen and West.

Oommen, T.K., 1990, *Protest and Change: Studies in Social Movements*, New Delhi: Sage Publications.

Rudolph, I. and Rudolph, S. 1987, *The Modernity of Tradition: Political Development in India*, New Delhi: Orient Longman.

_____, 1998, *In Pursuit of Laxmi: The Political Economy of the Indian State*, Orient Longman, New Delhi.

17

Indian Democracy and Personality Cult

The world's largest democracy is going to face its fourteenth general election and the first of this century. It is an opportune time for every conscious Indian to evaluate whether Indian "Democracy" has percolated down or it has remained only at the level of frequent elections, adult suffrage and making constitutional morality as the be-all and end-all of democracy.

To start with, the scene looks very ugly as the stars hobnobbing and power-seekers are shining in Indian democracy. Joining one political party and leaving the other without any commitment to political ideology or to the people is the most cherished game of the full-time politicians. Some 'not proved guilty' criminals also find it an opportune time to take refuge in the mainstream political parties. Above all, the way the two mainstream parties—the Bharatiya Janata Party and Congress-I—are welcoming, with open arms, the celebrated personalities from cinema, television, sports, erstwhile princely states etc. speaks volumes of domination of charismatic personality (ies) in Indian politics thereby suppressing the process of emergence of grassroot leaders at the national level, a must for the broadening of Indian democracy.

What is worrying for the world's largest democracy is that the personality (ies) from films, television, sports etc. devoid of any political ideology and commitment to the people are given party affiliation. Why I am forced to say that these personalities are devoid of any commitment to the people and ideology is because they have joined the bourgeois parties like the Congress, BJP, and SP only. Why have they not joined the Communist Parties like the CPI, CPI- M or a Dalit party like the

BSP? The domination of these personalities, especially the film personalities, ,has increased so much that they are regularly nominated to the Rajya Sabha, the Upper House of Parliament, which was once the citadel of the experienced and elderly politicians who contributed qualitatively in the day-to-day affairs of the emerging

Indian democracy. Today the aforesaid personalities are welcomed to exploit the emotions of the illiterate Indian masses and then in the next election a new personality is searched to be highlighted.

Further, this personality domination is writ large when the sons and daughters of famous politicians, princely families etc. are also admitted to the party and elevated to top party positions while the grassroots workers, who spend their whole life in the party, seldom get a place at the highest level. It is so comical to observe in contemporary Indian politics blood-relatives joining parties with opposite ideologies and yet proving their commitment to their respective ideologies and parties. Can political ideology alone influence the family values so deeply that a son is pitched against his own mother, a sister is pitched is against her own brother, a daughter-in-law is pitched against the other sister-in-law and so on and so forth, or is there something more to it?

A point can be made here that this dominance of a charismatic personality in Indian politics has a long history. It can be traced back to even the mythological period where a rigid social order restricted the international pattern in society and authorised a few to take up governance as their vocation; hence rendering the whole society as fatalistic. The following couplet from the *Geeta* amply proves the point.

Yada Yada Hi Dharmasya Gtani Bhavati Bharatha,...
Dharma Sanstha Apnarthaya Sambhaivami Yuge Yuge.

(Whenever the rule of law is undermined in society there will be one and only one incarnation for the destruction of unrighteousness and establishment of the rule of law.)

This couplet has a divine sanction and hence it carries lots of weight, especially in the countryside where the primordial loyalties are very strong and mythological sayings and stories govern the individual's life-style and psyche. These mythological sayings have taken vernacular forms and are recited regularly by the elderlies giving them the status of eternal truth. The impact of mythological sayings is increased when leaders belong to the *varnas* or castes located higher up in the hierarchy of the Hindu social order which gives them added charisma.

Since the inception of modern politics this phenomenon of personality cult has been used to the hilt in Indian politics. India entered an age of mass politics in 1920 when Mahatma Gandhi launched the first national civil disobedience movement. (Weiner 1957:7) Soon he started dominating the proceedings of the Indian National Congress and took whatever decisions he liked. Later on he was projected as the Mahatma and was also coronated with the title of the "Father of the Nation" He even legitimised the capitalists by accepting huge donations for running his *ashrama* and also the INC. Such was his dominance that he on his own decided the partition of the country, who will be the Prime Minister of India though the Congress Working Committee had a different choice.

After independence Jawaharlal Nehru became a colossal figure and, especially after the demise of Patel, it was difficult for anyone to break his personality cult. So dominating was his personality that in the absence of any opposition he used to write letters on his own and critique his policies. Before his demise he groomed his daughter to take over his mantle. Indira Gandhi took over the Congress' reins and by the 1970s the dominance of the personality cult in Indian polity assumed such heights that a slogan was mooted: "Indira is India and India is Indira".

Nobody could challenge the authority of Indira Gandhi till another personality challenged her. Again this personality was coronated with the epithet of *Lok Nayak.* Though Jayaprakash Narayan never assumed political power himself nor was he interested in it, his legacy was used and is being used even today for gaining political power by his followers. The 1980s again saw Indira Gandhi dominating the Indian polity and grooming her elder son, Rajiv Gandhi, to carry the legacy of the Gandhi-Nehru family. The charismatic personality of Indira came to the fore once again after her demise when people gave the slogan:

Jab Tak Suraj Chand Rahega Indira Tera Nam Rahega.
(The name of Indira live till the sun and moon exist.)

A novice like Rajiv Gandhi was made the Prime Minister just because he was the son of Indira Gandhi. After that he also won the Lok Sabha elections with a thumping majority with the help of her personality cult. As time passed the 1990s saw the ex-king, a Kshatriya by caste, Raja Vishwanath Pratap Singh coming to the centre-stage to challenge the legacy of the Nehru-Gandhi family. Again the slogan highlighted the charisma of Vishwanath Pratap Singh in Indian democracy which was by now forty years old:

Raja Nahi Fakeer Hai Desh Ki Takder Hai.

(He is not a king but a beggar! And the fortune of the country.)

This was till mid-1990s. After this all of a sudden veteran Opposition leader, Atal Behari Vajpayee's personality has been blown out of proportion by different actors in Indian politics. Till the 1990s he was simply a politician like any other politician. But soon he was projected as the most towering personality in Indian politics. His age became his biggest asset. Nobody even bothered to ask whether he has ever run the government. Rather, he was declared a visionary and champion of coalition politics, though a section of his party called him the 'mask' of the BJP. But during this period the irony was that the Opposition had no option but to fall back on another personality from the Nehru-Gandhi family to counter Atal Behari. Hence the late 1990s saw the war of two personalities in the representative democracy of India—one, Atal Behari Vajpayee and the other, Sonia Gandhi. Look at the slogans, which give us the dominance of these personalities during this period in Indian politics, which had by now celebrated its silver jubilee:

Raj Tilak Ki Karo Taiyari Jeet Gaye Atal Behari.

(Prepare for coronation, Atal Behari has won.)

Gaon Gaon Me Chali Bayar Sonia Gandhi Bahu Hamar.

(There is a wind blowing in every village that Sonia Gandhi is our daughter-in-law.)

If this was the scene at the national level State politics also saw the dominance of personality cult. Tamil Nadu showed the way. Two film personalities, M. Karunanidhi and M.G. Ramachandran, became the focal point of the State's politics. Similarly, Andhra Pradesh saw the ascendance of N.T. Ramarao, another film personality capturing political power. Tamil Nadu politics saw the domination of the personality of J. Jayalalitha when she became the Chief Minister though she was brought into politics by MGR to pull the crowed for his public meetings. In the same vein N.T. Ramarao's charisma has been encashed by his son-in-law, Chandrababu Naidu, and Biju Patnaiks's legacy is being enchased by his son, Navin Patnaik. To stretch the point further, even Dalit politics has also become captive of the personality cult. Earlier Kanshi Ram was projected *Ms* the true heir of Babasaheb Ambedkar; that is why a slogan was mooted:

Baba Tera Mission Adhura Kanshi Ram Karenega Pura.

(Babasaheb Ambedkar, your mission is incomplete, Kanshi Ram will fulfil it.)

Today Mayawati has been projected as the messiah of the Dalits in the country.

The impact of this personality cult is writ large on the forthcoming Lok Sabha elections of 2004 as the Bharatiya Janata Party has already projected Atal Behari Vajpayee as its Prime Ministerial candidate and floated a slogan:

Chauthi Bari Atal Behari.

(Fourth time Atal Behari.)

The aforesaid slogan undermines all the institutions and norms of the representative and democratic politics where different forums and processes are involved in the selection and election of an individual to the different offices of the government and party. But it is the sheer dominance of Vajpayee's personality that he has already been declared the Prime Ministerial candidate. Can this be called representative democracy?

To conclude, we can argue that the whole phenomenon of personality cult in the system of representative democracy has made the choice of leadership very limited. You are forced to choose from the lot which the parties project. And parties project the personalities keeping primordial loyalties like caste, region, religion and hereditary status in mind which have some element of charisma in them. The candidates are seldom projected on the universalistic values. This in turn reduces the breadth of the social base from which political elites are to be recruited rendering Indian democracy reduced to a narrow base. This is why we see that only a small strata have monopolised Indian politics since its inception. As has been rightly brought out by Singh (1994: 135).

Since still the majority of elite belonged to the upper castes, particularly the Brahmins caste, the elite structure could not be said to have been democratised in the real sense. Another fall-out of the domination of personality cult in Indian politics is that a number of institutions are compromised and the real issues related to the masses are thwarting the development of representative democracy and making it really participatory.

It is more astonishing that even the processes of modernisation and globalisation have not been able to break this domination of primordial loyalties which give birth to this personality cult in Indian politics, though it was envisaged that these would disappear with the passage of time. On the contrary, most of the modern institutions like film, TV, politics, bureaucracy, judiciary etc. have been used to monopolise power rather than to democratise the polity and society. Will Indian democracy transform itself into a government of the people by the people or will it remain a government of a hereditary class by a hereditary ruling class.

References

Weiner, Myron, Party Politics in India: The Development of a Multi-Party System, Princeton University Press, 1957.

Singh, Y. Modernisation of Indian Tradition, Rawat Publication, Jaipur, 1994.

18

Presidential Election in World's Largest Democracy: The Issue of Representation

It is really painful to see how the political elite of the country is making a mockery of public sensibilities while selecting a candidate for the post of the President of India. Overtly undermining the skills and acumen needed to run the highest office of the land they are giving credence of the primordial identities and loyalties of an individual for his/her candidature. Although all the political parties, with different ideologies, are pretending that they are committed to a national cause, they have failed to protect the dignity and authority associated with the President's Office.

Look at the Congress. The party bosses have very carefully chosen the Congress Presidential candidate, Smt Pratibha Patil, because she represents a particular region, religion, caste and most of all gender. It would be impossible for other parties to find a person representing so many institutions and identities. In the process, Smt Patil has already won friends from different ideological groups. By now it has become evident that she is a Marathi, married to a Rajasthani and that too from the *Shekhawati* region. These characteristics were necessary to neutralise the candidature of the Vice-President of India, Bhairon Singh Shekhawat, for the President's post.

The Congress' move has already won support from the *'Hindu Hriday Samrat'* Bal Thackeray's Shiv Sena on the pretext of 'Marathi identity' or 'Marathi pride' although they are both ideologically bitter enemies in Maharashtra politics. The Left parties are supporting Smt

Patil's candidature because of reasons known only to them. They rejected A.P.J. Abdul Kalam for a second term because they wanted someone with more 'political acumen' at the head of the state, although they had rejected a knowledgeable statesman like K.R. Narayanan for a second term. No doubt electoral arithmetic ensures that the UPA's candidate will become the next President of India. But it is a pity that a presidential candidate is chosen on the basis whether he/she is first the representative of the aforesaid institutions of the society. In the event Congress has undermined the specific qualifications required to occupy the highest office of the country.

On the other hand Bhairon Singh Shekhawat is going to contest the presidential election as an Independent candidate. The interesting part about Shekhawat is that the NDA led by the Bharatiya Janata Party, of which he used to be a member till a few years back, is supporting his candidature. Can ideological commitment of the Indian political class be so fragile that they can abruptly dissociate from it so easily whenever they want? Is an office above their ideology on the part of the BJP? How can a political party be so defensive about its ideology just for an office? Why did they not contest the elections and reveal how much support their ideology has? Why do they have to take refuge every time in coalition as they are doing in the State and parliamentary elections?

Another group, the so-called Third Front-in-the-making, led by the defeated Chief Ministers of various States also heading State parties, tried unsuccessfully to rope in A.P.J. Abdul Kalam again, without even bothering to take his consent before announcing his name. A.P.J. Abdul Kalam's case was also pleaded by the politically indifferent masses (who will never bother to cast their votes in an election by standing in the queue) by casting their votes through SMS polls on television. They all forgot how he erred in imposing President's Rule in Bihar last year.

It is too obvious that the aforesaid political parties were fighting an already lost battle. They were doing so only to play to their constituency, that they stand for secularism. As if by only projecting a Muslim candidate for the President's post one can establish one's secular credentials. It is with this symbolism only that last time the NDA led by the BJP was forced to nominate A.P.J. Abdul Kalam as the President of India after the Gujarat carnage. Otherwise, which political formation has the guts to nominate a person who has never participated in the process of democracy except for casting a vote? It is a fact that Abdul Kalam never contested any election from panchayat to Parliament. Even by nomination he did not occupy a political office like the Member of Legislative Council, Rajya Sabha or Governor etc. Even then he was elevated to the President's post. This was not the first time this symbolism or tokenism was used. Rather the Congress had used this long back when it nominated Dr Zakir Hussain and Dr Fakhruddin Ali Ahmed to the President's post.

In fact after the election of the first President of India, Dr Rajendra Prasad, every election for the post of the President in independent India has been used to meet the challenges emerging out of the problems of region, religion, language and caste. Election to the President's office has been successfully used to neutralise the people's alienation. As soon as a political party realises that a social group—based on region, or caste— is feeling discriminated against and is underrepresented in the echelons of power and this will be detrimental to the party prospects, it will try to nominate its representative to the post of the President. For instance, regional balance between the North and the South was maintained by appointing a President from the South as the Prime Minister used to be from the North. Dr Sarvapalli Radhakrishnan, V.V. Giri, Neelam Sanjeeva Reddy, R. Venkataraman, who were nominated to the highest office, were from the South. No doubt many of them were political activists as well. Even Dr Zakir Hussain was born in Hyderabad where his father, Fida Hussain, studied law and had a successful career.

'Similarly in the 1980s when the Punjab problem was at its peak the Congress appointed Giani Zail Singh—a Sikh—to neutralise the Sikh problem, during the Bhindranwale phase, with the help of the President's office. Lots of doubts were raised on his choice even then. In 1997 the Congress was forced to elevate K.R. Narayanan to prove its progressive ideology and neutralise the increasing influence of the Bahujan Samaj Party. Though Narayanan fully diserved to be the President of India because of his qualifications, it was projected that he was elevated to the post because he was a Dalit. The media reports suggest that his Dalit identity overpowered all his academic and political qualifications and throughout his tenure he remained the 'First Dalit President of India'.

This has happened with many other presidential candidates when their primordial identities have scored over their secular achievements and knowledge about social movements, political system, Indian Constitution, foreign relations etc. That is why the 'Indian President' has been reduced to a national head only. Things have come to such a pass that Pratibha Patil had a emphasise that 'I will not be a rubber stamp President'. But the reality is different, because the powers enshrined in the President's office are enormous which can effectively check both the executive and judiciary if they don't deliver. The only question is: how effectively can it be used? In this context it can also be asked: why have all our politicians not strengthened this office even after 60 years of India's independence?

Table 1: Names and Tenures of Presidents

S. No.	*Names of Presidents*	*Tenure*
1.	Dr Rajendra Prasad (1884-1963)	26 January 1950 to 13 May 1952
2.	Dr Sarvapalli Radhakrishnan (1888-1975)	13 May 1962 to 13 May 1967
3.	Dr Zakir Hussain (1897-1969)	13 May 1967 to 3 May 1969
4.	Shri Varahagiri Venkat Giri (1894-1980)	3 May 1969 to 20 July 1969 and 24 August 1969 to 24 August 1974
5.	Dr Fakhruddin Ali Ahmed (1905-1977)	24 August 1974 to 11 February 1977
6.	Shri Neelam Sanjiva Reddy (1913-1996)	25 July 1977 to 25 July 1982
7.	Giani Zail Singh (1916-1994)	25 July 1982 to 25 July 1987
8.	Shri R. Venkataraman (1910-2009)	25 July 1987 to 25 July 1992
9.	Dr Shankar Dayal Sharma (1918-1999)	25 July 1992 to 25 July 1997
10.	Shri K.R. Narayanan (1920-2005)	25 July 1997 to 25 July 2002
11.	Dr A.P.J. Abdul Kalam (1931-)	25 July 2002 to 25 July 2007

Therefore, if India has to transform itself into a vibrant democracy then each of its institutions has to perform effectively so that greater checks and balances can be created within the different institutions of democracy. This will happen if our politicians move beyond symbolic representation of people in the name of religion, region, caste etc. and loyalty of a candidate towards a political party as the main criteria while nominating them to prestigious offices. The political elite should not be permitted to use different offices of democracy to suit their ends for long.

19

Saffronisation in Democracy

The Indian society is a religious society no doubt. But the past three months have seen an unprecedented rise in religious celebrations within the internally differentiated Hindu communities. We saw the *kazuarians* visiting Hardwar to fetch Ganges water. *Krishna-ashtmi* had its own spell. Then came the *Amarnath Yatra* in the difficult terrain of the Himalayas of course amid tight security provided by the Indian Army. *Kumbh Mela* in Nasik at the banks of river Godavari attracted one and all along with *Ganesh Chaturthi* with the idols of Ganesh being immersed in the Bay of Bengal with chants of *Ganapati Bappa Moiya.* Then we had *Navaratri* associated with *Durga Puja* and *Dandia (Garbha)* this month. Thereafter we observed *Dussehra* with *Ram Lila* and the burning of Ravana. These are to be followed by *Diwali* towards the end of October. We should not forget the annual *Ajmer Sharifs Urs* at the *mazar* of the *sufi* saint who won India with love and not by the sword.

These celebrations have some common denominators. One, the media (print and visual) gave all of them extended coverage. Each TV channel had a special time-slot for their regular coverage. Second, the individuals and government spent a huge amount of money in these celebrations. Imagine the budget of Nasik Kumbh 2003: a whopping Rs 448 crores which was only Rs 21 crores in 1991-1992. And for what? For helping people to take a faith-based bath! Similarly, take one pandal of *Durga Puja* in the Marxist bastion of Kolkata, which costs Rs 25 lakh. If we go by these standards of expenditure on each event, then we can very well imagine the total expenditure. Not only that, we should also give a thought to the morale of the administrative machinery and the Army. The police are primarily responsible for maintaining internal security and the Army for defending our borders but they are time and again forced to control the crowd involved in these religious activities.

Another common feature related to these celebrations is the criminal silence of rationalists and mainstream intellectuals on the legitimacy of these celebrations. Though they did not overtly support these religious celebrations and the exorbitant expenditure involved in them, they did not criticise them either. Therefore, by logic their silence amounts to covert support to these activities. We have read so many articles by them criticising any extraordinary expenditure by the government or by individuals. These conscience-keepers give a number of arguments about the poverty and low human development index (HDI) of India. Depending on the seasons, winter, summer or monsoon, they will write how the government or X or Y can spend so lavishly when so many Indians are dying from cold or heat waves or from floods! You can add drought and epidemics etc. in their list. But today, why are they all silent on the exorbitant expenditure incurred on the aforesaid religious ceremonies? Has the HDI of India gone up? Are people not dying of hunger or from floods? If yes, then why this silence?

Further, look at the TV channels, which are flooded with serials based on religious themes. If religion is not directly present in them we will find either magical inputs in the serials or some superhuman power in the main characters of the serials. All these artificial traits, which are usually out of bounds of human power, are shown in the serials related to children. The young generation is being forced or lured by these fantasies. If TV channels are not sparing the kids, the so-called spiritual *swamis* are not sparing the literate, semi-literate, urban and semi-urban gentry. Their number is increasing by the day. The whole process is unique. The spiritual guru sits on an air-conditioned platform and gives his *pravachana* (sermon) and the poor followers sit on the ground in the hot summer and dance to his tune. Listen to these sermons in the *astha* channel and you will find what they preach. The worst part of these programmes is that even the dignitaries holding high offices of the land go and bow down in front of these so-called spiritual leaders publicly giving them the legitimacy. One can imagine the impact of such practice on the general public. Many a time the general public justify their acts by giving examples of these dignitaries.

Now the issue is: how can one utilise public office for personal faith or pleasure? The intellectuals should condemn this, but nobody does.

The aforesaid discourse of selective legitimisation of the Hindu religious ceremonies by the media and the intelligentsia has two dangerous implications. One, we are undermining the spirit of Article 51-A (h) of the Indian Constitution which assigns to the Indian citizen a fundamental duty "to develop the scientific temper, humanism and the spirit of inquiry and reform". Can we name even one event, except for the science conferences, which is open to professionals, which helps our general public to inculcate the scientific fervour? Not even one serial is shown which is really based on scientific knowledge. Instead, we have to look to specialised channels like National Geographic which is too heavy for children. Can't we teach science through entertainment? I think if we do that, we would be able to attract our younger generation towards science and technology which is the need of the hour in this era of globalisation and technology-driven information revolution.

Another fall-out of this mad race for religious functions, serials and spiritual leaders is that we are undermining the diversities within the Indian society. We are basically perpetuating only one aspect of the Indian culture and that too the great tradition of the upper strata of the Hindu society. Therefore, in the name of India we are putting foreward the Hindu minority worldview. For instance, the media has seldom or very rarely highlighted the celebrations of the Dalits and Tribals. Take the case of the fair at *Chaitya Bhoomi* in Nagpur, Maharashtra on *Dussehra* day. This fair is regularly held since 1956 when Ambedkar embraced Buddhism. Lakhs of Buddhists visit this place marked by a weeklong fair. A number of cultural events take place during this period specially relating to Dalit folk culture. Dalit literature, posters of Dalit icons, cassettes of Dalit songs, etc. are sold here giving it the shape of a big market. This fair and the celebration on this day depict the differences between the Dalits and Hindus. While Dalits/Buddhists celebrate this day as *'Dhamina Chakra Parivartan Divas'* and relate it to Buddha's social revolution in ancient India, the Hindus relate it to Rama's victory over Ravana.

Has anybody heard about the celebrations connected with Birsa Munda, the tribal leader, Jatra Oraon, who led the Tana Bhagat movement against the landlords in Chotanagpur? Very recently we heard so many intellectuals denouncing *tantra* as spreading superstition. But the same intellectuals were hell-bent on justifying *purohiti* and Astrology as a stream of knowledge. Why this dualism? Just because *tantra* challenges the Brahmanic supremacy and hegemony by permitting the lower strata of Hindu society to provide leadership? I am not trying to justify *tantrism*. But definitely I am trying to plead that if the whole society is submerged in the aforesaid religious ceremonies in the name of Indian culture and faith than why not recognise *tantrism* also as a stream of knowledge?

Having defined the negative impact of these ongoing religious ceremonies and their over-exposure in the media, I would like to put a word of caution to the general and conscious citizens. That is, the aforesaid phenomenon is giving rise to a specific consciousness among the Hindus that is more oriented towards physical symbols of the religion rather than its ethos. This consciousness suits the *Hindutva* forces, who are committed to project Hinduism as a monolithic whole and Indian society as a Hindu society. Therefore, they can easily use these religious ceremonies and consciousness for political purposes as and when they require it. Hence, we should evaluate the aforesaid process with a different perspective. By discarding them merely as a process of "saffronisation" will not do any good to our cause. We must explain to the masses what exactly lies beneath this process of "saffronisation" because to me, it is too sophisticated a term to explain the heinous and agonising existential realities which a nations suffers from.

Look at the symbols used till now to mobilise the Hindus—Temple, Cow, *trishul,* Sadhus, Dharm Sansad, *Ratha Yatras* etc. to quote just a few. To whom do these symbols belong? Of course, not to the Dalits, Tribals, or OBCs who have been cleverly co-opted into the "Hindu society". Rather, they belong to the so-called twice-born Hindus who are only a minority. It is this minority which has appropriated these symbols and projects itself as if it is speaking for a Majority though they do not allow the Dalits, Tribals and OBCs to hold religious offices at par with the twice-born castes. For example, can any Dalit, Tribal, or OBC become a Shankaracharya of any Matha or for that matter the head of the Sangha? It is different that the saffron forces use a few OBCs to lead the movement. But one should know that they are only functionaries following the dictates of their masters and if they digress from the path assigned to them they will be thrown out. The process of co-option of the non-twice-born castes is just a strategy to pitch them against the minorities so that they can do any illegitimate thing in the name of the "majority" and the minorities are also forced to live in perpetual fear because of this false projection of "Hindu Majority". Therefore, one is forced to conclude that "saffronisation" in reality is nothing but Brahminism which ultimately wants to keep its hegemony intact. So to prepare ourselves to face the challenges of the *Hindutva* forces we have to put brakes on these religious ceremonies and serials and also explain the real content and intent of the process of "saffronisation". One should not forget that religions give rise to solidarity and conflict both. It is up to us how we use them.

20

How Representative are Social Sciences in India?

The structural location of Dalits has placed them at a disadvantage while accessing education. In ancient India the structure of professional organisation of education was hereditary and hence closed to Dalits. Their educational status did not change during the medieval period either. During the British period, the State, the principal political party, the Congress and the civil society clandestinely worked to ensure the exclusion of Dalits from education.

The British had three reasons for not supporting education among Dalits *(Dr. Babasaheb Ambedkar Writings and Speeches Vol.2,* Education Department Government of Maharashtra, 1982, Mumbai). One, they thought "Education and Civilisation may descend from the higher to the inferior classes." Second, if education spreads among Dalits then, "nothing would prevent their aspiring to the highest offices open to native talent— to Judgeship, the Grand Jury." And third "if our *(British) system of education* first took root among them (Dalits), it would never spread further." The Congress party's aversion to Dalit education is reflected in the words of Annie Besant:

"The children of the depressed classes need, first of all, to be taught cleanliness outside decency of behaviour... Their bodies, at present are ill-odorous and foul with the liquor and strong smelling food out of which for generations they have been built up; it will need some generations of purer food and living to make their bodies fit to sit in the close neighbourhood of a school-room. Hunter Commission in 1882 revealed opposition of civil society towards the Dalit education by stating that upper castes all over the British India protested against imparting common education to Dalits along with the so-called upper castes." ("What Congress and Gandhi have done to the Untouchables", "Mr. Gandhi and the Emancipation of Untouchables", *Writings and Speeches, Vol. 9,* Education Department, Govt, of Maharashtra, 1991, Bombay, Against this, missionaries, the British Army, Phule and Ambedkar gave Dalits access to education. Ambedkar argued, "...Fortunately or unfortunately, the East India Company needed soldiers for their army.. .it could find none but the untouchables.... In the army... there prevailed the system of compulsory education for Indian soldiers ... The education received by the Untouchables in the army... gave them new vision and value". Trained in a Scottish missionary school, "in 1848, Phule, opened a school for girls and the low and untouchable castes in Pune,1853. Phule formed a society for increasing education among Mahar, Mangs and others. The society opened two schools for untouchables." Ambedkar on 8th July 1945 founded the 'People's Education Society' and then in 1946 he established Siddharth College of Arts and Science. In 1947, he submitted a memorandum "States and Minorities" to the Constituent Assembly for making special arrangements for the development of education among Dalits. Apart from other demands Ambedkar sought money for foreign education of the Scheduled Castes— a provision of Rs 10 lakhs annually. Later he introduced Article 46 in the Indian Constitution for the promotion of educational interests of the SCs and STs by the State.

In 1954, the Ministry of Education through chief secretaries of all the state governments made provision for 20 per cent reservation of seats in educational institutions for SCs and STs, which was changed to 15 per cent for SC and 7.5 for the STs in the year 1982. Nonetheless,.over 50 per cent of Dalits continue to be illiterate with a high drop out rate of 76.63 in standards I-X. No doubt literacy rate among Dalits is increasing at higher pace in comparison to the general castes yet the gap continues to be very high. This gap cannot be attributed to a lack of capabilities, but to the fact that Dalits have been late starters. Till 1978-79 only 5.9 per cent of Dalits could be admitted in engineering courses and a paltry 7.1 per cent were admitted to other higher educational subjects. Dalits have been excluded from the institutions of education not only as students but also as teachers. The scant presence of Dalit teachers in the ten central universities is a case in point. Out of 1457 Professors and 1438 Associate Professors/Readers, only 08 and 10 respectively belong to the Dalit community. At the level of Assistant Professor/Lecturers, even though 15 per cent of the seats are reserved for Dalits, only 51 out of 1578 posts, i.e. only 03 per cent, are appropriately filled. The condition of academic institutions in various IITs, state Universities and affiliated colleges is worse (see Sixth Report of National Commission for Scheduled Castes and Scheduled Tribes, 1999-2000 & 2000 - 2001, New Delhi).

In 1999 a professor, who has extensively worked on issues of caste, asked after my presentation at a seminar on 'Dalit Identity', "What is the difference between Jai Shri Ram and Jai Bheem, as both are religious symbols?" I explained to the learned professor that Jai Bheem referred not to Bheem of Mahabharata but the first name of Bheem Rao Ambedkar, now a greeting symbol of Dalits. This instance highlights the misunderstanding about Dalit issues in Social Sciences in India and how Dalits end up being represented as dirty, drunkard, devoid of any merit and good for nothing. They are reduced to an appendage of Indian society and sarcastically called *'Sarkari Brhamans'* or *'Sarkari Damad'*.

The Indian economists, on the one hand have failed to record the causes of relative poverty and inequality between Dalits and so-called upper castes. Neither have they taken note of the contribution made by Dalit labour in running the economy of the country: the midwife, landless agricultural labourers, sweepers, hide cleaners and factory workers, all belong to Dalit community. If we quantify the labour of these people then we will realise the real value of their labour. Why have Indian economists failed to recognise the contribution made by the Dalit labourers in building and running the Indian economy?

Moreover, economists apply the concept of 'class' to measure the economic status of the people. Though there is a general understanding that all poor are equal, it can be easily argued that the unique amalgam of caste and religion leads to a differential crystallisation of the class of poor of the so-called upper castes and of so-called lower caste. That is why we can argue that causes of poverty of Dalits and upper castes are also different as they depend on their structural location in the society. For instance, a penury stricken Rajput or Kshatriya will never plough his land even if he is financially broke, as he fears losing his caste. On the other hand if a poor Dalit wants to open an eatery shop in the country side he will not be allowed to do so. Similarly poor of different castes are treated differently. A poor Brahman begs and blesses the donor. On the contrary the cobbler who polishes the shoes and a sweeper who cleans excreta are treated with contempt. Caste affects the economic status, yet economists treat all poor as equals and formulate universal policies of poverty alleviation.

Political scientists have failed to record participation of Dalits in Indian politics. From casting their votes to democratic demonstrations, it is Dalits who respect Indian democracy the most. Hence they have a much larger agenda of nation building through the maintenance of Indian democracy. By establishing their own political parties Dalits have taken the Indian democracy much closer to the masses and have stopped Dalits from joining the Naxal movements by holding them in the democratic politics. The political scientists have failed to understand the basic nature of Dalit politics. Dalits politics is not a monolithic whole. It can be divided into dependent and independent Dalit political leadership. That is why they have not been able to appreciate the contributions of independent Dalit leadership like Independent Labour Party, Scheduled Caste Federation, Republican Party of India, Dalit Panthers, Bahujan Samaj Party etc. On the other hand political scientists have stigmatised Dalit politics as divisive and failed to study the limitations of instruments of— democracy, which has proved detrimental to the development of Dalit movement.

Sociologist Kathleen Gough has argued that there is chasm between the cultures of untouchables and Brahmins ("Brahmin Kinship in Tamil village", *American Anthropologist, 1956).* According to her, there is a tacit opposition between the inhibiting 'culture' of the Brahmins and the free 'nature' of the untouchables. Both differ in their attitudes towards sexuality and aggression towards elders and peers. Engaged in the practical business of earning a living through manual labour, the low castes care more for health and prosperity in this life. T K Oommen argues that, "There has been a cognitive black-out in Indian social science, until recently, as far as knowledge regarding the life-world of Dalitbahujans. The fact that the life-styles of upper castes and Dalitbhujans vary dramatically in terms of food habits, worship patterns or gender relations is tacitly acknowledged. But instead of squarely recognising these variations and explaining why they exist, the dominant tendency in Indian Sociology, at least until recently, has been to suggest that the Dalitbahujans are abandoning their way of life in favour of the life-styles of caste Hindus." (*Understanding the Indian Society: The Relevance of Perspective from below,* Department of Sociology, University of Pune, 2001). Further, Indian Sociologists have not done quantitative or qualitative analysis of the processes of exclusion and deprivation of the Dalits in Indian Society in general and 'Hindu social order' in particular. How has it resulted in loss of cultural capital and hence the subjugation of Dalits? The exclusion of the Dalits from the modem institutions of democracy i.e. Parliament, Bureaucracy, Judiciary, Media etc is not there.

Ankersmit argues (in Keith Jenkins's *On 'What is History': From Carr and Elton to Rorty and White,* Routledge, 1995, London and New York) that history text consists of many individual statements made by historians after careful selection. The result is that a certain 'picture of the past'—an icon—is fabricated. In the Indian context, Ranjit Guha noted this selectiveness of Indian Historians. He argues that, "The historiography of Indian nationalism has for a long time been dominated by elitism... elitism shares the prejudice that the making of the Indian nation and the development of the consciousness- nationalism is exclusively elite achievement... The history of Indian nationalism is thus written up as a sort of spiritual biography of the Indian elite." (*Subaltern Studies-I, Writings on South Asian History and Society,* OUP, Delhi). Similarly Sumit Sarkar has also argued that this "historiographical elision has been most powerful in respect of caste" (*Writing Social History,* OUP, 2005, New Delhi). In her book, *Beyond the Four Varnas: The Untouchables in India,* Prabhati Mukherjee exposes the "hesitation and reluctance ... among Indologists and historians to study the past history of the untouchable."

Historians blacked out the Dalits and their contributions in the annals of Indian History. The references are few and far between. For instance., Stephen Cohen's *The Indian Army, Its Contribution to the Development of a Nation (OUP, 2004, Delhi) makes mentions of Chamar and Regiment*: "... Mahars, an untouchable caste of present-day Maharashtra... were a sizeable portion of the armies of the Mahratta chieftain Shivaji... Heavily recruited in the pre-mutiny years, the Mahars constituted a fifth to a quarter of the entire Bombay Army."

Most mischievious has been the wilful censoring of Ambedkar's historical role; with historians reducing him to the status of a mere Dalit leader. At their most generous, a few of the 'progressives' concede him the status of a Constitution maker. In the process historians have deliberately forgotten Ambedkar's role as a nation builder. So extreme was the negation of these social reformers that Dalit politics led by Kanshi Ram had to construct the pantheon of Dalit leaders, which included Jotiba Phule, Narayana Guru Swamy, Sahuji Maharaj, EV Ramaswamy Naicker Periyar and Ambedkar.

One would have expected the psychologists to understand the construction of consciousness of Dalits and different groups within them. For instance, how the specific life experiences of Dalit women—their vulnerability to the triple exploitation of class, gender and caste—as against women in general creates a specific Dalit female consciousness. Dalit activists assert that the rape of Dalit women is not only a brutal sexual act but is also mediated through their caste location. If we understand the psychology of Dalits then we will be able to understand the difficulties faced by them in the process of their integration in the mainstream of society.

Indian literature largely excludes Dalit issues. M N Wankhede notes that, "a Marathi writer's understanding of life is restricted by his birth and upbringing in a particular caste and class and he is unable to come out of his own little pond. He has never seen that outside there is a vast world—a suffering, distressed, struggling, howling world, burning with anger from within like a prairie fire." ("Friends, the day of irresponsible writers is over", in Arjun Dangle (ed.) *Poisoned bread,* Orient Longman, 1992, New Delhi). Dalits were forced to write their own experiences and in the 1960s Dalit literature movement in Maharashtra was born.

Usage of politically incorrect language can be another basis of exclusion. Social scientists continue to deploy stigmatised categories like 'lower castes', 'exterior castes', 'untouchables', 'harijans' etc. for the Dalits, whereas the usual references to the so-called upper castes are couched in more refined language: 'twice born', *'dvija'* etc. This is unpardonable, especially since recent years have seen an impetus for politically correct language for erstwhile stigmatised communities: 'blacks' for 'negroes', 'sex-workers' for 'prostitutes' and so on. However, Indian social scientists carry on regardless.

It is important to seek the reasons for the exclusion of Dalit issues from Indian Social Sciences. We might be reasonable in asking how many leading social scientists have researched in Dalit localities; and how many studies have taken place from the perspectives of Dalits to understand the basic.

21

Literature and Self Representation: A Case of Dalits

This paper is a humble attempt to record how Babasaheb Ambedkar and Dalit assertion has been represented in the popular Hindi writings, especially in the Hindi Poems written by the Dalits themselves and autobiographies. We have tried here to record how Babasaheb Ambedkar and his writings have influenced the lives of the millions of Dalits in many different ways. Babasheb Ambedkar has become instrument in bringing about change in the lives of Individual Dalits and group of Dalits alike? How deeply has Ambedkar influenced consciousness of millions of Dalits, which is depicted in their compositions, not only through his persona but also through his writings has been recorded in the paper? An attempt has been made here to probe how Dalits have tried to understand on the one hand the basic structures of Indian society like-caste and village. On the other hand how have they made an attempt to understand the cultural values like equality, fraternity, power etc. through the writings of Ambedkar. In other words, we have tried to capture the fact how Ambedkar becomes an agency of social change and assertion fact by analysing different compositions of Dalits. The paper briefly touches towards the end of the paper the various types of compositions which have questioned the sanctity of the sacred texts of Hindu social order.

Introduction

Let us accept the fact that Babasaheb Ambedkar has been victim of the process of reductionism. In this the mainstream media, academia and intelligentsia has played a dominant role. This whole process has reduced him to the status of 'a Dalit Leader'. Some progressive intellectuals have at the most called him 'Chief Architect of the Indian Constitution'. In turn his contributions in the realm of understanding individual, caste, Hindu social order, Problems of Hindu Women and Indian minorities etc. in a world his contribution to the process of nation building from an alternative perspective has been wilfully blacked out. Thanks to the Dalit movement led by the Dalit themselves, which has given visibility to Babasaheb Ambedkar. This has forced the mainstream academia to nominally include Ambedkar in the subject matter of social sciences.

It is not only social sciences which have blacked out Ambedkar, literature considered to be the mirror of society of that time has also not given space to Ambedkar. A fact highlighted eloquently by Gauri Vishwanathan. She writes, "The privileging of Gandhi as an emblem of nonpartisan feeling has, as its inverse, the demonisation of Ambedkar as a purveyor of sectarian politics. The view that, "the national hagiography in India has rarely conceded a space for Ambedkar alongside Gandhi" is born out by the amazing excision of Ambedkar from several well known literary works about untouchability. One of the best known of these, Mulk Raj Anand's untouchable (1935), is written in the time period of Ambedkar's quarrels with Gandhi over the communal award and published inexactly the same year as Ambedkar's decision to convert" (Visvanathan 2001:2000).

Ambedkar's absence from the novel is all the more important to note because, "The novel is said to have educated the conscience of its English readers about the moral evils of assigning ritual pollution to untouchables and rendering them outsiders, but it makes no mention of Ambedkar at all. Instead the novel celebrates Gandhi as the savior of the untouchables" (Visvanathan 2001:220). Therefore Vishvanathan concludes, "Anand's narrative alienates and marginalises the assertion Dalit will, and totally ignores the debate initiated by Ambedkar on the same issue *(ibid)*. How Ambedkar has been excluded from school texts has been highlighted by Om Prakash Valmiki in his autobiography 'Jootha' when he narrates that he new Gandhi, Tagore, Subash, Chandra Shekhar Azad etc. and had 12 years of school education but no one has ever mentioned name of Ambedkar. I think it is a universal experience of every Dalit youth, who is denied the exposure to Ambedkar on the other hand.

Ambedkar has not been excluded from the curriculums of higher texts alone, he has been excluded from the school texts as well. This fact has been highlighted by Om Prakash Valmiki in his autobiography 'Joothan'. He has narrated that though he spent 13 years in a school and came to know many Indian leaders from Gandhi to Sarvakar but could never heard the name of Ambedkar. I think it is a universal fact as far as Dalit youths are concerned because the Institutional education never ever has a lesson on Ambedkar and they do not come to know about him. What a pity. Dalit youths grow without any Icon hailing from their own community.

Dalit Literary Representation of Ambedkar

Away from the exclusion of Ambedkar from the mainstream literature, the Dalits have written ocean of literature in most of the Indian language keeping Baba Saheb Ambedkar at the center of their creative composition. Ambedkar gets a mention in every types of composition of Dalits whether it is prose, poetry or autobiography written by a Dalit. That is why great Buddhist scholar used to say:

> "People want to forget Gandhi but the government never allows to forget him. Government wants to forget Ambedkar but people never all to forget him"

In fact he has been hailed as the harbinger of social change in the society at large and Dalit society in particular. He has been accepted as unchallenged icon who has made difference in the lives of millions of unsung and un-notices Dalits. Here I will restrict my self to Hindi poems and other forms of Dalit literature in Hindi. The persona of Ambedkar is such that every conscious or unconscious Dalits want to passes him. Look at this couplet, which has become a universal formulation and any body can fit his name in it to associate himself with Ambedkar. The couplet goes on to say:

Every kid belongs to Bheem (*Bachha Bachha Bheem Ka)*
Of Vivek Kumar's Team (*Vivek Kumar Ki team Ka*)

Any body can fill his or her name to complete the couplet. Now this formulation is becoming more and more popular in civil society also though earlier it was very among the political parties in the north India from locale to national.

Breaking the stereotypes:

Dalits have been stigmatised with a stereotype images like dirty, drunker, devoid of merit. But dalits have tried to break this stereotype images by 'carving' out an omnipotent image of Babasaheb. Look at this poem 'Baba Mahan' or 'Baba the Great' by anonymous writer which has become part of public memory and can be heard in almost every Dalit public meeting or cultural gatherings:

Unanimous

Words to Dumb (Gungo Ko Jubari)

Ears to deaf (*Bahron Ko Kaan*)

Respect to Dalits (Dalkiton Ko Sammari) Equal rights to women Alms of husband to Kastoorba Alms of life to Gandhi Constitution to India

Knowledge of Buddhist philosophy to the world Such was Baba the great!

(Mahilaon Ko Adhikar Samari) (Kastoorba Ko Pad Daan)

(Gandhi Ko Praan Daan)

(Bhart Ko Samvidhan)

(Vishva Ko Baudh Darshan Ka Gy an) (.Aise The Baba Mahan)

(Translated by Vivek Kumar from Hindi)

Now let us see how Ambedkar has been received by Individual Dalits. How is he revered by the Dalits as an icon? Here again let us look at some of the Poems, which have added even theoretical formulations like Revolution, equality, Nationalism etc. This is a poem by Sudesh Tanvar published in 'Ambedkar in India', in March-April 2002 issue, a monthly magazine published from Lucknow, Uttar Pradesh regularly since 1999. Look at the poem:

Ambedkar

Ambedkar is fire of
Hearth is light of lamp
is fire of revolution
Ambedkar
is ointment of affection is
ocean of compassion is path
of equality Ambedkar
is philosophy of unity is
quintessence of Nationalism is

Religion of Humanity

(Translated by Vivek Kumar)

These adjectives or formulations assume different meaning for Dalits as we take into account the fact that Dalits were deprived of all these. The fire in the earth and light in the lamp was not there for them or it was rarity because of poverty. Then they were denied of humane gestures like affection, comparison and equality because they were not treated as human beings. And therefore Dalits look these elements in Ambedkar. There is expectation from him because he is responsible for ensuring them in the constitution and through his movement. And then the writer goes from particular to universal. He argues that Ambedkar has universal values too; these are unity, Nationalism and humanism. Humanism is specifically related to Buddhism.

Understanding the Basic Structures of Indian Society through Ambedkar

Dalits were motivated to write because they have read Ambedkar sometimes consciously and unconsciously. The writings of Ambedkar left so deep imprint on their consciousness that they composed poems through his writings. Through these compositions these writers have tried to understand on the one hand basic structures like-Caste and village of the Hindu society and on the other hand they have also tried to understand its cultural elements like-religion, untouchability, boycott, freedom, fraternity. In fact these facts have been directly drawn from his essays like-Annihilation of Caste, Outside the Fold. Away from Hindus, Hindus and want of public conscience', The Hindu social order: Its essential principles etc.

Let us see how a Dalit writer, tries to understand the basic structure of caste through Ambedkar's writing 'Annihilation of caste'.

Jati (Caste)

Caste has killed the morale of the Public

and has destroyed the sentiments of the religion ..

what is the caste of a Hindu?

Is it its people?

Is it its responsibilities?

His loyalty lies only towards his Caste

Qualities are subject to Caste

There is no reward to competence

No appreciation for the competent

No Hindu will ever accept
The leadership of a great man (Except a saint)
He will accept
Only the leadership of a person of his caste
A Brahmin will follow only a Brahmin leader.
A Kayastha will follow only a Kayastha leader.
Competence is praiseworthy
If he is a member of the high caste
Important is neither competence, non-incompetence
Important is the caste
The love fur caste only.
Does't it makes the Hindu a traitor?

Let us understand the Indian village through the Ambedkar's writing via a Dalit Poet. Here it is necessary to understand the structure of Indian village because this gives an alternative perspective. Most of the writings on Indian village are influenced by 'Charls Metchalf version of 'Indian Villages as Republics' or Gandhi's version of 'Gram Swaraj'. Because of these versions Indian village is eulogised and the critical understanding of Indian village does not exist. Even Indian Anthropologists and Sociologists have failed to carry out a study of Indian village from the locale where the Dalits live. Though they have studied the Indian village but it has been from upper caste perspective and also they lived with the upper castes while they were carrying out their research. That is what Sociologists Andre Beteille wrote, "I did my field work in Sripuram while living with the people as one among them. I was permitted to live in the *agraharam*, in a Brahmin house-a privilege ...I dined with the Brahmins and had access to most of their houses.. .1 was identified with the Brahmins by my dress, my appearance, and the fact that I lived in on their houses...I soon discovered that it made me suspect in the eyes of the Non-Brahmins and Adi-Dravidas...My access to these groups was, therefore, far more limited than to the Brahmins. I went to their streets to elicit answers to specific questions. I was not able to move with them freely as with Brahmins. Among the Adi-Dravidas there was an additional difficulty...My visits to an Adi-Dravida streets had...to be made discreetly... Consequently my data for the Adi-Dravidas and also to some extent for the Non-Brahmins are of a poorer quality than for the Brahmins. Had I lived with the Adi-Dravidas this study this study would perhaps have had a different focus. A somewhat different picture of Sripuram" (Beteille 1971 9-10). Therefore we should understand the version of village given by Ambedkar because possibly this is the first time the reality of Indian village was being so thoroughly exposed from insider's perspective:

Village

The Indian Hindu Village is known as a republic

And they are Proud

On its internal structure

In which there is

No democracy,

No equality

No fraternity.

This is a republic of high castes for high castes

For untouchables, it is the imperialism of the Hindus.

It is a colony

For the exploitation of the untouchables

Where there are no rights for the untouchables.

Services, with timeless patience and passivity

Is the take of the untouchables in this village

Either they have to do or die.

How polluted is this Hindu slaughter house

This is a fact that can't be challenged

For this fact is its truth. (From Outside the Fold)

So this is the reality of Hindu Village a reality which was never revealed before. I think social scientists can learn from this composition if they want to give the real picture of the Indian village. Let us see how does a Hindu social order function? This poem again has been extracted from Babasaheb,s writings on Village.

Does the Hindu social system Recognise fraternity?

Christian and Muslims believe

That all human beings are the creations of God.

But according to the Hindu belief God, from different part of his body Has, created different human beings.

Thus, from his mouth have been created the Brahmins...

And Kshtriyas from his arms

Vaishyas have been created from his stomach

And Shudra from his feet

Hence, no fraternity is there

Between Brahmins and kshatriyas

Between kshatriyas and vaishyas

Between vaishyas and Brahmins

Between Shudras and Brahmins

From a different father

(From 'The Hindu social order: Its essential principles, Ambedkar: 1987).

What about necessity of power for the Dalits. There are types of power and which type of power is essential for the Dalits has also been discussed in the poem.

Satta (Power).

It is Power alone

Which makes one the ruler over other.

Its is power alone

That is required to eliminate power.

The ethical use of power

Can be a problem

But without the power of one, the power of other cannot be destroyed.

Power can have economic character or political

Labourers have control over the economic power,

Which lies in strikes.

Untouchables also come under the category of labourers

But they are dispossessed of any economic power

Hence, the untouchables should have political power

Which will, of course, be less

Than the all-pervasive socio-economic power of the Hindus.

The untouchables should remember

That their political power shall be of no use

If they depend upon Hindus for their representation

Because, the political life of Hindus breeds

On discrimination against untouchables

For their own socio-eco benefits ('A warning to the untouchables')

Babasaheb becomes the Agency of Change

An icon who is revered by he Dalits, Babasaheb is held own who shows the path for change. From individuals to group he has affected the life of Dalits in number of ways. Number of writers have accepted the fact how Babasaheb has changed their life. D.R. Jatav in his autobiography powerfully explains how deeply he was influenced by Babasaheb's life and wanted to become like him. And he wanted to take a Ph.D degree just because Doctor' should be added in front of his name like Babasaheb. He writes, "I had heard name of Babasaheb Dr. Ambedkar, in my village, from an illiterate man. He used to say that Bombay's will come to free all of us from the scholar of social slavery... Pandit Motilal (a teacher) presented me a book named 'Dr. Ambedkar-life and mission' written by Dhananjay Keer. Dr. Babasaheb Ambedkar's life-story inspired and encouraged me...resultantly desire to do a part graduate become strong.... April 1957 I passed M.A... Actually: after reading and analysing Dr. Ambedkar's life, mission and his writings, I had decided to do a Ph.D like him. (Jatav 2002: 21-27).

Similarly, Omprakash Valmiki in his autobiography reveals how Ambedkar's reading has changed his thought process and consciousness. He writes, "As I was flipping its pages, Hemal said, 'You must read this book'. The name of the book was Dr. Ambedkar: A Biography, its author was Chandrika Prasad Jigyasee. Ambedkar was an unknown entity to me then. I know about Gandhi, Nehru, Patel, Rajendra Prasad, Vivekanand, Tagore... Savarkar and so on, but was completely ignorant about Dr. Ambedkar... I asked Hemal, 'who is this Ambedkar?' 'We' talk after you have finished the book'...there was nothing special in the opening pages. But-the further I went into the book, I felt as though a new chapter about life was being unfurled before me. A chapter about which I had known nothing. Dr. Ambedkar's life-long struggle had shaken me up. I spent many days and nights in great turmoil. The restlessness inside me had increased. My stone-like silence had suddenly begun to melt. I proceeded to read all Ambedkar's books that I found in the library... My reading of these books had awakened my consciousness. These books had given voice to my muteness. It was during this time in my life when an anti-establishment consciousness became strong in me" (Valmiki 2003: 71-72).

In the same vein Biharilal Harit argues that Bheem flag a symbol of assertion will bring for reaching changes in the society by securing different rights to Dalits and frustrating the people involved in the selfish law of the land:

Hail bheem flag will secure lost rights; Hail bheem flag will instigate untouchability; Hail bheem flag will make remember Pride.

Hail bheem flag will wake the whole community Hail bheem flag will frustrate the selfish.

(Translated by Vivek Kumar from *Harit*: 2006)

In his songs Ramesh chandra Buddha has shown what Ambedkar has said about changing the religion. Basically this is a process of deconstruction of established institutions of Hindu Social Order. In turn it is construction of a new identity and symbol for the Dalits. This song has been translated and incorporated in the book Multiple Marginalities. The author goes on to say:

Embrace the religion of Buddha, This is what Ambedkar said.

Leave: Ram and Krishna Brahma and Vishnu Gauri and Ganesh

For they serve the purpose of exploiters,

Follow the religion of Buddha And make your life meaningful with education organisation and the path of struggle.

In another song he shows his optimism how change is going to where with the help of Babasaheb Ambedkar showing the path. In this song again the composer denounces the symbols of Hindu Social Order. This song has also been incorporated in the book Multiple Marginalities:

We did not get freedom

From the Vedas and Puranas of the Hindu.

The poor have got the light,

From the sacrifices of Baba

and the missionaries of Ambedkar Through the fire in them.

A new revolution is seen being born

In every corner of India.

It is interesting to note here even if the authors are looking the elements of change in other Dalit poets, even they have compared those writings with Ambedkar's writing for instance Dharamveer in his analysis of saint poet Ravi Das versus of change compared it with Babasaheb Ambedkar's 'Annihilation of Caste'

There is caste within caste within Caste like the leaves of Banana Ravidas says there cannot be unity till caste is annihilated.

Every one is lost in the question of caste this has finished humanity

Dharamveer calls these couplets as the basic trust of 'Annihilation of caste', which of course is document of change published by Babasaheb Ambedkar.

Ambedkar and Dalit Assertion through Literature

Assertion is to claim what ever is legitimately due to the person or the group. It is very not to hurt others or usurp what is due for others. Dalits want to claim their space through erecting the statues of their icons. But this is not liked by the so-called upper castes and they discrete these statues. But Dalits do not take things lying; they get angry if their symbol is desecrated. But their anger is beyond control if Babasaheb Ambedkar's statue is disrespected or desecrated. Dalit assertion in this context can be seen as a marker of social change. They do not look in the mood of petition rather thy protest. The writer establishes that what does Ambedkar stand for nation and then for Dalits.

Whom you are Insulting?

Whom you are insulting?

Who has given matchless Constitution to you

Who has lit the flame of Humanity

Who talked about Human rights

You are garlanding shoes thinking

Ambedkar's statue

It is not statue of Ambedkar only

Symbol of honor of Dalits

Symbol of Pride of Dalits

Symbol of Dalit Identity
Is symbol of Humanity.
Dalits are not going to be mute now
Humanists will not keep quite
The movement will come as earthquake
Now rebellion will rise
Property of the nation will be destroyed
Then Nation will be destructed.

(Translated by Vivek Kumar from Prasad, 2005: pp. 90-91).

Assertion and Questioning the Sacred Texts of Hindu Social Order

It was Ambedkar who motivated Dalits to question the sacred texts of Hindu social order (Ambedkar 1979). In his essays 'Riddles of Hinduism' Ambedkar (1988) has evaluated the characters of Heroes of Ramayan and Mahabharat that is of Rama and Krishna (the two great heroes and icons of Hindus). Taking clue from him Dalits have written many books in Hindi for questioning the basic values enshrined in it. A collection of compositions '*Bhartiya Savidhan Baman Valmiki Ramayan*' (Indian Constitution versus *Valmiki Ramayan*), *'Bhartiya Savidhan Baman Manusriti* (Indian Constitution versus *Manusmriti), 'Bhartiya Savidhan Baman Mahabharat* (Indian Constitution versus *Mahabharat*), *Ramyan Ke Pramanikta* (Authenticity of *Ramayan*), *Mahabharat Ke Pramanikta* (Authenticity of *Mahabharat*), *Ramayan Ke Mahapatra* (Heros of Ramayan), *Mahabharat Ke Mahapatra* (Heroes of Mahabharat), and *Bhartiya Sanvidhan Banam Hindu Sahitya* (Indian Constitution versus Hindu Literature) have been written by K.M. Sant of Uttar Pradresh. His basic argument is that Caste-ism, Brahmanism, Feudalism have grown because of State power and the Hindu social order has provided strength to these values.

The author exposes these systems based on inequality and hatred and compares with the egalitarian values like-equality, liberty, and fraternity enshrined in Indian Constitution. That is why he compares all the Hindu literature with the Indian Constitution and takes pride in it because it has been written by none other than Babasaheb Ambedkar. In reality these books have created lots of discomfort among the believers. And has hurt the feelings of the followers of 'political Hindutwa' in the society at large. The author has been charged by the High Court of Madhya Pradesh for his composition is testimony to the above fact. Now the author is fighting a case in the court of law. But his writings have given enough material to Dalits to question the authenticity of these sacred texts of the Hindu Social order. People further wonder whether these are only cooked stories or these have occurred in reality. The whole exercise has deconstructed and reconstructed many myths about these caste Hindu texts and heroes.

Conclusion

In this manner we can see the range of imagination, creativity and reflectivity of Dalits in their composition, which emerges out of their relationship with Babasaheb Ambedkar. There composition are full of imagination and innovation and reflect their confidence and assertion. They have not only produced knowledge they have tried to theorise and philosophies their thoughts and cognitive thinking. In the process Dalits used a vocabulary, which has conceptual categories used in mainstream academia. Further, Dalits with their writings associated with Ambedkar have tried to construct and deconstruct number of identities and symbols which was not possible earlier. Through this they have successfully established new center for them it is of course Babasaheb.

References

Ambedkar, B.R., Annihilation of Caste (1923-96) In Dr. Babasaheb Ambedkar Writings and Speeches Vol. 1. Education Department, Government of Maharashtra Mumbai, 1979.

_____, 'The Hindu Social Order: Its Essential Principles' (pp. 95-115), In Dr. Babasaheb Ambedkar Writings and Speeches, Vol. 3. Education Department, Government of Maharashtra, Mumbai, 1987.

Riddles of Hinduism, in Dr. Babasaheb Ambedkar Writings and Speeches, Vol. 5, Education Department, Government of Mharashtra, Mumbai, 1988.

_____1989, 'Out Side The Fold' (pp. 19-26) in Dr. Babasaheb Ambedkar Writings and Speeches Vol. 5, Education Department, Government of Maharashtra, Mumbai.

Beteille, Andre, 1971, Caste, Class, and Power-Changing patterns of Stratification in a Tanjore Village, University of California Press, Berkly.

Bharti, Kaval, Dr. Ambedkar Ki Kavitayen (Poems of Dr. Ambedkar) in Badri Naraian (eds.) Multiple Marginalities, Manohar Publications, New Delhi, 2004, (pp. 192-237).

Dharmveer, Guru Ravidas, Samta Prkashan, Delhi, (2003), (p. 20).

Jatav, D.R., Mera Safar Meri Manzil: Ek Atmakatha (My Journey My

Destination an Autobiography) Samata Sahitya Sadan, Jaipur, 2002, (pp. 21-27).

Prasad, Satrughna, Agnishikha, Navabharta Prakashan, 2005 (pp. 90-91).

Tanwar, Sudesh, 'Ambedkar In India', in March-April, Lucknow, U.P. 2002.

Valmiki, Om Prakash, Joothan: A Dalit's Life, Translated from the Hindi by Arun Prabha Mukherjee, Samya, Calcutta, 2003, (pp. 71-71).

Veeni Lai Harit, Sheoraj Singh Bechain's Hindi Dalit Sahitya: Ek Prasthbhoomi, in, Devendra Chaube (eds.) Hindi Dalit Sahitya Ka Maya Saundrya Sashtra, 2006 (p. 144).

PART-V: DEMOCRACY AND DEVELOPMENT

22

Social Development and Planning in Developing Countries

This chapter explores India's efforts at social development through various policies since the 1950s, including the series of five-year plans. Reviewing India's social development efforts reveals how a relatively young nation—emerging from the yoke of colonialism, cultural heterogeneity, religious pluralism, and caste hierarchy—evolves an independent model of "mixed economy" and attempts to meet the dual challenge of incorporating its excluded groups and modernisation.

Introduction

Social development policy and planning in India emerged within a specific sociopolitical context. The colonial legacy, overwhelming proportion of rural population, high levels of poverty, high birth and death rates, and rampant illiteracy characterised Indian society. The rigid social order with its family, caste, religion, and village ties was not open to any sudden changes. Furthermore, India's partition took away the energy and resources meant to be put toward developmental activities. It is in this context that the societal goals of planning have emerged in India. The leaders of independent India included not only economic aspects of planning, but also noneconomic aspects such as health, education, population control, political participation, and so on. India's emphasis is on sociocultural, not merely economic development.

Policy Formulation and Dominance of Political Leaders

According to Arjun Sengupta (2001, pp. 121-161), "The question relating to policy making, that is, whether it is relevant or not, the motivation behind it, and so on, are normally answered not exactly by what was actually happening in the country. They depend also on the perceptions on development of political decision makers who were forming the policies. Economic policy making is basically derived from the politics of policy making and the politics of policy making is derived from the political leaders' view of the kind of policies that will serve their ends." For instance, Pandit Jawaharlal Nehru, the first prime minister of India, dominated planning policy in India. The three basic tenets of his policy were industrialisation, self-reliance, and Socialism. According to Sengupta (2001), "Industrialisation was Nehru's basic approach to India's transformation. Nehru articulated this approach from his understanding of history in general and India's history in particular, based on the national movement for independence. From the very beginning the urge to develop the living condition of the poor, the deprived was linked to independence. . . . Nehru believed that industrialisation . . . ensured independence and it benefited the poor" (p. 123). He also believed that industrialisation will lead to modernisation of the country. And by "industrialisation," he meant heavy industrialisation and not small-scale or cottage industries. He was referring to a factory system that uses capital intensively, that uses machinery equipment and modern technology, which will help to modernise India (Sengupta, 2001).

Indira Gandhi was of the opinion that by identifying oneself with the national movement, the poor and deprived can remain in power (Sengupta, 2001, p. 129). She took steps against princely states, effected nationalisation of banks and nationalisation of coal, then introduced the antipoverty programme, the "Twenty Point Programme." After 1980, when she returned to power, she tried to reform the economy. According to Sengupta (2001, p. 132), she tried to liberalise the economy, but this liberalisation was to be achieved in such a manner that she would not be accused of deviating from her commitment to the poor or compromising the agenda set during the national movement. Liberalisation in this context meant relaxing constraints of controls of license raj. In other words, licensing is probably done only for ten to fifteen big investments by big business houses (Sengupta, 2001, p. 132).

History of Planning in India

The goals of development are enshrined in the Constitution of India. The constitution aims to build a secular and democratic polity means a social order that generates equality, liberty, and justice to every individual, irrespective of caste, race, gender, and place of residence. Specifically, planning in India derives its objectives; social premises from directive principles of state policy enshrin in the constitution. In order to achieve these goals or directives, government devised an institutional mechanism and mobilised the human and material resources. Here, public and private sectors viewed as complementary. The private sector covers not only organise industry, but also small-scale industries such as agriculture, housing and construction. Although in the past economic planning envisage, a growing public sector with massive investments in basic industries, the emphasis on the public sector is less pronounced. The planning commission was set up in 1950 to prepare the blueprint of development, taking an overall view of the needs and resources of the country. The planning commission has stated the following for development: "To initiate a process of development which will be living standards and open out to the people new opportunities for richer and more varied life" (Government of India, 1952).

Dubashis (1987, pp. 37-38) describes India's approach to planning the following manner:

(a) Indian plans are comprehensive and balanced and include both public and private investment. Growth of all sectors of the economy is encouraged.

(b) The Indian approach can be called democratic planning, different from totalitarian planning. In democratic planning, people regularly and effectively organise and develop through active participation. In totalitarian planning, people's participation is not encouraged.

(c) India's approach to planning is aimed at setting up a socialistic pattern of society. Both economic and social aspects of development are considered.

(d) India's approach to development has strived to combine the economic, technological, human, and institutional components of development. For instance, attention has been paid to improvement of technology adopted by village and cottage industries.

(e) India's approach to planning tries to reconcile planning with democracy and increased production with equitable distribution. It upholds both human values and the pursuit of material advancement.

Highlights of India's Five-Year Plans

In India, each five-year plan has had a different emphasis and objectives, therefore it is necessary to evaluate each plan individually to understand the direction of planning in India. There have been ten five-year plans in India, and each of them has been unique in the spheres of development. For instance, the first five-year plan (1951-1956) had twin objectives. One was to correct the disequilibrium in the economy caused by World War II and the partition of the country, and the second was to initiate a process of balanced development. Similarly, the second five-year plan (1956-1957 to 1960-1961) sought to promote the establishment of Socialism in India. This form of development would envisage social gains and establishment of greater equality in income across the population. The third five-year plan (1961-1962 to 1965-1966) aimed at self-sustained growth. The fourth five-year plan (1969-1970 to 1973-1974) was designed to raise the standard of living of the people through programmes designed to promote equality and justice. Between the years 1966 and 1969, three annual plans were formulated. The fifth five-year plan (1974-1975 to 1977-1978) emphasised achievement of self-reliance and adopted measures for raising the consumption in people living below the poverty line. The sixth five-year plan (1980-1981 to 1984-1985) emphasised eradication of poverty after assessing the achievements and failures of previous plans. The seventh five-year plan (1985-1986 to 1989-1990) focused on food-grain production, employment opportunities, self-reliance, and social justice (Government of India, 1988).

Planning for Socio-cultural Development

The schemes of development in this chapter demonstrate how the principles of Socialism, equality, social justice, and democracy have been incorporated into assorted development schemes (table).

Social Development of Scheduled Castes: A Case Study

Dalits, India's ex-untouchables, also referred to as the Scheduled Castes, account for 16.3 per cent of India's total population, according to the 2001 census (Premi, 2006). Historically, Dalits have been subjected to various kinds of social discrimination and economic deprivation. Cumulative deprivation suffered by the Dalits is tacitly supported by the Hindu social order, which takes refuge in its sacred texts to justify the seclusion of one-fourth of the Indian population. This is why Scheduled Castes continue to have such bad socioeconomic indicators (see Table 1). It is true that structurally Scheduled Castes were forced to live outside the main living area in the villages and were not allowed to practice an occupation of their own choice. If anyone attempted to do so, he or she was punished by caste and village *panchayats.*

Table 1: Schemes of Development in India

Protective Discrimination	*Rural Development*
1. Scheduled Castes 2. Scheduled Tribes 3. Women	1. Community development programmes 2. *Panchayat* raj institutions with 73rd and 74th constitutional amendment 3. Cooperatives
Antipoverty Programmes	*Urban Development Programme*
1. Training Rural Youth for Self Employment (TRYSEM) 2. Integrated Rural Development Programme (IRDP) 3. National Rural Employment Programme (NREP) 4. Jawahar Gram Samridhi Yojana (JGSY; earlier Jawahar Rozgar Yojana [JRY]) 5. Indira Awas Yojana (IAY) 6. Mahatma Gandhi National Rural Employment Guarantee Scheme (MGNREGP)	1. Slum clearance 2. Housing for poor 3. Small-scale industries

Source: Government of India (n.d.).

Protective Discrimination

To ameliorate the Dalits' condition, the Indian constitution under Article 16 emphasised equality and a policy of protective discrimination better known as the policy of reservation. Reservation has been provided for the Dalits since India's independence in three areas: political reservation of seats in parliament (Lok Sabha) and state assemblies (state legislatures), urban, and rural local bodies; in public jobs, central and state services, public sectors, banking sector, and the insurance sector; and in school and college admission and related facilities in educational institutions. This policy has produced significant results, though the evaluation of its precise impact on the Dalits in the country is over-due. Political reservation under Articles 330 and 332 (which were to (lapse after ten years after the commencement of the constitution have been extended till 2010) and 243-D and 243-t, which provide reservation in rural and urban local bodies, have been fully implemented the reservations in the central and state governments have been not according to the allotted quotas of jobs for the Dalits under Article 3 of the constitution, which has no time stipulation (see Table 2).

Table 2

S. No.	*Names of the States*	*Population (2001)*	*Literate Population (2001)*	*(1993-1994)*	*(1990-1991)*
1.	Andhra Pradesh	16.2	53.5	34.92	86.00
2.	Arunachal Pradesh	0.6	67.6	—	—
3.	Assam	6.9	66.8	29.86	62.42
4.	Bihar	15.7	28.5	62.91	89.39
5.	Goa	1.8	71.9	—	81.07
6.	Gujarat	7.1	70.5	38.62	71.29
7.	Haryana	19.3	55.4	35.07	78.12
8.	Himachal Pradesh	24.7	70.3	27.70	67.78
9.	Jammu & Kashmir	7.6	52.9	—	79.09
10.	Karnataka	16.2	38.06	54.00	75.03
11.	Kerela	9.8	82.7	34.01	51.05
12.	Madhya Pradesh	15.2	58.6	55.41	61.58
13.	Maharashtra	10.2	71.9	52.10	71.96
14.	Manipur	2.8	72.3	—	81.70
15.	Meghalaya	0.51	56.3	—	30.57
16.	Mizoram	Neg.	89.2	—	—

S. No.	*Names of the States*	*Population (2001)*	*Literate Population (2001)*	*(1993-1994)*	*(1990-1991)*
17.	Nagaland	NSC	—	—	—
18.	Orissa	16.5	55.5	48.2	81.54
19.	Punjab	28.9	56.2	25.02	79.34
20.	Rajasthan	17.2	52.2	43.50	82.07
21.	Sikkim	5.0	63.0	—	91.51
22.	Tamil Nadu	19.0	63.2	52.77	77.32
23.	Tripura	17.4	74.7	—	87.29
24.	Uttar Pradesh	21.1	46.3	58.50	72.20
25.	West Bengal	23.0	59.0	41.51	88.81
26.	Delhi	16.9	70.8	—	65.36

Status of a Religious Minoritias (Muslims) in India

There is no universally agreed-on definition of minority in India. Min status is a matter of self-ascription as well as an objective definition. According to Weiner (1998), "India contains such a medley of religious caste and linguistic groups that the sense belonging to a min depends upon where one lives or how much power and status one and one's sense of community threat" (p. 461). In this context, We has tried to carve out four types of minorities in India on the basis of communities' self-perception. These are linguistic, religious, caste, tribal minorities. This chapter will concentrate on religious minority.

The numerical strength of different types of religious minority according to the 2010 census is presented in Table 3. Muslims are largest religious minority in India. According to the latest census, Muslims accounted for 138 million out of India's total population of approximately 1 billion (Premi, 2006). Furthermore, the same census suggested that today the share of Muslim population is 12.9 per cent, up by percentage points since 1961 (Premi, 2006). This rise between 1961-2001 is a consequence of the higher-than-average growth rate of Muslims.

In 2001, 35.7 per cent of the Muslim population were living in urban areas, compared to 27.8 per cent of the overall population.

Table 3. Information Regarding Representation of Scheduled Castes in Different Services

Class of Service	*Central Services*	*Public Sector Undertaking*	*Public Sector Banks and Financial Institutions*	*Insurance Sector*
A	11.29	10.35	12.51	13.2
B	12.68	11.05	14.88	12.4
C	15.72	18.93	24.46	17.2

Source: Government of India (2004, December, pp. 40, 41,172-174,177).
Note: Data are reported with respect to 15 per cent reservation services. Reservations work to eradicate differences between lower castes and tribes in India by reserving a certain percent of jobs or placement in various services fields in India.

Table 4. Population Distribution by Religions, 2001

All Religions	100
Hindu	80.9
Muslim	12.9
Christian	2.4
Sikh	1.9
Buddhist	0.8
Jain	0.4
Other religions and persuasions	0.6

Source: Premi (2006, p. 170).
Note: Data exclude Jammu and Kashmir.

The Indian Constitution protects minority rights through the inclusion of the nondiscrimination and equality clause. The rights include (l) equality in the eyes of the law (Article 14); (2) nondiscrimination on grounds of religion, race, caste, sex, and so on (Article 15); (3) equality of opportunities in public employment (Article 16); (4) the right to six freedoms (Article 25); and (5) freedom to manage religious affairs (Article 26). These are available to any member of a minority community. Another strategy for protection for minorities is the collective rights that are available to them as groups or communities. These rights were designed to allow minorities to preserve their language, religion, and culture; therefore, they are grouped as "cultural and educational rights" under Articles 29 and 30.

Nevertheless, various studies (Sachar Committee, 2006) show that Muslims have fared poorly in certain aspects of socioeconomic development (see Table 5). Muslims in India remain grossly underrepresented, deprived, and excluded from the mainstream socioeconomic spheres compared to other religious minority communities including Christians, Sikhs, Buddhists, and Jains (Shariff & Azam, 2004).

The Sachar Committee report suggests a "need for transparency, monitoring and data availability" if Muslims are to be uplifted. (Sachar Committee, 2006, pp. 237-254). Furthermore, the report observes, "While equity in the implementation of programmes and better participation of the community in the development process would gradually eliminate this perception of discrimination there is a need to strengthen the legal provisions to eliminate such cases" (Sachar Committee, 2006, p. 239).

Social Development and Population Growth

Population growth affects social development through the size of the population and its distribution across age groups. The growth rate indicates a large proportion of children due to a higher fertility rate; the decline in mortality rate and rise in longevity indicate a rise in the size of the working and elderly populations. The increase in the rise of the dependent population adversely affects the dependency ratio that accompanies a growing population in the lower- as well as upper-age structures of the general population. The combined effect of population

Table 5. The Socioeconomic and Educational Profile of Muslims in Various Indian States

S. No.	*Names of the State*	*% Muslim Population (2001)*	*% Literate Muslim Population (2001)*	*Urban Poverty Line among Muslims (2004)*	*Rural Poverty Line among Muslims (2004)*
1.	Andhra Pradesh	9.2	76.5	49	10
2.	Arunachal Pradesh	—	–	–	–
3.	Assam	30.9	56.0	13	38
4.	Bihar	16.5	51.8	57	52
5.	Chattisgarh	2.0	90.5	62	42
6.	Delhi	11.7	72.3	29	0
7.	Gujarat	9.1	82.9	34	13
8.	Haryana	–	55.8	46	26
9.	Himachal Pradesh	2.0	66.1	1	4
10.	Jammu & Kashmir	6.70	58.7	11	3

growth, limited work opportunities, unemployment, and underemployment increase the dependency burden in some Indian states, particularly in Bihar, Uttar Pradesh, Rajasthan, and Madhya Pradesh (Haq, 2007). The social base of the family is weakened by high dependency because it reduces family income and savings, and limits capital formation, in turn affecting the opportunities and quality of life of these individuals. This may explain why India has such a low human development index, and as of this writing is placed at number 134 out of 187 ranked countries in the world (www.hdr.undp.org).

Growth and Outcomes

According to *Economic Survey* (Government of India, 2006-2007, p. 1), "Vigorous growth with strong macroeconomic fundamental has characterised developments in the Indian economy in 2006-2007. Growth of 9.0 percent and 9-2 per cent in 2005-2006 and 2006-2007 respectively surpassed expectation. While the up-and-down growth pattern in agriculture continued the growth estimated at 6.0 per cent and 2.7 percent in 2006-2007, and service maintained, its vigorous growth performance, there were distinct signs of sustained improvements on the industrial front." The *Survey* further says (p. 205), "Progress towards sustained improvement in the quality of life of the people in general and the poor in particular continued as reflected in the UNDP's global Human Developmental Report (HDR) for 2006 which ranks India in terms of the Human Development Index (HDI) at 126 ... out of 177 countries of the world. In terms of the Gender Development Index (GDI), however, India showed a marked improvement from the 105th rank in 2000 to 96th rank in 2004." In spite of these figures of development, the stark reality revealed by the National Sample Survey Organisation (2005) provisional data for the year 2004-2005 indicate that the poverty ratio at the national level was 27.8 per cent if the uniform recall period (URP, in which the consumer expenditure data for all the items are collected from a thirty-day recall period) is used, and about 22 per cent if the mixed recall period (MRP, in which the consumer expenditure data for five nonfood items—clothing, footwear, durable goods, education, and institutional medical expenses—are collected from a 365-day recall period, and the consumption data for the remaining items are collected from a thirty-day recall period) is used *[Economic Survey* [Government of India, 2006-2007, pp. 207-208]). Bhaduri (2006, p. 53) suggests that "higher productivity is desirable not merely to cut production cost, but because higher productivity would provide us with more goods and services for a better standard of living for all. This can happen only if higher productivity goes with more employment and satisfactory wages. From this point of view, a minimum wage in the vast unorganised sector of India is not merely an addition to cost, it is also a major source for expanding domestic demand."

References

Bhaduri, A. (2006). Development with dignity: A case for full employment. New Delhi: National Book Trust.

Dubashi, P.R. (1987). Development: An overview. In K.S. Shukla (Ed.), *The Other Side of Development.* New Delhi: Sage.

Government of India. (1952). First five-year plan, planning commission, New Delhi. Retrieved from http://planningcommission.nic.in/plans/planr fiveyr/default.html

Government of India. (1988). *India 1987, A Reference Annual.* Ministry of Information and Broadcasting: New Delhi.

Government of India. (2001). Sixth report of national commission for Scheduled Castes and Scheduled Tribes, 1999-2000 and 2000-2001, New Delhi. Retrieve from http://ncst.nic.in/index2.asp?slid = 48i&sublinkid = 279&langid = 1

Government of India. (2004, December). Sixth Report. National Commission for Scheduled Castes and Scheduled Tribes, 1999-2000 and 2000-2001, New Delhi.

Government of India. (2006-2007). *Economic Survey.* Ministry of Finance, Economic Division. New Delhi: Government of India Press.

Government of India (n.d.). Five year plans. Planning Commission of India Retrieved from http://planningcommission.nic.in/plans/planrel/indexy.pl state = planbody.htm

Haq, E. (2007). *Sociology of Population in India.* Delhi: MacMillan India.

National Sample Survey Organisation (NSSO). (2005). Indebtedness of farnmily household, 59th round. *Report No. 498, Ministry of Statistics and Programme Implementation.* New Delhi: Government of India.

Premi, M.K. (2006). Population of India in the new Millennium: 2001 *census.* New Delhi: National Book Trust.

Sachar Committee. (2006, November). *Report: Social, economic, and educational status of the Muslim community of India.* Prime Minister's High level Committee, Cabinet Secretariat.

Sengupta, A. (2001). The planning regime since 1951. In N.N. Vihar (Ed.), *India in the twentieth century.* New Delhi: National Book Trust.

Shariff, A., and Azam, M. (2004). *Empowerment of Muslims in India.* New Delhi Institute of Objective Studies.

Weiner, M. (1998). Indian minorities: Who are they? What do they want? P. Chaterjee (Ed.), *State and Politics in India.* New Delhi: Oxford University Press.

23

Caste Development and Corruption

The recent debates on corruption and agitation against it have raised many questions. However, without defining the contours of 'Corruption' and its structural location in the Indian society. It has also brought the theoretical debate on what is a movement and nature of democratic assertion into the centre stage. The clandestine support of media and political parties to a movement led by so-called 'Civil Society' raises the issue of legitimacy to the 'Civil Society' in Indian society. Therefore it is pertinent to understand and analyse these aforesaid issues. This paper is humble attempt from perspective below. Before we come to analyse the nature of agitation led by Kishan Rao Hazare in New Delhi we will analyse the nature and structure of corruption in Indian society. Corruption can be defined both in a generic and narrow terms. Let us begin with the first one.

Defining Corruption: Broader Definition in Indian Context

In generic sense corruption can be defined as a mechanism by which, a numerically small section of society collectively or individually denies majority of its people a plethora of rights and privileges whether it is 'Human Rights for dignified existence', 'equality: economic, political and social', 'liberty of occupation, residence and religious practices, fraternity etc. By doing this numerically smaller group monopolises religious, political, economic, educational and judicial institutions etc. Historically this mechanism is created, at the inception of the society, through religious texts and sanctions. Later they are legitimatised socially by theories of Dharma and Karma. The traditional structures created, in this fashion; do not die in modern times. But they remain alive changing their form and style of functioning and influence keeping the monopoly of the numerically small section of the society intact. The existing dominance in and composition of modern institutions of governance, production, and education in India amply prove the point.

Corruption: The Narrow Definition

However in contemporary times in India the so-called leaders against corruption have promulgated a very narrow definition of 'Corruption'. According to this definition 'corruption can be defined as misuse of a government or public office for personal gains'. In other words how a government servant or a politically elected member, or a judge misuse his office is called corruption. This is very reductionist and sweeping definition because of different reasons. One, this definition has taken cognizance of corruption in government offices only. That means this assume that by nature people are honest but they become corrupt when they join the government institutions. But the fact is that individuals are not born in Parliament, Bureaucracy, or judiciary. They are born in society which socialises them before they join institutions of governance or public life. That means we can argue that the institutions by nature are not corrupt rather there is something wrong with the people who man them or run them.

In this context, it is important to note that this definition does not take note of corruption induced by social sector. This is the second lacuna of the narrow definition of corruption. For instance, every year numbers of women are burnt alive because of dowry. After burning their bride the groom's parent bribe the police so they are not caught. One can call it a crime. But I will call it social corruption because of greed certain people commit this act and then indulge in corrupt practice. Similarly, corrupt practice comes to fore when huge offerings of gold and silver are made temples without any transparency? Nobody gives a receipt of donation neither one knows whether a person has paid income tax on that gold. Further, temple income is also not taxed even though temples have gold worth trillions of rupees. Thirdly, the narrow definition does not take into account of corruption that exists in and because of private sector and Civil Society organisations. Again the fact is that corporate sector and big Industrial houses have lobbyist to get them government contracts and bribe the government employees to grant them concessions in the tax, excise and import duty by making laws for legitimising their act. Industrial houses do not pay their labourers even their minimum wages. They now have higher and fire policies as well. Is this not corruption? But this narrow definition of Corruption does not take all this into account. However the narrow definition of corruption reveals certain important facts. Most importantly this definition reveals that corruption is a caste phenomenon.

Is Corruption a Caste Phenomenon?

Generally it is propagated that corruption is a faceless enemy. However, according to the analysis of both the broader and narrow definition of corruption we can argue that corruption is not a faceless enemy but has an identity of caste. According to broader definition of corruption, corruption can be defined as, "a mechanism by which, a numerically small section of society denies majority of its people a plethora of rights and privileges whether it is 'Human rights for dignified existence', 'equality: economic, political and social', 'liberty of occupation, residence and religious practices, fraternity etc. By doing this numerically smaller group monopolises religious, political, economic, educational and judicial institutions etc." Going by the aforesaid definition of corruption, who are the people who have made such structures in ancient period which denied majority of people from plethora of rights for thousands of years? Who were the people who monopolised the institutions of governance, education, and production? Of course, the so-called 'upper-castes'! They could do this because they misused their ritual and social position in the society. And hence they were responsible for a corrupt social order from its inception which was in-equal and devoid of equality, liberty and fraternity (Ambedkar 1994).

If that was the case in ancient period when there were no modern institutions of governance what was the condition in colonial period during the British. In this context Phooley had written long ago in 1873 that:

> "The Brahmin despoiled the lower classes not only in his capacity as a priest, but also in the capacity of a Government officer, as the Brahmins had monopolised all higher places of emoluments, the village police Patil being a tool in his hands. He was the temporal and spiritual adviser of the *ryots*, the money-lender in their difficulties...In the capacity of a *Mamlatdar*, a supervisor exploit him, in the Engineering Department, an officer in the Revenue and Public Works Departments he was there to exploit him, league with the Kulkarni, or the lawyer or the money-lender who were

> Brahmins. So there was nepotism, bribery and jobbery because of the domination of one caste in the administration" (Keer 1974: 116).

In the same vein Ambedkar has also highlighted the relationship between caste and corruption. According to him:

> "The Police and the Magistrate are sometimes corrupt. If they were only corrupt, things would not perhaps be so bad because an officer who is corrupt is open to purchase by either party. But the misfortune is that the police and Magistrate are often more partial than corrupt. It is this partiality to the Hindus and his antipathy to the untouchables, which results in the denial of protection and justice to the untouchables" (Ambedkar 1982:105).

In the contemporary times even if we consider the narrow definition of corruption then what picture emerges? According to narrow definition of corruption, corruption can be defined as, 'misuse of public office for personal gains'. In this context let us analyse who are the people who dominate and monopolise the modern and secular institutions viz. Polity, Judiciary, Bureaucracy, Industry, University and Media? Again the answer is the so-called Upper-castes! This can be proved on the basis of composition of the three institutions namely- Judiciary, bureaucracy, and Media. The available data clearly shows that these institutions are totally monopolised by the so-called upper-castes (for Judiciary and bureaucracy see 4th National Commission for Scheduled Caste and Scheduled Tribe report 1996-7 and 1998-9, pp. 20-22). According to this report there are only 3 per cent of SC and ST in High Courts as Judges and Additional Judges. Now there is no SC and ST Judge in Supreme Court of India. Further this report says that Brahmins, Rajputs, Kayasthas, and Banyas constitute approximately 83 per cent of Class-I government and Non-government services. SCs, STs, OBCs and Minorities roughly constituted only 13 per cent and rest were other castes. That means in these institutions again so-called upper-castes are directly responsible for corruption.

Corruption and Socialisation

True individuals do not become corrupt in a day or two. Rather there is a long drawn direct and indirect process of socialisation for the same in the society and culture where they live. If we take the Hindu society in particular then we can find institutions, ways and means in which people are socialised from the childhood which facilitates the practice of corruption in the society. The individual and groups are not only socialised into the institutions which gives them legitimacy to exploit the others but the individuals socialised in such a way that they willingly pay without making any fuss. For instance the young ones are socialised by observing their parents willingly making an offer in cash or kind to priests at the time of multiple rituals performed in the home or in the temples. Children are also told to offer to gods and goddesses whenever there is an exam or some result of competitive exam is about to come. For instance Phooley in his book, Cultivator's Whipcord (1883) has described:

> "...how a Brahmin priest persecuted a Shudra farmer all the year round from cradle to cremation, from pregnancy to pilgrimage, and how all this exploitation was done under the cloak of religion and its unending rites and rituals" (Keer 1974: 183).

In their youth they are socialised to demand dowry in marriage and keep demanding from the bride's family for all their lives. And parents of girls are socialised to pay dowry helplessly. It is not only the individuals are trained to offer and demand but they are trained for not giving what is due to someone. For instance in the villages the so-called upper castes have a habit of not paying for the labour of the Dalits and other artisan classes. Landlords do not pay minimum wages to landless labourers. The Priests are not supposed to work and produce instead socialised to survive on the hard labour of others and accumulate capital in the temple as their private property without using it for public good. That is why Indian temples have been found to possess gold and silver worth trillions of dollars beside ready cash. The moneylenders specifically the *Vaishyas* are trained to lend loans to villagers at an exorbitant rate of interest. They exploit the masses by manipulating their records as the masses were illiterate and powerless. Even dacoits make offerings to Goddess Kali for big haul. Above all the Hindus are also socialised the way out of sin by these corrupt practices. The way is simple. Keep your gods-goddesses happy by offerings or keeping fast, chanting Mantras and by taking dips in holy-river like Ganges. In medieval ages *Nazrara* (Trailer), *Shukrana* (Thanks Giving), and Zurbana (Fine) continued to socialise people in illegal practices. In modern times the huge gifts the elite' exchange on the eve of the different Hindu festivals especially on Diwali is akin to socialisation and initiation in the corruption.

In this way we can argue that Indians have many structures and processes which train individuals to indulge in corrupt practices later in the life. And they do not hesitate to give or take bribes.

Economic Development in the Era of Globalisation and Corruption

It can be observed easily that corruption has increased in Indian society since the pace of economic development has increased. It became visible especially after the process of globalisation came to stay in India along with its other elements of economic liberalisation and privatisation. This can be observed easily after 1990s with the advent of Multinational Corporations and Information Revolution brought new rules in the market. Various institutions were created to deal with the demands of the time. For instance a number of regulatory bodies were created to look after the demands of these industries. Secondly, the government of India tried to disinvest from its so-called sick public sector units. No norms existed before and new norms have not yet become effective and therefore there was complete namelessness and hence the businessmen, politicians and bureaucrats connived to reap the benefit of this situation. Each deal became suspect deal that could not be exposed. Harshad Mehta (1992), Ketan Parekh, Satyam Scam, Hawala Scam, Commonwealth Scam, The Coal Scam', The 2G Spectrum Scam, The Land Scams to name just a few emerged within twe-years of the process of globalisation and neo-liberal economy. It is not that Indians were not involved in corruption earlier to the process of globalisation. However now because of media exposure and huge amount of money involved in exchange of the deals that they got exposed again and again.

Corruption : Withdrawal of State and Ascendence of Private Sector

It can be easily hypothesised that each policy in the era of globalisation forced the state to withdraw. It looked that the corruption increased because the Private Sector wanted to replace the state from different spheres of services so that it can capture it. One can identify at least a dozen of area in which state instead of providing better and effective services kept on withdrawing. It seemed as if it was a calculated effort that if the State will not give good services then automatically citizens will move towards better provider of the services and it happened the same. The different sectors of Government could not provide good communication facilities/Indians moved to private sector. From mobile phone to internet the private sector soon started dominating and it is no co-incidence that the sector saw one of the nation's biggest scam. The state could not give good healthcare and therefore those who could afford took good health- insurance and moved to private sector hospitals. Private transporters including cheap airways and SUVs enjoying every type of fuel subsidies are pocketing the profit. Today government is not able to give clean drinking water (the private sector is ready to buy the rivers). It has already bought our coal mines and other natural resources. This all could take place because of greed and corrupt nature of certain sections of the Indian population. Hence, one can argue that the development and neo-liberalism has really increased the chances of corruption and also the quantity of it.

Having defined the structures and phenomenon of corruption let us analyse the nature of mobilisation against the corruption that took place in August 2011.

II

An Un-Representative and Un-informed '*Anshan*' (Sit-up): A Sociological Perspective

To begin with the agitation *(Anshan)* on single point agenda of Kisan Baburao Hazre (He is not Anna to me) caught the imagination of many for different reasons in Mid-August of 2011. Some called it a movement; some named it as *'Doosari Aazadi Ki Ladai'* (second freedom struggle) yet another group compares it with Jai Prakash Narain's movement of *'Sampoorn Krant'* (Total Revolution). There was huge support of people in Delhi and different parts of the country. Apart from real world support people are supporting through virtual world-web-sites, face-book, twitter, SMS also. The visual media with its power of construction of history projected that it is a nation-wide phenomenon by showing coverage from different parts of the country simultaneously on the same screen. However media gave very little or no space to alternative and dissenting voices. There has been one sided projection of the sit-up at least from private channels.

Anshan or Andolan (Agitation or Movement)

Hence there is an immediate need to highlight facts about these dissenting voices. First of all this '*Anshan*' (sit up) cannot be called a '*Aandolan*' (movement). Because a movement is an organised effort of large group of people based on an ideology and organisation, with leaders in command, to change or sustain a system (Rao ed.1979). This is not an organised effort of people, this is self-driven and self-motivated population with different ideologies on which Kisan Baburao Hazare does not have any control. This was evident by the fact that different groups were having their own ideological slogans and symbols. For instance members of 'Youth for Equality' were shouting slogans against reservation which has nothing to do with corruption. When asked, a leader said we cannot stop such frivolous groups. The lack of ideology of the participants came to fore as the agitation progressed. And it was exposed fully when the individuals who were at the forefront of the movement started making frivolous comments about their concerns. One person asked for the plebiscite on Kashmir, another misused his office for his personal gains and yet another used the national medal for so-called public good. The zenith of lack of ideology came to fore when one of the participants was thrown out of the team because he was allegedly spying for government. The same member later after mailing the whole mobilisation at Ram-Lila ground with misuse of donation, went to join the popular show 'Big Boss'. Number of other credible members resigned from the group because the few leaders of the agitation on their own decided to participate in the political campaign against a political party. Can we really call such a gathering of people a movement?

Not the Second Freedom Struggle

We should not is our 'Freedom Struggle' as well by calling this agitation as the 'Second Freedom Struggle'. Plethora of writing exists on freedom movement highlighting its nature, meaning and significance in the history of our nation. Even then we can highlight some points which will sensitise us about our freedom movement in the context of on-going sit up. By a conservative assessment 'Freedom-struggle' was a long drawn struggle for approximately one century if we take 1857 as first war of independence. It is impossible to even give an approximate figure of people who sacrificed their lives and contingent comfort. The Oppression and exploitation during colonialism which Indians suffered is second only to the Black Slaves of Africa and America. The string of movements cannot be counted during this struggle which gave us political independence. The gift of the freedom movement being assertion of sovereign existence of the Republic with a democratic Constitution, which took almost three years to be completed with representatives of different ideologies, caste, religion and class present and debating.

No Comparison with JP's Movement

In the same vein this 'Anshan' cannot be equated with 'JP's' movement either. Because that was not a *'Anshan'*, rather it was an out and out political movement against a government which was centralising power and was abrogating the democratic rights of the people by arresting people. Further it succeeded in preserving and renewing the constitutional structure which government of the day seemed to be destroying. After a long drawn political movement which trained number of future political leaders, a new age of politics was born in India. However, in this present mobilisation, government is giving space and permission for 'Dharna', on its own, after just one arrest. Secondly, there is no hope that a political party will be formed after victory in 'Anshan'.

Unrepresentative Character of the Agitation

The claim that this *'Anshan'* (sit-up) represents the aspiration of the whole nation is also farce. We should recognise that sociologically, nation comprises number of social and religious groups. How, can this *'Anshan'* be national in character if it did not represent the diversity existing in the country? Initially, when the *'Anshan'* was launched to negotiate with the government all the five members of the core group were males. And two members even of the same family. There was no representation of women, Scheduled Castes, Scheduled Tribes, and religious minorities. Today, omission of Scheduled Castes and Scheduled Tribes cannot be done on the basis of merit because at this point in time many qualified individuals are available among these sections. That means the core committee of team Hazare is self-appointed. Neither have they been democratically elected nor have people appointed them. Neither have they represented Civil Society. On a national TV channel debate, Krejiwal had replied to my query that they do not represent Civil Society. The height of absurdity was reached when in the same show, on my query, Kiran Bedi had told meaning of Civil Society as *'Sabhya Samaf* as if the political class is uncivilised. This is the level of understanding of the leaders of this *'Anshan'*.

People's Support and Question of Legitimacy to Social Action

Now one can ask that when it is not a national movement, then why so many people did come to participate in it. The answer is, corruption is a faceless enemy. Nobody knows the identity of a corrupt person. Even those who have been deeply involved in corrupt practices get legitimacy by protesting in the first row. Therefore, it is easy to come and protest against the state. If you call the same crowd for a movement of social justice, against the atrocities on Dalits, for the distribution of resources in the society etc. they will all run away. Why! Because then the enemy has a face and identity. The face may be one's own community, one's own caste or even one's religion. So this crowed is a hypocrite. They are mere spectators who are not conscious; rather they are driven by fashion. Secondly, numbers do not necessarily imply that an act is legitimate and patriotic. Can the demolition of Babri Masjid be justified because it was demolished by a large crowd? Can we justify the caste-ist protests against the 'Mandal Commission Recommendations' on both the occasion in 1990 and 2006? Or can we call Lakhs of spectators in and outside the Eden Garden for India and Pakistan match as patriotic? Above all how can we call a crowd of a few lakh of people in a population of 1200 million, as representative of national aspiration?

Another flaw of this Hazare's 'Anshan' is that he and his team have very narrow definition of corruption which should be brought under the proposed bill. The corruption of government sector which emanates from the misuse of public office is only to be checked. The team does not take cognizance of rampant corruption in day to day life of the society. Starting from denial of human rights to number of groups to access to institutions of governance and resources, etc. all amount to corruption. Then the corruption in corporate sector, media and above all the corruption of international and national Non-governmental and Civil society organisations all has been left by alone by team Hazare in the proposed Lok Pal Bill. This raises a serious debate. Specifically, the deprived sections are asserting that the present '*Anshan*' is deliberating targeting only those institutions where a little caste and religious diversity is reflected. They are not taking note of Industrial houses where still monopoly of few families exploit the natural resources of the country and lobby to influence the government to launch favourable policies to benefit them.

Hero Worship A Danger to Democracy

The irony of this '*Anshan*' is that it is based on a personality. Larger than life image of Hazare is being presented to the masses by the media professionals and event managers involved in the '*Anshan*'. The way the whole stage of the '*Anshan*' site has been designed and managed is testimony to the aforesaid fact. The giant poster of Gandhi and then Hazare in Gandhi cap sitting all alone at the top of the stage is not a coincidence. It is a well thought out strategy to project Hazare as the brand of '*Anshan*' Jan Lok Pal bill. Further to popularise the idea from the day one of the '*Anshan*' T-shirts with Hazare's Photograph, Gandhi Caps with 'I am Anna' written and printed posters of Hazare were distributed across the big cites, say, Delhi, Mumbai, Chennai, Bangalore etc. The lacuna in this type of mobilisation is that this process leads to 'hero worship or Bhakti'. In this way a 'Great Man's' image is constructed and all of us lay our freedom in his feet. That is why John Stuart Mills has cautioned those who want to maintain their democracy must not, 'lay their liberties at the feet of even a great man or to trust him with powers which enable him to subvert their institutions'. Taking cue from him Ambedkar cautioned the parliament while presenting the Constitution that, 'Bhakti in religion may be a road to the salvation of the soul. But in politics, Bhakti or hero-worship is sure road to degradation and to eventual dictatorship' (Ambedkar 1994: 1215-16). That is why Hazare's '*Anshan*' is based on mistrust. Mistrust of parliament, mistrust of government and mistrust of judiciary. He is so adamant that he wants the whole nation to trust him although he is not ready to trust parliament with 543 duly elected members of Lok Sabha and 242 in Rajya Sabha. This means in turn he does not trust millions voters who have elected their leaders according to constitutional provision? The most crucial aspect of this election is that if these elected representatives do not perform they can be removed by simply casting a vote at least once in every five years. How can we remove Hazare who has not even passed the test of democracy by going to people in the manner in which constitution of India desires?

That is why Babasaheb Ambedkar said that if we want to maintain democracy not merely in form, but also in fact we have to hold on to constitutional methods. It means we have to abandon the bloody methods of revolution. It means that we must abandon the method of civil disobedience, non-cooperation and *Satyagrah.* These methods are nothing but grammar of anarchy. How can we undermine established democratic institution of our nation which is the only hope for the world's largest democracy?

Conclusion

So what are the conclusions we can draw from the above analysis of structures and mechanisms of corruption? Firstly, there has to be a broad definition of corruption in Indian Society which can highlight the structures and mechanisms of corruption. This definition should include corrupt practices in every spheres of society. The narrow definition does not explain the evolution, development and processes of initiation in the phenomenon of corruption. Neither it gives picture of corruption existing in different spheres of society. From the above analysis we can also conclude that corruption is not a faceless entity rather it can be identified in Indian society with institution of caste. It can easily be called a processes associated with the castes which dominated and monopolised the institutions like political, economic, religious, educational, production etc. These castes deny the so-called lower castes access to these institutions. Even if they are inducted they remain in minority and at peripheries in the institutions of governance. Corruption does not have legitimate structures and caste only; there is processes of initiation in a particular act of corruption in India. Hence, individuals do not hesitate in indulging in the real act of corruption when he begins to perform his role in public life. On the other hand the ongoing campaign against corruption is not a movement rather only an agitation which with its narrow definition of corruption is only trying to delegitimise the democratic institutions which have shown diversity in inducting the diverse groups. The agitation was the product of the government creation as it gave legitimacy to the group without verifying its credentials and its organisational strength. The agitation was given boost by the traditional and new-media (Internet and SMS). The media constructed its image as national with the power of its reach. It also rationalised its terms and condition by highlighting the suitable terms in the channel-room discussions. Some of the television anchors played the role of an aggrieved party by scuffling the voice of any type of decent. They telecast the agitation round the clock without the voice of dissent making it look as if the whole of the country is supporting it. Another element which should be kept in mind that all these mechanisms under the garb of the 'Civil Society' movement is another mechanism to create new-elite from the erstwhile dominant castes of the society. Last but not the least it is forgone conclusion the LOK PAL cannot remove corruption from Indian society unless we treat the exploitative nature of our society which is caste ridden and hierarchical.

References

Ambedkar, B.R. 1982, Dr. Babasaheb Ambedkar Writing and Speeches, Vol. 2, Education Department, Government of Maharashtra, Mumbai, 1994. Dr. Babasaheb Ambedkar Writing and Speeches, Vol. 13, Education Department, Government of Maharashtra, Mumbai.

Keer, Dhananjay, 1974, Mahatma Jotirao Pholey: Father of Indian Revolution, Popular Prakashan, Bombay.

Rao, M.S.A. (ed.) 1979, Social Movements in India: Studies in Peasants, Backward Classes, Sectarian, Tribal and Women's Movements, Manohar Publication, New Delhi.

24

Cultural Heterogeneity and Exclusion in India

For some politicians it is difficult to understand India's diversity and appreciate it too. The lesson taught in our school days that there exists 'unity in diversity' in Indian society is taught even today in our schools and colleges. Although the slogan emerged at a particular point in time yet it is as relevant as it used to be in the past. However, very few know the basis of this 'unity of diversity' contained in this slogan, which was coined by British historian Vincent Smith and later on popularised by our first Prime Minister, Jawaharlal Nehru. The basis of unity is unique because it did not emerge out of similarity. Unity in this slogan does not mean uniformity. This unity is organic in nature, because this emerges from differences. Very much like the unity of different organs of the human body. As in an organism, although the organs of the body are different in their shape, size and function yet they contribute to the maintenance of the body; similarly in Indian society, there are so many social groups which are of different shape, size and perform different functions but they all contribute to the maintenance of the Indian society.

Each group has contributed in its own capacity since time immemorial to running the country's economy, polity and society. For instance, a very small religious group like the Parsis has contributed in a significant way to the development of the country's economy and science and technology. This helped India to maintain its scientific capability. Who can forget the labour of the Sikhs of Punjab for producing tonnes to wheat to feed the country, of course with the help of the migrant Bihar and Uttar Pradeshi labour. The Dalits and tribals have contributed their labour, acting as landless agricultural and industrial labourers, in running the economy and polity of this country. Moreover, what is known as Indian art and culture today comprises Buddhist, Jain, Mughal and British architecture as well as Madhubani and tribal paintings. Can we forget the role of Abdul Rahim Khan-e-Khana and Raskhan in popularising the Hindi language? If Pandit Bhimsen Joshi, Pandit Jasraj have enriched the Indian classical singing, the Dagar Brothers popularised the Dhrupad style of singing which starts with Sanskrit *shlokas.* The *jugalbandi* of Ustad Bismillha Khan's *shehnai* and *tabla* of Ustad Zakir Hussain take Indian music to different heights. This list can be unending but I think these examples are enough to make the point that it is the collective effort of Indians which runs the country.

However, diversity is the reality of Indian society. But what we have to understand is that no one community has deliberately created this diversity. Rather, it is natural in nature. The Indian diversity has evolved through eight interrelated and inter-connected epochs. If we take the Indus valley civilisation as the starting point, then the first epoch of the Indian society starts with the advent of the Aryans, which created a hierarchical social order and hence the diversity. The second epoch comprises Jain and Buddhist revolutions. The advent of Islam both through *Sufism,* that is, through peaceful means, and the 'kings' conquests' is the fourth epoch. The coming of the Europeans, the British victory and the establishment of colonial rule mark the beginning of the fifth epoch in making India more diverse culturally and religion-wise. The trauma of partition of the country the transfer of huge populations on both sides of the artificial but political borders is the sixth epoch of Indian history. The commencement of our democratic Constitution along with the process of modernisation, which included the establishment of big industries and dams, can be termed as the seventh epoch in the making of India as we see it today. This epoch is significant because after centuries Indians got the identity of free citizenship. The different identities of region, religion, caste, etc. became subservient to this identity of the citizen, at least in the spheres of constitutional rights and state run programmes and policies. The eighth epoch in the making of contemporary India started with the process globalisation along with its sub-processes of liberalisation, privatisation and information revolution.

In turn these aforementioned epochs have given birth to diversities of different types. That is why people of all major religions of the world—Hinduism, Islam, Christianity, Sikhism, Buddhism, Jainism, Zoroastrianism, Bahai live in India. Along with these religious groups there are a number of sects and cults and other divisions in all the religions found in India. It is interesting to note the religions are internally differentiated. Further, according to B.S. Guha's classification, people of six racial stocks live in India. However, linguist Grierson reported 179 languages and 544 dialects in India. However, according to the 1971 census there were 1652 languages spoken as mother tongue. Knowing fully well this linguistic diversity the framers of the Indian Constitution gave certain languages a co-national status. The Constitution of India now recognises 22 languages, spoken in different parts of the country, namely, Assamese, Bengali, Bodo, Dogri, Gujarati, Hindi, Kannada, Kashmiri, Konkani, Maithili, Malayalam, Meitei, Marathi, Nepali, Oriya, Punjabi, Sanskrit, Santhali, Sindhi, Tamil, Telugu and Urdu. The intellectuals always play down the caste system as if it shows them the mirror of their so-called tolerant society. However, the reality is that Indian diversity becomes more acute because of the presence of approximately 6000 castes in it. The Mandal Commission alone listed 3743 castes plus there are 1000 Scheduled Castes as well. If we add to these castes, sub-castes and sub-sub-castes, it is very difficult to comprehend this diversity. Although intellectuals keep on down playing the existence of caste in society, stressing on the difference between caste assertion and caste in Indian politics, there is 'caste in Indian politics', 'politics of caste' and casteism writ large in Indian society.

The most worrisome aspect of this diversity in Indian society is that it is accompanied by exclusion as well. Although this exclusion because of different diversities is part and parcel of Indian society, it is not discussed among the masses in general and in classrooms in particular. We are told on and off about the unity in diversity but rarely are we told about the hegemony in diversity. If we analyse the nature of the exclusions in Indian society we will find its different forms with different basis. There is exclusion on the basis of cultural heterogeneity. In this type of exclusion groups are excluded because they differ on the basis of cultural diversities even though they belong to same country and religion.

The cultural region becomes very important in this type of exclusion. But the positive aspect of this type of exclusions is that it is always temporary in nature. That is, it passes out quickly and is never successful in driving out the people en masse from the host society. The latest outburst of a politically naive leader against the North Indians in Mumbai is one of the recent examples of such exclusion. We can observe ourselves that although the people from UP and Bihar are Indians and a majority of them belong to the same religious group, they are not welcome in the alien culture. However, it is certain that this politics of hate against North Indians will not last long and will die its own death. Nobody would have taken note of it had the media not aired it continually for several days. One can recall the Shiv Sena's example. It came to power on the plank 'Mumbai for Marathis' but soon its leadership added religious exclusion, which has a different basis. The leadership took a plank of the *'Hindu Hriday Samrat'* for mobilisation and consolidation. Similarly, the allergy of the Dravidian parties in South India against Hindi did not last long as well. Both the Dravidian parties aligned with a party which swears in the name of Hindi and *Hindutva.*

In comparison to exclusion based on cultural heterogeneity the exclusion on the bases of gender, that is, between men and women, hierarchy and externality are more dangerous. Fifty per cent of the Indian population had been excluded because of gender only. Female foeticide is the latest form of exclusion. Further, around a quarter of the Indian population is excluded in Indian society on the basis of hierarchy, that is, on the basis of their caste. Here, especially in the case of ex-untouchables or Dalits, who are considered a part of the Hindu religion and belong to the same country, they are excluded from the main part of the village, certain occupations and day-to-day life interaction. They are now excluded from modern institutions like education, judiciary, bureaucracy, market and media. Another form of exclusion, which occurs in Indian society, is because certain people follow certain religious faiths which have a foreign origin. The exclusion of Muslims and Christians is the most glaring example. Even though they have been living here for generations and contribute with their labour in the process of nation-building, they are often told to got out of this country as they do not belong to this land. These types of exclusions are more permanent and harmful in nature. Their permanence is evident from the fact that in spite of a number of movements and campaigns since time immemorial they continue to survive and persist in society. Therefore, while celebrating diversity we should be more concerned about the exclusions based on gender, religion, caste and tribe. One should not worry too much about the exclusions emerging out of cultural heterogeneity. On the other hand the media should boycott such attempts of power hungry people creating hype to heighten the exclusions. The TV channels should be aware of the fact that, after all, India has survived all these years only celebrating its diversity and whosoever has tried to undermine this diversity for homogenisation has become history in due course of time.

25

The Reformist Role of Buddhism: Dalits and Their Development

An aspect of Buddhism which is of great interest to me is its revival and development among the Dalits in India. Dalits are referred by various names in the Indian society viz. Untouchables, Scheduled Castes, Harijans, Parayans, Adi-Dravida, and occupy the lowest position in the caste hierarchy—the hub of Hindu Social Order. Owing to their positioning in the social structure, Dalits have had to suffer 'cumulative deprivation'— social, economic, political, religious and so on. As this deprivation was legitimised by the sacred scriptures, Dalits could not challenge it and remained subjugated, exploited and isolated. But as time went by, they started waging a war for the amelioration of their condition. Though history testifies that Dalits have asserted their legitimate rights in different realms of society since time immemorial, I will restrict my narration to my experiences about the assertion of Dalits in the religious realm.

As a young Dalit, I grew up in the fold of Hinduism. Members of my family, though treated as untouchables, followed the practices of Hindu religion, and most of them still do so. They observed the same Hindu festivals and rituals as the so-called Upper Caste Hindus did and spent their time, money and energy on them. They took holy dips on different occasions in river Gomti, undeterred by the fact that it has been polluted to such an extent that even the Lucknow Water Works Department finds it hard to treat it. The social ceremonies from birth to death via marriage saw a half-baked priest reciting *Sanskrit shlokas* incorrectly and going scot-free, proving my family members' total submission to, and blind faith in a process about which they knew nothing. The lavish expenditure they incurred on these religious festivals and ceremonies could easily incapacitate a rich man. But the pathetic part is that this expenditure has become indispensable among the Dalits. Come what may, they will have to spend it, even if they have to borrow. And borrow at a higher rate of interest.

The continuous cycle of festivals in India kept my relatives and my family in perpetual debt. Caught in the debt trap, they could never come out of their economic drudgery. They could not accumulate any surplus capital to invest in the future of the younger generation. I still remember, though faintly, the '*Brahmin-Bania*' nexus—a proverb quite popular among the literate Dalits who often blamed this nexus for their poverty. I could not relate to it in those days, but now I can understand the mechanism of Dalit exploitation. The *Bania* lends, and the *Brahmin* legitimises. The paradox of subjugation of my people on the one hand, and exploitation on the other, within the system started vexing me as I grew up. Gradually, I became disillusioned with the Hindu Social Order.

I cannot state precisely when exactly I became a Buddhist but it is certain that my education and the Dalit assertion in Uttar Pradesh helped me gain an insight into Buddhism. As I grew up and did my graduation, I started attending the small meetings and talks organised by the Dalits. Each meeting started with *Buddh Vandana* (Prayer of Buddha) *Tisaran* and *Panchshila, Buddham Sarnam Gachhami, Dhammam Sarnam Gachhami, Sangham Sarnam Gachhami* (I take refuge in Buddha; I take refuge in the Dhamma; I take refuge in Sangha) ... as a layman I used to repeat the prayer, in the crowd, without knowing its meaning. For long, I used to think that the prayer is in Hindi. I later read in a book that the language of the prayer is Pali and not Hindi. Another thing which attracted me to Buddhism was a string of conversion ceremonies organised by Dalits in different parts of the country. I attended many of them, particularly in Uttar Pradesh. Gradually, I started reading more about it and learnt about the role of Iyothee Tass and Babasaheb Ambedkar in reviving the ancient religion of India and using it as an emancipatory tool for the Dalits. Buddhism became a natural choice for me as it was becoming increasingly popular among educated Dalits in contemporary Indian society.

Buddhism touched my life deeply when as a rebel, in my family, married according to Buddhist rituals. My family and relatives witnessed such a ceremony for the first time in their lives and were amazed by the simplicity and minimal expenditure involved in it. The second incidence, which shocked them, was the funeral procession of my mother. In Hindu society, whenever a funeral procession starts, the people accompanying it chant *Ram Nam Satya Hai* (Ram's name is truth). But somewhere I had heard that according to Buddhist rituals, on such an occasion, people chant '*Buddham Sarnam Gachhami, Dhammam Sarnam Gachhami, Sangam Sarnam Gachhami*' (though still I have not referred any text for this). Therefore, I started chanting these words and so did the others. I do not claim that these practices of Buddhism have become established in my family and community, but I am sure they made many of them conscious about these elements being present in Buddhism. I came to know afterwards that many other people have also tried it. In this manner, a silent revolution is taking place among Dalits which is leading to the revival of Buddhism. But this revival of Buddhism in India has a history too.

The revival of Buddhism in India is synonymous with Ambedkar's conversion to Buddhism in 1956, which is misleading. Evidence proves that Buddhism was used by Dalits to enhance their self-esteem and change their identity in Tamil Nadu way back in 1898. Aloysius (1998) reports that Pandit Iyothee Thass (1845-1914) with other Dalits organised the *Sakya Buddhist Society* in Madras in 1898. Their decision to seek out and reclaim their lost religious identity was unambiguously aimed at moving Dalits from their present enslavement towards future emancipation. He narrates that in 1907, the society began a weekly newsmagazine to educate fellow Dalits. In this magazine, Buddhism was presented as the religion of the oppressed. Branches of the society were opened, initially, in Bangalore and the Kolar Gold Fields, and then elsewhere in northern Tamil Nadu. This movement spread primarily among urban Dalits and remained small. It rejected the rituals, beliefs and traditions of the Hindu caste system, which was guided by Brahminism. In its place, it propagated Buddhist ceremonies, weekly meetings and celebrations for the community. Right conduct was consistently upheld as the essence of religion, the goal of which was *mukti* or emancipation (Aloysious 1998: 134). This movement withered away because of the emergence of Dalit politics and the rigid British policies not to extend the facility of reservation to the Buddhist converts from Dalits. Moreover, this movement could not spread in other parts of the country. Though it is difficult to say at this point in time that this movement had any influence on Ambedkar or not, but it did play an important role in keeping Buddhism alive in India.

According to many Dalits, it is a myth that Babasaheb Ambedkar converted to Buddhism on 14 October 1956 in Nagpur along with *lakhs* of his followers. They argue that it is true that he took *deeksha* on the said date, but it was a happy homecoming for him because he always maintained that Dalits were originally Buddhists and because of their rivalry with Aryans, who practised *Brahminism*, they were forced to leave their original religion. In 1948, he published *The Untouchables: Who were They and Why They Became Untouchables* (Ambedkar 1990:239-370). His book asserts that the Untouchables (now Dalits) were originally broken men, stray survivors of the indigenous tribes conquered by invading sedentary agriculturists, the Brahmans. These men came to live on the outskirts of villages as labourers for the conquering agriculturists. They were hated by the Brahmins in the villages because they were Buddhists, and Buddhism was antithetical to Brahmanic religion, which at that time practised cow sacrifice. When Brahmins saw that they were losing masses of non-Brahmins to Buddhism, which forbade the slaughtering of the cow but not meat-eating, they were forced to engage in one-upmanship to regain their leadership from the Buddhists.

They gave up meat eating, became vegetarians, and declared the cow sacred, which it was not to the Buddhists. Thereafter, the broken men became Untouchables. Because of their poverty, they were forced to eat carcasses of the now sacred cow and by doing so, they became polluted outcastes. In this way, we can say that Ambedkar identified the contemporary Dalits with the ancient Buddhists. Ambedkar also supplied the rationale for this identification. Lynch observes, 'The Untouchables, descendants of the Buddhists or broken men are the true autochthons, carriers of true and only valid Indian tradition. Their destiny then demands that they revive their cultural heritage and that they regain their ancestral patrimony' (Lynch 1974:142). That is why, it is believed by the Dalits, that Ambedkar not only appealed to the Indian Dalits to convert to Buddhism, but also did so to the Sri Lankans as well. Keer writes, 'Ambedkar then addressed a meeting in the town hall at Colombo and appealed to Untouchables there to embrace Buddhism. He told them that there was no necessity of their having a separate organisation. He also urged Buddhists in Ceylon (as Sri Lanka was known at that time) to accept the Depressed Classes in Ceylon and look after their interests with paternal care' (Keer 1990: 423).

In Ambedkar's article entitled 'Buddha and Future of his Religion' which he contributed to the Mahabodhi Society Journal, Ambedkar summarised his thoughts on Buddhism as follows: (1) The society must have either the sanction of law or the sanction of morality to hold it together. Without either, the society is sure to go to pieces. (2) Religion, if it is to function, must be in accordance with reason, which is another name of science. (3) It is not enough for religion to consist of a moral code, but its moral code must recognise the fundamental tenets of liberty, equality, and fraternity. (4) Religion must not sanctify or ennoble poverty (Keer 1990: 421). With this core thought on Buddhism, and foreseeing the future of the Dalits in it, Ambedkar declared that he would dedicate himself to the propagation of the Buddhist faith in India. And he succeeded in doing so when he got the chance. In this regard, Keer (1990: 481-2) argues, 'Ambedkar also declared that he would propagate Buddhism in India when equipped with proper means for the task. As maker of the Constitution, he had already achieved several things to that end. He described the provision for the study of *Pali* made in the Constitution, the inscription of a Buddhistic aphorism on the frontage of the imposing Rashtrapati Bhawan in New Delhi, and the acceptance of the Ashok Chakra by Bharat as her symbol, as personal achievements. Government of India had declared Buddha Jayanti a holiday mainly through his efforts . . . Besides, he had established two Colleges, one at Bombay and the other at Aurangabad, where about 3,400 students were studying and where he could encourage Buddhism.'

Last, but not the least, no one can forget Ambedkar's conversion along with his huge army of followers, which gave a fillip to the religious conversion to Buddhism later on and a jolt to everyone at the helm of affairs. To keep the Dalits and followers of Buddhism, he wrote a book named *Buddha and His Dhamma* and along with *Tisaran* and *Panchshila*, he added twenty-two oaths as the part of the prayer. These oaths embodied the total rejection and renunciation of Hinduism and the complete acceptance of the Buddhist creed. Since then, we can see that Buddhism has been spreading among Dalits in India, slowly but surely.

Since Ambedkar converted to Buddhism, more and more Dalits are being attracted towards this religion, shedding their previous religious faith. Today, according to a rough estimate, Buddhists number approximately seven million, that means in forty years i.e. since 1961, their population has doubled. *Bodh Viharas* of different shape and size have been established in different parts of the country. In 1960, especially in Agra, such was the enthusiasm among the Dalits that they converted twenty to twenty-two Hindu temples into Buddhist temples (Lynch 1974: 164). Today, their number is increasing day by day. Not only that, a number of organisations have mushroomed in the name of Buddha where Dalits come together and debate on various issues relating to Buddhism or the Dalit community. A noticeable feature of this conversion to Buddhism by the Dalits is that, except in the initial period when Babasaheb converted to Buddhism, it attracts more and more educated Dalits. This is in contrast to Hinduism and other religions in India where the illiterate masses are subsumed for salvation. It is also true that the conversion to Buddhism takes place without any allurement and force from any outside agency.

The impact of Buddhism has grown in the daily lives of Dalits. Today, even marriages are solemnised in accordance with the Buddhist rituals. The religious choice of Buddhism has become so overpowering that Dalits have broken the marriages of their daughters if the bridegroom's side has refused to comply with it. The portrait of Buddha has become a must among Dalits, whether it is a seminar or a birthday party or a marriage. In fact, garlanding the Buddha's statue or portrait and the recital of *Buddha Vandana* in the beginning of every programme has become an established ritual among Dalits. Further, you can find Buddha's idol in the drawing rooms of most of the literate or semi-literate Dalits. Soon after Ambedkar attained *Nirvana* on 6 December 1956, a fair is held every year on the day of Dussehra in the same venue where Ambedkar took *Deeksha* on 14 October 1956 along with lakhs of his followers in Nagpur, Maharashtra. The number of Dalits visiting this fair is increasing every year. Dalits—rich or poor, literate or illiterate—throng here in large numbers from different parts of the country.

Though Gokhale (1993:187) eloquently portrays the impact of Buddhism on the Mahars of Maharashtra, but the same can easily be said about other sections of Dalits living in different parts of the country in order to understand its growing influence. According to her, 'The conversion thus has created a new set of symbols and myths and produced a new consciousness within the Mahar-Buddhist community. It has instilled a sense of pride and self-affirmation' among the former Mahars. They felt released from the tyranny of the caste-Hindus. They have acquired the *manuski* (humanity, self-worth), denied to them as Untouchables. This newfound sense of equality and dignity has had repercussions 'particularly in the villages.'

Similarly, Wilkinson (1972: 98), argues, 'Change of religion has liberated them (Mahars) from the stigma of untouchability, thus enhancing their self-confidence to a great measure. Many of them explained that the economic benefit after conversion was mainly due to their giving up the rituals and ceremonies for which a considerable amount was spent. Not being burdened with all these conventional expenses, they could use the money thus saved for bettering their economic condition.' But this does not mean that after embracing Buddhism, Dalits have abandoned Hinduism completely. Yes, there are evidences where Dalits practise Hindu rituals along with Buddhism. It has only been forty-five years since Dalits started reasserting their faith which they were forced to abandon centuries ago. With time, they are shedding their Hindu rituals.

Significantly, the spread of Buddhism among Dalits has transcended national boundaries. In ancient India, King Ashoka, after the Kalinga war, sent his son, Mahendra, and daughter, Sanghmitra, to different parts of the world for spreading the message of Buddha. And since then, Buddhism has been flourishing in many Asian countries like China, Japan, Thailand, and South Korea, along with the Indian subcontinent. In the recent past, with the Dalit migration to different parts of the world, Buddhism has spread to other countries as well. One can observe a steady migration of trained Dalits to countries like the US, the UK, Canada, Malaysia and so on. They celebrate *Buddha* and *Ambedkar Jayanti* regularly in these countries. A Dalit non-resident Indian emphasised that these rituals have inculcated solidarity among Dalits who have migrated. For example, in the UK, over one lakh and fifty thousand Dalits, approximately, celebrate *Buddha and Ambedkar jayanti* (www.ambedlzar.org). Similarly, after the 'First Dalit World Conference: A Vision Towards a Casteless Society' held in Malaysia on 10 October 1998, Dalits world-over feel that among the Dalits, Buddhism can be a uniting force.

Recently, in India, Lord Buddha Club is deeply involved in the conversion of Dalits to Buddhism. The club has organised a number of programmes of conversion throughout the country. This was an exercise to galvanise the Dalits at the grass-roots level and to prepare at least one million Dalits to convert to Buddhism on the famous Ramleela Ground at New Delhi in 2001. But it is stated that, because of the state intervention to avoid any collision, the ceremony could not take place on the scale propagated. But it is true that a few thousand did convert to Buddhism. Recently, Kanshi Ram, the president of Bahujan Samaj Party (BSP), the only party with a national stature led and dominated by Dalits, has announced that he will organise a 'Conversion Rally' to Buddhism in 2006.

This can be a significant event in the history of Buddhism because BSP has a substantial following in the country, especially in the northern part. And even if a small portion of its supporters convert to Buddhism, it would boost the numerical strength of Buddhists in the country. We can conclude that the future of Buddhism among Dalits in India is taking deep roots as time is passing by. On the basis of the above analysis, we can say that it will spread further, as the level of education, politicisation, and consciousness among Dalits grows proportionately.

Importantly, the Dalits have made various efforts to enhance their social status. Three major strands can be seen in this regard. One, they took refuge in different religions by the process of conversion. They converted mainly to Islam, Christianity, Sikhism and Buddhism. Secondly, they tried to establish their independent religion with the plea that they were the original inhabitants of the Indian society and different from Hindus (Aryans). Hence, the Dalits launched a number of movements such as the Adi-Hindu, Adi-Dravid, Adi-Dharm in the first half of the twentieth century. Lastly, Dalits tried to develop their own sects in the name of Dalit Saints and declared themselves different from the Hindus. They called themselves *Raidasis* or *Ravidasis, Kabir Panthis* and *Satnamis*. But their sects were not considered outside the fold of Hindu social order and remained more or less within it. A striking feature about these efforts for the enhancement of social esteem by the Dalits is that conversion to Buddhism was chosen as the last resort. Despite this, it has come to stay among them and is spreading day by day. We hardly hear about Dalits converting to other religions and establishing new sects in India.

References

Aloysius, G., 1998, Religion as Emancipatory Identity: A Buddhist Movement among Tamils under Colonialism, *New Age International Publishers, New Delhi.*

Ambedkar, B.R., 1990, The Untouchables: Who were They and Why They Became Untouchables', *Dr Babasaheb Ambedkar Writings and Speeches*, Vol. 7, Education Department, Government of Maharashtra, Bombay.

Gokhale, Jayashree, 1993, *From Concessions to Confrontation: The Politics of an Indian Untouchable Community*, Popular Prakashan, Bombay.

Keer, Dhananjay, 1990, *Dr Ambedkar: Life and Mission*, Popular Prakashan, Bombay.

Lynch, O.M., 1974, The Politics of Untouchability: Social Mobility and Social Change in a City of India, *National Publishing House, New Delhi.*

Wilkinson, T.S., 1972, Buddhism and Social Change among Mahars, in T.S. Wilkinson and M.M. Tomas (eds.) *Ambedkar and the Neo-Buddhist Movement*, Christian Literature Society, Madras.

List of Acknowledgements

...........2001, Untouchability in Uttaranchal, Economic and Political Weekly, Vol. xxxvi, No. 49, December, Mumbai.

............2003, Uttar Pradesh: Politics of Social Change, Economic and Political Weekly, Vol. XXXVIII, No. 37, Sep.13-19, Mumbai.

............2003, Emergence of Dalit Youth: Some Sociological Reflections, in Vinod Chandra (ed.) Construction and Reconstruction of Indian Youth, J.N. Postgraduate College, Lucknow.

............2004 b, Reformist's Role in Renuka Singh (ed.) The path of Buddha:

Writings on contemporary Buddhism, Penguin Books, New Delhi.

............, 2005 -a, Understanding the Politics of Reservation, Economic and Political Weekly, Vol. XL, No. 9, February 26- March 4, Mumbai.

............, 2005 b, Violence and Youth: Carving Out an Independent Agenda for Youth, Indian Journal of Youth Affairs, Volume 9, No. 2, Vishva Yuvak Kendra, New Delhi, July-December.

............, 2005, Units 'Caste: Views from the field' in course material) for MA Sociology

Prgramme -MSO 004-Sociology in India for Indira Gandhi Open University (IGNOU, New Delhi.

............, 2005, 'Unit on Ambedkar and Lohia on Caste' in course material for MA Sociology

Prgramme, MSO 004-Sociology in India for Indira Gandhi Open University (IGNOU, New Delhi.

............, 2006, Education: A perspective from below: Viewing Social Sciences from a Dalit perspective, Biblio, September- October, New Delhi.

............2007 b, Behind the BSP victory, Economic and Political Weekly, Vol. XLII, No. 24, June 1-7, Mumbai.

............, 2007 c, Literary Representation of Ambedkar" A survey from

Hindi Literature, Creative Forum: Journal of Literary & Critical Writings, Vol. 20, No.2, July-Dec2007, Bahri Publications, New Delhi.

............, 2008, Democracy and Self- Representation, Mainstream, Vol. XLVI No. 42, October 4, 2008, New Delhi.

.... 2010, Teaching Caste and the Hindu Social Order: Dalits in Indian Sociology, in Maitrayee Chaudhuri (ed.), Sociology in India: Intellectual and Institutional Practices, Rawat Publications, New Delhi.

............, 2013, Social Development and Planning in Developing Countries, in Shewta Social Work and Social Development: Perspectives from India and the Unites States, Lyceum Books INC, Chicago.